THE GEEKS' GUIDE TO WORLD DOMINATION

[BE AFRAID, BEAUTIFUL PEOPLE]

THREE RIVERS PRESS
NEW YORK

THE GEEKS' GUIDE TO WORLD DOMINATION

[GARTH SUNDEM]

Library of Congress Cataloging-in-Publication Data

Sundem, Garth.
The geeks' guide to world domination / Garth Sundem.—1st ed.
        p. cm.
1. Curiosities and wonders—Humor.   2. Geeks
(Computer enthusiasts)—Humor.   I. Title.
PN6231.C85S86 2009
031.02—dc22
2008036037

ISBN 978-0-307-45034-0

Printed in the United States of America

Design by Maria Elias

11

First Edition

To Kristi. Geeks have hope.

CONTENTS

ACKNOWLEDGMENTS
xxxi

INTRODUCTION
xxxii

GREAT MOMENTS
IN DADA
1

"PROOF" THAT 2 = 1
2

SEVEN KICK-ASS
MARTIAL ARTS MOVES
YOU CAN DO WITHOUT
INJURING YOURSELF
2

SEVEN COMMON
JEOPARDY! CATEGORIES
3

SIX ENGLISH PHRASES
YOU CAN SPELL ON
A BASIC CALCULATOR
3

VERY COOL PARASITIC
BEHAVIORS
4

**THREE APPLICATIONS
OF GAME THEORY**

5

**FIVE SECRET SOCIETIES
YOU CAN JOIN**

5

**HOW TO ASK FOR
THE RESTROOM IN
TWELVE LANGUAGES**

7

**CONSTELLATIONS
OF THE NORTHERN
HEMISPHERE
IN SUMMER**

8

**FIVE CLASSIC THOUGHT
EXPERIMENTS YOU CAN
DO WITHOUT GETTING
OUT OF BED**

8

**SIX CHESS OPENINGS
WITH COOL NAMES**

11

**ASIMOV'S THREE LAWS
OF ROBOTICS**

12

**THE THREE BASIC
PRINCIPLES OF
ECONOMICS**

12

**FIVE LATIN PHRASES
TO SHOUT WHILE
RIDING INTO BATTLE**

13

**A SAM LOYD
PICTURE PUZZLE**

13

**SIX BAR BETS YOU
CAN WIN**

14

**FIVE UNSOLVED
PROBLEMS IN
MATHEMATICS**

16

**THREE MULTIPLICATION
TRICKS YOU CAN DO
IN YOUR HEAD**

17

**GET RICH
(NOT SO) QUICK:
COMPOUND INTEREST
CALCULATOR**

18

A SAM LOYD ALGEBRA PUZZLE

19

THREE REAL-WORLD PROBLEMS YOU CAN SOLVE WITH THE PYTHAGOREAN THEOREM ($A^2 + B^2 = C^2$)

19

THE QUOTABLE YODA

19

NINE AUSTRALIAN ANIMALS MOST PEOPLE THINK ARE FAKE

20

HOW TO BOX-STEP

21

FOUR RULES OF LOGIC

21

HOW TO COUNT CARDS: THE MIT BLACKJACK TEAM

22

HOW TO READ A CHINESE ABACUS

22

HOW LONG YOU CAN SLEEP ON YOUR ARM WITHOUT LOSING IT

23

THE HIGHEST-SCORING WORDS IN SCRABBLE

23

HOW TO BREW YOUR OWN BEER

24

THREE SPELLING RULES YOU LEARNED AND THEN QUICKLY FORGOT

25

THE TINKERTOY COMPUTER

25

THINGS THAT WILL MAKE YOUR BRAIN HURT I: EINSTEIN'S SPECIAL RELATIVITY

26

PATENT YOUR INVENTION IN SIX EASY STEPS (!)

27

THE WORLD'S BEST CORNFIELD AND HEDGE MAZES
28

SEVEN MATERIALS-SCIENCE BLUNDERS THAT BECAME EVERYDAY PRODUCTS
29

GREAT MOMENTS IN PSEUDOSCIENCE
30

USELESS STATS OF FAMOUS PIRATES
31

THE BASICS OF EXTRATERRESTRIAL DETECTION
33

A SAM LOYD PICTURE PUZZLE
34

TEN SPORTS REQUIRING ALMOST NO PHYSICAL EXERTION
35

FOUR OF HISTORY'S GREATEST HEISTS
35

SIXTEEN ESOTERIC TEXT MESSAGE ABBREVIATIONS
37

TÊTE DE VEAU: A RECIPE FOR A TRULY DISTURBED FRENCH FOOD
38

TWO LIKELY OPTIONS FOR A SECOND EARTH
39

THINGS THAT WILL MAKE YOUR BRAIN HURT II: EINSTEIN'S GENERAL RELATIVITY
39

WHAT RICHARD FEYNMAN KNEW ABOUT SAFECRACKING
39

THE CLASSES REQUIRED FOR MIT'S B.A. IN ELECTRICAL ENGINEERING AND COMPUTER SCIENCE
40

**FIVE CLASSIC
MACGYVER HACKS**

42

**SIX PEOPLE WHOSE
OBITUARIES WERE
PUBLISHED BEFORE
THEIR DEATHS**

43

**WWF STARS
OF THE 1980S**

43

**INTERNET POKER:
BY THE NUMBERS**

44

**FINGER AMPUTATION
DATA**

46

**THE BEST COLLECTIBLES
FOR INVESTMENT
PURPOSES**

46

**NINE SHADOW PUPPETS
YOU CAN MAKE WITH
YOUR HANDS**

47

**BEWARE, MLB HURLERS:
TED WILLIAMS MAY
BE BACK**

48

**HOMOPHONES,
HOMOPHENES,
HOMOGRAPHS,
HOMONYMS,
AND HETERONYMS**

48

**A DIAGRAM OF THE
CAFFEINE MOLECULE**

49

**A SAM LOYD
LOGIC PUZZLE**

50

**GREAT MOMENTS IN
*MORK & MINDY***

51

**THE TOOLS OF THE
WORLD'S LARGEST
SWISS ARMY KNIFE**

51

**GUITAR TABLATURE
FOR THE OPENING
OF AEROSMITH'S
"WALK THIS WAY"**

54

**SIX UNQUESTIONABLY
TRUE CONSPIRACIES**
54

**HIGHLIGHTS OF
EARLY MATHEMATICS
EDUCATION**
55

**SYMBOLISM OF THE
REVERSE SIDE OF THE
ONE-DOLLAR BILL**
56

**THE QUOTABLE
*HE-MAN AND
THE MASTERS
OF THE UNIVERSE***
56

**HOW TO HAVE SEX
ON SECOND LIFE**
57

SUDOKU STRATEGY
57

**MORAL LESSONS
BROUGHT TO YOU
BY THE MONSTERS
OF *THE ODYSSEY***
59

**CAFFEINE LEVELS IN
DESIGNER COFFEE**
59

**A SAM LOYD
PICTURE PUZZLE**
60

**THREE STEPS TO
SUCCESSFUL EXORCISM**
61

**NOTABLE EMERGENCY
USES OF DUCT TAPE**
62

**THE GREAT MYTH OF
THE METRIC SYSTEM**
63

**THE SCOUTING
HIERARCHY**
63

**GREAT MOMENTS
IN PRE-1980
KUNG FU MOVIES**
64

**A BIT OF CARD-BASED
MATHEMATICAL
FLIMFLAMMERY**
64

**THE CLASSIC
LOGIC PROBLEM**
65

THE RULES OF PIG LATIN
66

**FIVE COOL CONSTANTS
FROM THE WORLD
OF PHYSICS**
66

**FOUR GREEK MYTHS IN
EXACTLY 200 WORDS**
67

**THE 10 MOST VALUABLE
COMIC BOOKS**
68

**THE QUOTABLE
CHE GUEVARA**
68

**FIVE BRILLIANT RUSSIAN
NOVELISTS YOU'VE
NEVER HEARD OF**
69

**GREAT CARS IN
007 FILMS**
70

**HOW TO MAKE AND
USE A QUILL PEN**
70

**POLTI'S 36 DRAMATIC
SITUATIONS**
71

**FIVE USEFUL PHRASES
IN KLINGON**
72

**TEN SOMEWHAT
ARCANE DIAGRAMS
OF PULLEY SYSTEMS**
72

**WINE VARIETALS:
GET SNOOTY QUICK**
73

**THE BASICS OF
GEOCACHING**
74

**CONVERSION:
CELSIUS TO FAHRENHEIT
TO KELVIN**
74

**A SAM LOYD
LOGIC PUZZLE**
75

HOW TO MAKE A LASER
75

SPEED READING MADE EASY
76

THE 10 ALL-TIME GEEKIEST WRITERS
77

SOMEWHAT ABSTRACT EMOTICONS
78

ARE YOU FAT? DETERMINING BODY DENSITY THROUGH HYDROSTATIC WEIGHING
78

THE FINGER CALCULATOR TRICK
79

CHINESE NAMES OF POPULAR TAKE-OUT FOODS
79

33 SONGS YOU CAN PLAY ON GUITAR WITH ONLY THE FOLLOWING THREE CHORDS
80

THREE TWO-PLAYER PAPER-AND-PENCIL GAMES
81

CLASSIC EYE-BENDERS FROM THE WORLD OF GESTALT PSYCHOLOGY
82

GREAT THINKERS WHO HAVE MET TRAGICOMICALLY GRUESOME ENDS
84

IMPORTANT LINKS FOR USE WITH THE SIX DEGREES OF KEVIN BACON
85

AI AND THE END OF HUMAN RELEVANCE
85

THANKSGIVING DINNER IN 30 MINUTES OR LESS
87

APOLYTON UNIVERSITY: B.A. IN BS OR NEW-WAVE IT DEGREE?
88

TWELVE HARRY POTTER SPELLS FOR USE IN DUELING
89

THE SIMPLEST ELECTRIC MOTOR
89

PATTERNS IN THE PERIODIC TABLE OF THE ELEMENTS
90

A SAM LOYD MATHEMATICS PUZZLE
92

A BIT OF PSEUDO-INCOMPREHENSIBILIA FROM A PAPER MY FRIEND WROTE
93

DRAGONS IN MYTH
93

SECURITIES SAVINGS ACCOUNTS: IRA VS. 401(K) VS. MUTUAL OR INDEX FUNDS VS. BONDS
94

HACKING 101
96

FOUR CLASSIC TYPES OF RAT MAZE
96

THE PREDICTIVE POWERS OF THE IOWA ELECTRONIC MARKETS
97

MANGA, ANIME, AND THE GRAPHIC NOVEL
98

THE LESS-KNOWN FICTION OF J. R. R. TOLKIEN
98

THE FOUR LAWS OF THERMODYNAMICS
99

ROBOGAMES AND OTHER ROBOTICS COMPETITIONS
99

FUN QUOTES FROM THE WORLD'S TOP DICTATORS
100

COOL INVENTIONS OF THE ANCIENT CHINESE
101

NASA'S CENTENNIAL CHALLENGES
101

THE PREDICTIONS OF NOSTRADAMUS
103

THE TRAGIC CASE OF LEE SEUNG SEOP
103

MALE/FEMALE RATIO AND BAND TRIVIA FROM AMERICA'S TOP UNIVERSITIES
104

FOUR PRETTY CONVINCING UFO SIGHTINGS
105

STARTING PAY BY COLLEGE MAJOR
106

THE MYSTERIOUS NUMBER PHI
106

THE 121 CURRENT BOY SCOUT MERIT BADGES FROM MOST TO LEAST GEEKY
107

THE NINE TAXONS USED TO CLASSIFY ALL LIVING THINGS
109

A SAM LOYD PICTURE PUZZLE
109

FIVE VERY GOOD PLACES TO EAT PIE (THE DESSERT)
109

ESSENTIAL EQUATIONS: DETERMINING THE ALCOHOL CONTENT OF HOME BREW
110

HEIGHT/WEIGHT CHART
111

A FILM-CANISTER CANNON NEARLY GUARANTEED TO REMOVE EYEBROWS AND/OR BLOW OFF FINGERS
112

COMMON PROGRAMMING LANGUAGES
112

FAMOUS SWORDS OF HISTORY, MYTH, AND LEGEND
114

THE THREE MOST COMPREHENSIBLE IRRATIONAL NUMBERS
114

NICKTOONS AND CARTOON NETWORK SHOWS THAT ARE PERHAPS BEST APPRECIATED BY ADULTS
115

CALCULATING MONTHLY MORTGAGE PAYMENTS AND FUTURE INVESTMENT WORTH
116

DECIMAL, BINARY, AND HEXADECIMAL
116

ATTRACTING SEARCH ENGINE ATTENTION
117

WHAT'S SO FRICKING COOL ABOUT THE HUMAN GENOME PROJECT?
118

THE BENDS: RULES FOR DECOMPRESSION
119

A SAM LOYD MATHEMATICS PUZZLE

120

POWERFUL THINK TANKS AND THEIR IDEOLOGIES

120

EVERYDAY APPLICATIONS OF QUANTUM MECHANICS

122

AT-HOME EYE EXAM

122

FROM THE OFFICIAL RULES OF ROCK, PAPER, SCISSORS

123

SIX SOMEWHAT FIENDISH CHESS PROBLEMS

124

THE CLASSIC PONZI SCHEME

124

POKERBOTS

125

NINE KNOCK-KNOCK JOKES LIKELY ORIGINATING IN WISCONSIN

126

THE FIVE CANONS OF RHETORIC

127

CATCHPHRASES FOR THE MANAGEMENT OF EMERGENCY SITUATIONS

128

HOW TO CREATE A DUNGEONS & DRAGONS CHARACTER

128

A SAM LOYD MATHEMATICS PUZZLE

129

SOMEWHAT ESOTERIC MACINTOSH KEYSTROKES

130

FIVE NOT-TO-BE-MISSED TECH CONVENTIONS

130

MAP:
RECORDED FINDINGS OF
GIANT SQUID
131

THE BASICS OF NUCLEAR
ENERGY
131

THE DEWEY
DECIMAL SYSTEM
132

THE FINE ART OF
THUMB TWIDDLING
132

THUMBS II:
WRESTLING CHEATS
AND THE TWF
133

HOW TO MAKE
CHAIN-MAIL ARMOR
133

MORSE CODE
134

MECHANICS OF THE
THEATRICAL FLY SYSTEM
135

THE LONGEST AT-LEAST
HALFWAY BELIEVABLE
DESCRIPTOR FOR
DESIGNER COFFEE
135

THE NINE MEMBERS
OF THE FELLOWSHIP
OF THE RING
136

A SAM LOYD
MATHEMATICS PUZZLE
137

A STRANGE THING
SOMEWHAT
NEAR REDMOND,
WASHINGTON
137

THE PETERS PROJECTION
VERSUS MERCATOR MAP
137

REFRACTION:
HOW TO POP A CAP
IN A CARP
139

AHAB :
MOBY-DICK ::
SHIMOMURA : _____
140

**THREE BASIC
TAP-DANCE STEPS**
141

**TRAGICOMIC EVENTS
IN THE LIFE OF FABIO**
141

**BE AFRAID. BE VERY
AFRAID: THE CPSC'S TOP
FIVE HOME HAZARDS**
142

**TONGUE TWISTERS IN
LANGUAGES OF FEWER
THAN A MILLION
SPEAKERS**
143

**HOW TO WRITE YOUR
NAME IN ELVISH**
144

**CAFFEINE TOXICITY:
HOW MUCH IS
TOO MUCH?**
144

LEGO ART
145

**THE SCIENTIFIC METHOD
THE NASA WAY**
145

**A SAM LOYD
MATHEMATICS PUZZLE**
146

**FOUR VERY DIFFERENT
"BEST" AMERICAN
BOWLING ALLEYS**
146

**CORNELL UNIVERSITY'S
"I TOUCHED CARL
SAGAN" CONTEST**
147

**FOUR RECIPES USING
ONLY FLOUR, BUTTER,
EGGS, MILK, AND WATER**
147

**MOVIES FOR THE
MATHEMATICALLY
MINDED**
149

**THINGS YOU WILL FIND
WHEN YOU MISTYPE
"MIT" INTO A SEARCH
ENGINE**
149

BEACHES AT WHICH YOU ARE MOST LIKELY TO BE EATEN (BY SHARKS)
150

THE DIGITAL PINHOLE CAMERA AND THE END OF ART
151

EIGHT U.S. TOWNS WITH SEXUALLY EXPLICIT NAMES
152

TWO IMPORTANT SUGGESTIONS FROM THE WORLD ROCK, PAPER, SCISSORS SOCIETY'S RESPONSIBILITY CODE
152

CLONE YOUR PET IN FIVE (NOT SO) EASY STEPS
152

PING-PONG DIPLOMACY
153

SIXTEEN CLASSIC BUSINESS AND ECONOMICS BOOKS
154

THE SEVEN BEST COLLEGE PRANKS OF ALL TIME, IN NO PARTICULAR ORDER
155

THREE BILLION-DOLLAR BUSINESSES THAT STARTED IN GARAGES
155

SEVEN MUST-SEE SIGHTS ON THE GEEK WORLD PILGRIMAGE
157

HOW TO LOAD A PAIR OF DICE
157

IF IT FEELS GOOD, DO IT: JEREMY BENTHAM'S HEDONISTIC CALCULUS
158

PENCIL-AND-PAPER ROLE-PLAYING GAMES: GENRES AND MAJOR EXAMPLES
159

NOTHING BUT A GIGOLO
159

SLINKY TRICKS
160

A SAM LOYD MATHEMATICS PROBLEM
160

GREAT FEATS OF RUBIK'S CUBISM
161

CHEMICAL EQUATION PUZZLES: IF THESE ARE FUN, YOU ARE A GEEK
162

BEWARE YOUR FOOD
163

PHOENIX CHAMBER OF COMMERCE: "YES, BUT IT'S A DRY HEAT"
164

WHATEVER HAPPENED TO HARRY ANDERSON FROM *NIGHT COURT*?
164

ULTIMATE FREEDOM: GOING COMMANDO
165

HOT WHEELS CARS RELEASED IN 1968 AND 1969
166

VALUE-BASED FANTASY FOOTBALL: DEFT, NOT DAFT, IN THE DRAFT
167

OH SHIT! IT'S THE SCIENCE FAIR!
168

QUASIMODO: MASTER OF PERMUTATIVE GROUP THEORY
169

IM AT YOUR OWN RISK
170

GREAT MOMENTS IN CITIZEN JOURNALISM
171

**THE QUOTABLE
BILL GATES**
172

**TELEPORTATION
USING EINSTEIN-
PODOLSKY-ROSEN (EPR)
ENTANGLEMENT**
173

**ROCK, PAPER, SCISSORS:
ALTERNATE SYMBOLS**
174

**A SAM LOYD
PICTURE PUZZLE**
175

**CARTOON WOMEN
WHO HAPPEN TO BE
VERY HOT**
176

**HIGHLIGHTS FROM THE
NATIONAL ASSOCIATION
OF ROCKETRY'S SAFETY
CODE**
176

**THE HIDDEN HISTORY OF
ICONIC SPORTS
TEAM NAMES**
177

**HYPNOSIS 101:
HOW TO MAKE
YOUR FRIENDS ACT
LIKE CHICKENS**
178

**80S DANCE MOVES THAT
DESERVE RESURGENCE**
179

**TOUCH-TONE TUNES:
THE KEYS TO SUCCESS**
179

**THE EVOLUTION OF
LINK, THE GAMING
CHARACTER**
180

**MacGYVER WINE
MAKING**
181

**THE MATHEMATICS OF
SPAM FILTERS**
182

**PETER PIPER PICKED
A KEPPLER-POINSOT
POLYHEDRON PATTERN**
182

AUDIENCE PARTICIPATION GAGS REQUIRING PROPS IN *THE ROCKY HORROR PICTURE SHOW*
184

THE LONGEST WORDS IN MANY LANGUAGES
185

CREVASSE RESCUE USING COOL PULLEYS
185

ORIGAMI FROG HIGH JUMP CHALLENGE
186

THREE MORE PENCIL AND PAPER GAMES
188

A SAM LOYD LOGIC PUZZLE
189

COFFEE ALTERNATIVES
189

THE COOL THING ABOUT DIVIDING BY SEVEN
190

PERSON NEVER SEEN IN THE SAME ROOM AS BATMAN
190

SELECTIONS FROM THE SOCIETY FOR CREATIVE ANACHRONISM'S RULES FOR ARMED COMBAT
190

THE WORLD'S WORST SOMEWHAT-MODERN NATURAL DISASTERS
191

THE WORLD'S WORST SOMEWHAT-MODERN NATURAL DISASTER MOVIES
192

A BRIEF HISTORY OF LASER WEAPONS
193

RARE NORTH AMERICAN BIRDS AND WHERE THEY CAN BEST BE SEEN
194

MARITIME SIGNAL LANGUAGE
194

THE QUOTABLE *XENA: WARRIOR PRINCESS*
195

A RECORDER FINGERING CHART
195

INTERESTING BITS OF EGGSHELL PHYSICS
196

ALTERNATE PATHS TO SUCCESS
197

SUPERHEROES, THEIR NEMESES, POWERS, SECRET BASES, AND WEAKNESSES
198

THE MATHEMATICAL DEFINITION OF AN EULER BRICK
199

I CAN'T BELIEVE IT'S A LOOPHOLE!
199

OCARINA SONGS FROM *THE LEGEND OF ZELDA*
200

TOILET TRAIN YOUR CAT
200

TURTLE ART
202

THE JOYS OF FANGRAPHS.COM
202

SIX STEPS TO COLLEGE ACCEPTANCE
203

FOLDING INSTRUCTIONS FOR A MASSIVELY COMPLEX PAPER AIRPLANE
204

ARE YOU HOT? YOUR COMPUTER KNOWS
204

A SAM LOYD LOGIC PUZZLE
205

THE TURING MACHINE
205

A SAMPLING OF YIDDISH WORDS ADOPTED INTO THE COMMON LEXICON
206

THE PROBLEM WITH SEMAPHORE
207

BODY TRICKS WE LEARNED IN MIDDLE SCHOOL THAT INDUCE ZOMBIFIC POSSESSION AND/OR ALTERED STATES OF CONSCIOUSNESS AND PERCEPTION
208

SLIGHTLY COMBATIVE AND/OR VIOLENT TWO-PERSON GAMES
208

BECOME A BILLIONAIRE TODAY THROUGH THE POWER OF NO-LOSE BIDDING!
209

THE QUOTABLE *KUNG FU*
210

IT'S THE GREAT CIRCLE (CHARLIE BROWN)
210

THE BASICS OF GOLDEN AGE GEEK BRITCOM
211

THE NECESSARY HOME SAFETY DEVICES
211

UNDERSTANDING THE SUBPRIME MORTGAGE DEBACLE
212

FOUR PAIRS OF VELCRO SHOES AVAILABLE NEW FOR BELOW $34.99
213

DEVELOPMENTAL MILESTONES
214

DAVID COPPERFIELD'S ATTEMPT TO DISCOURAGE THE HUDDLED MASSES
215

ODE TO NPR
215

A TIMELINE IN PICTURES: BADLY BROKEN ARM
216

ANOTHER LOOK AT PSEUDOSCIENCES
216

THE QUOTABLE *X-FILES*
217

THE ANSWER TO THE ULTIMATE QUESTION OF LIFE, PART I
217

THE ANSWER TO THE ULTIMATE QUESTION OF LIFE, PART II
217

THE 0.15 OF A TOPIC: THE ANSWER TO THE ULTIMATE QUESTION OF LIFE, PART III
217

BRAINS, BRAINS!
218

HOW TO PROGRAM UNIVERSAL REMOTE CONTROLS
218

SINUS INFECTION, BEGONE!
219

YE OLDE WEB ACRONYMS
219

THE WORLDS OF NORSE MYTHOLOGY
220

ARCH PHYSICS
220

HOW TO TAP A MAPLE TREE AND CONDENSE SYRUP
221

HOJUJITSU ROPE RESTRAINT
222

WHISTLE PHYSICS AND AIRPLANE WINGS
222

SPECIES IN D&D, MIDDLE-EARTH, *WINNIE-THE-POOH*, AND MAGIC: THE GATHERING
223

PIMP YOUR CUBICLE: FIVE MUST-HAVE GADGETS
223

THE RUBE GOLDBERG MACHINE
224

ELEVEN WAYS TO MAKE MONEY ONLINE
225

A MASSIVELY COOL DIAGRAM OF A SYNAPSE
226

A SAM LOYD SLIDING-TILE PUZZLE
226

PANGRAMS IN MANY LANGUAGES
227

DATING TELLS
227

THE QUOTABLE *FUTURAMA*
228

SPECIES COUNTERPOINT
228

THERE IS NO EASTER BUNNY
230

RACISM AND GENOCIDE IN THE MMORPG LINEAGE II
231

FUTURE COOLNESS AS PROMISED BY NASA
232

INFORM AND INTERACTIVE FICTION
232

SPAM HAIKU
234

**BLINKENLIGHTS:
COURTESY OF IBM, 1955**
234

**BEER'S CONTRIBUTION
TO THE FIELD OF
STATISTICS**
235

**THE ROCK, PAPER,
SCISSORS MATING
STRATEGY OF
THE SIDE-BLOTCHED
LIZARD**
235

**HEAD PICKLING THE
OLD-FASHIONED WAY**
235

**WORLD LEADERS
WHO ALSO HAPPEN
TO BE HOT**
236

**APPENDIX:
VERY GEEKY
PUZZLE ANSWERS**
239

ACKNOWLEDGMENTS:

Thanks to my web of friends willing to point in the direction of splendid geekery: Rob Bentley, Jer Goldman, Louie Yang, Rich Katz, Ariel Kemp, Constance Steinkuehler, Derek Lam, Ben Sacks, Jocelyn Hendrickson, Jeremy Masters, Joe Gosen, Jamileh Jemison, Bill Pikiewicz, et al. Thanks also to my family, who weathered the perfect storm of this geekery inserted into every conversation for a year without dumping or disowning me. (Of course, much of this geekery is my family's fault, anyway.) Thanks to Julian Pavia, Philip Patrick, Carrie Thornton, Adam Korn, and the rest of the Three Rivers gang (the house with the highest geek-to-editor ratio of any major publisher). Thanks, too, to agent extraordinaire Jennifer Griffin, who leaps tall buildings in a single bound. Finally, thanks to my Labrador, Gus, for ensuring I continue to see the light of day (even if only for the time it takes him to create acidgenic bald spots on the lawn).

INTRODUCTION

Welcome to my GEEK brain.

It has exactly 314.15 information slots. While I wish there were more slots, alas, there are not. And while I wish these slots were packed with things like mathematical proofs of Millennium Prize problems, the mechanics of teleportation using Einstein-Podolsky-Rosen entanglement, and the physics behind NASA's new plasma propulsion engine, this is not the case either. Instead, elbowing out useful, enriching, or scientific facts are folding instructions for a jumping origami frog, lists of English words you can spell on a basic calculator, and haikus written in praise of SPAM (the pork product of questionable lineage), all of which threaten at any second to burst through my facade of normalcy like parasitic aliens from John Hurt's chest. Geek attack: Picture it. It's not pretty.

And, for better or for worse, I'm not alone.

Today's ubiquitous geek is like a massive musical mixing board, with various geeks turning up or turning down different dials, boosting—for example—80s pop arcana or programming languages or fantasy football stats or behavioral economics or quotes from *This Is Spiñal Tap* (the last of which have the relevant dial turned up to 11). We don't all boost the same dials and we certainly don't appreciate being *defined;* however, there is one constant that applies to all brands of geek—in all of us, *these dials are turned way up*. In fact, our geek informational dials are turned up to the point that they sometimes drown out our ability to function smoothly in the social world; in other words, with our geek specialty of choice thumping away inside our brains at maximum decibels, things like social niceties, our wardrobes, our anniversaries, and our ability to contribute to dinner conversation without injecting weird factoids from the mating strategies of clownfish can be effectively silenced.

Take heart, dear geek: With the world evolving toward ever-higher levels of required specialization, more and more people are turning up their information dials to the point of usurping their ability to function normally. In short, more people are becoming geeks.

To illustrate this geekification of modern society, imagine—if you will—a middle-school rocket club. One kid follows the directions, carefully penciling in exact fin placement and then, after allowing the required drying time, painstakingly sanding, painting, and applying decals until the finished rocket is a mere blip in a wind tunnel. All another kid wants to do is send a live payload as high as possible—into the clear plastic cockpit of a three-stage D-engine rocket, he packs intrepid (and potentially ill-fated) caterpillars, each with a name like Buzz or Chuck or Neil. A third kid has a vision: a center fuselage flanked by auxiliary tubes, each with a separate nose cone, the whole contraption having the potential to arc gracefully skyward or, three feet off the launch pole, to start spinning wildly, explode spectacularly, and negatively affect hearing in the faculty adviser's left ear.

Yes, I knew these kids. (Today, the first is in the Stats department at Oxford, the second is an entomologist specializing in system change due to catastrophic events, and the third is an environmental architect.) OK, I was one of them—I oscillated between keeping a meticulous flight log and pirating the rocket engine gunpowder for use in more terrestrial pyrotechnic experiments. Thanks in part to genetics—my dad is a former president of the American Accounting Association—I also programmed choose-your-own-adventure stories in BASIC, circa 1987, eagerly anticipated the logic puzzles in the next installment of *Games* magazine, and designed multilevel dungeons on graph paper. In an especially cruel twist, my mother is a psychoanalyst, so I was especially aware how these pursuits were likely to affect my social and emotional development (adversely).

Back to geekification:

In the sepia tones of yesteryear, we rocketeers remained geek kings and queens of only the rocket club (and—in the spirit of full disclosure— later the jazz band and the math and chess clubs. Wow, this is actually rather cathartic). Today, with highly specialized knowledge of all sorts driving the world, it is as if more and more people are clamoring for inclusion in these clubs. Everyone now wants and needs information, leading to a much wider pool of adoration for the alpha geeks in each discipline.

It may be no revelation that yesterday's geeks rule today's world. A quote widely misattributed to Bill Gates: "Don't make fun of geeks because one day you will end up working for one." But with most of society now acting as phytoplankton at the base of the ecosystems in which geeks are alpha predators, we are not only driving the traditional geek fields, but we're starting to drive *cool* as well.

For example, imagine a twenty-four-year-old dude with an uneven peach-fuzz beard, wearing a green foam $E = mc^2$ hat, a red Che Guevara shirt, and Converse All Stars, and listening to an iPod while riding a long-board to his job as a Web designer. By any definition, this person is a geek. This person is also very, very cool. He probably owns an island in Second Life and has an algorithmic tattoo, too. Women want him, and men want to be him. (We assume he dates a girl with piercings.) And with this shift in cool, we see that instead of struggling to join society at large as we have always done in the past, now society at large is joining us.

OK, now that you are versed in hypothetical, external geekification, it's time for a bit of self-examination (no, you needn't undress). Does what you know affect how you act? In light conversation, do you unintentionally inject your personal geekery? Does this make things a little awkward? Last Friday, instead of trudging through another of these awkward conversations, did you decide to order Chinese again (and eat it while watching *Red Dwarf* reruns and/or blogging about it)? Do your friends and family buy you books with "geek" in the title?

If you answered yes to any of these questions, you're a geek. Go ahead and skip to this book's first entry. Go on, you know you want to.

But maybe you thought, *Oh shit! After reflection I'm not a geek and will thus be relegated to a lifetime of groveling at the feet of my great geek overlords. Oh how I wish I could be a geek too!* Or you might've answered, *Oh shit! I used to be a geek but have spent the last fifteen years perfecting a veneer of social competence in order to pimp real estate and have thus let my geek credentials lapse. Whatever shall I do?*

Never fear: you hold in your hands the secrets you need to function—again or for the first time—as a geek. In fact, if you read and enjoy this book, you will necessarily be transformed into a geek by the simple act of partaking in the geekiest of geek activities: the enjoyment of knowledge for its own sake (Descartes: "I think, therefore I am [a geek]"). With this book, you, too, can gain the cultural knowledge necessary to peek behind the Wizard's curtain—to glimpse the Matrix—and can thus join in the experience of *total world domination*. Think of this book like a benevolent werewolf, ready to give you a friendly nip in the jugular; come next full moon, you'll be howling too.

And then, during the geek uprising, when your IT guy rediscovers his Klingon spirit and the Web-widgets girl down the hall goes *Xena: Warrior Princess*, you will be able, when the pogrom reaches your cubicle, to demonstrate complex handmade shadow puppets against the whiteboard and recite pi to at least the fifth digit, thus proving your allegiance and claiming your rightful spot in the coming Geek World Order. (Which, you have to admit, is worth the price of a book.)

[THE GEEKS' GUIDE TO WORLD DOMINATION]

GREAT MOMENTS IN DADA

Hugo Ball suggested one could achieve eternal bliss by saying the word Dada until losing consciousness. Tristan Tzara, in an inspired moment that is itself Dada, described the art as an armadillo and advocated caution. Geeks know that Dada, like the number 42 and Beatles records played backward, explains everything worth knowing.

Compass
Man Ray, 1920

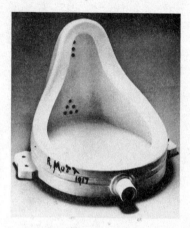

Fountain
Marcel Duchamp, 1917

L.H.O.O.Q.
Marcel Duchamp, 1919

"PROOF" THAT 2 = 1

Does two *actually* equal one? Does this proof demonstrate the failing of math as a rational science and thus the end reason, logic, and an ordered society? Or is there a trick? (See answer in Appendix.)

$$a = b$$

$$a^2 = ab$$

$$a^2 - b^2 = ab - b^2$$

$$(a - b)(a + b) = b(a - b)$$

$$a + b = b$$

$$b + b = b$$

$$2b = b$$

$$2 = 1$$

SEVEN KICK-ASS MARTIAL ARTS MOVES YOU CAN DO WITHOUT INJURING YOURSELF

ESCAPE FROM BEAR HUG

An attacker has grabbed you from behind. Rise up on the balls of your feet while grabbing either of your attacker's arms. When your attacker pushes down against this action, use the downward momentum—bend quickly to your knees and hurl the attacker over your shoulder.

ESCAPE FROM HOLD WITH KNEE STRIKE

An attacker standing in front of you has grabbed both your wrists. Grab his/her wrists and twist outward while pulling your attacker into a vicious knee strike. Hi ya!

RICE BALE REVERSAL

From the front, your attacker butts his/her head into your abdomen like a football tackle. You are like water—go with the flow. Grab your attacker as you roll to your back and use the momentum to chuck him/her into next week.

HOOKING BLOCK, PALMHEEL STRIKE

An attacker punches at you from the front. Wave your right arm away from your centerline (wax off), catching the oncoming strike and pulling your attacker toward you, where you meet his/her head with the heel of your left palm.

MIDDLE BLOCK, BACKFIST

An attacker punches at you from the front. Wave your right arm toward the centerline (wax on), diverting the blow, and then counter immediately with the back of your right fist.

FORWARD FOOT SWEEP

You have locked arms with your attacker. Push forward with your left hand while using the inside of your left foot to sweep inward against the outside of your attacker's left foot. Now pull back toward you and release the right hand to spin your attacker to the ground.

LARGE OUTER REAPING

You have locked arms with your attacker. Quickly use your left foot to step on your attacker's left foot. Now, step behind this foot pile with your right leg and swing it back stiffly into your attacker's pinned left leg. Give a shove and a twist to send your attacker to the ground.

SEVEN COMMON JEOPARDY! CATEGORIES

In the geek pantheon (note: geek, not Greek), Ken Jennings sits directly next to the Silver Surfer, and for many, Alex Trebek rules from behind his podium, radiating lightning bolts of pure intellect. Come on, you know you've pictured it—standing there with a smug look on your face as the maddening theme music changes key. You've probably even stayed awake at night evaluating optimal Final Jeopardy betting strategies. But before you take that leap to fame, fortune, and the Tournament of Champions, you will actually have to know something about the following categories:

1. Name's the Same (A: Bernanke and Stiller. Q: Who is Ben?)

2. Before and After (A: "I'm Gonna Knock You Out" rapper and author of the Silmarillion. Q: Who is LL Cool J. R. R. Tolkien?)

3. Potent Potables (A: Gin, lemon juice, sugar, club soda, orange, and a cherry. Q: What is a Tom Collins?)

4. Rhyme Time (A: A large truck. Q: What is a big rig?)

5. Crossword Clues (A: An early tennis simulation game—4 letters. Q: What is Pong?)

6. U.S. Presidents (A: Survived a gallstone operation without anesthetic or antiseptic. Q: Who was Polk?)

7. Common Bonds (A: Paul McCartney, Princess Diana, and Hillary Clinton. Q: Who are people surreptitiously replaced by androids?)

SIX ENGLISH PHRASES YOU CAN SPELL ON A BASIC CALCULATOR

This requires an old-school calculator—preferably purchased for less than $3.29 and on which the solar powered display flickers when you sit under fluorescent lights. Enter numbers using the following code: 0 = O, 1 = I, 2 = Z, 3 = E, 4 = h, 5 = S, 6 = g, 7 = L, 8 = B. Don't forget to spell backward, so that when you turn the calculator upside down, the words/phrases read correctly.

SHE OGLES SLOBS
58075 53760 345

BOOZE IS BOB'S HOBBIE
318804 5808 51 35008

GOSH SHE IS SO OBESE
35380 05 51 345 4506

HELLISH BLOB OOZES GOO
006 53200 8078 4517734

BLESS HIS IGLOO
00761 514 55378

HELLO BOOBIES
5318008 07734

VERY COOL PARASITIC BEHAVIORS

• Many parasites depend on their host's behavior in order to successfully reproduce. Instead of leaving this behavior to chance, some parasites actively manipulate their hosts to produce the desired behavior. For example, after infecting a rat, the *Toxoplasa gondii* parasite needs to be transferred to a cat's belly to reproduce. To do this, the sneaky parasite rewires its rat host to ac-

AMONG the many, many other geeky goodies from the world of biology is the truth about the clownfish, or *Amphiprion akindynos* to you and me. It turns out Nemo is an expert gender bender. The pugnacious little buggers live in groups in which mating occurs only between the dominant male and female. When the female is eaten by a barracuda or otherwise dies, her mate changes sex to become the next dominant female. Sorry, Nemo—after a couple weeks, it would technically be a new *dad* you are looking for.

tively seek the smell of cat urine. Obviously, this tends to put the rat in dangerous proximity to the source of said urine, and when the rat gets eaten, the parasite completes its necessary transfer. *Cordyceps* fungi infect insects and steer them to higher ground where, when the insect dies and the fungus bursts forth, the fungus spores will be more effectively dispersed by wind.

• Another parasite—this one a mite of wasps—is transmitted sexually, after which it acts as a sperm plug to prevent further fertilization (and thus competition).

• The candiru fish has seen the pop-culture spotlight for obvious reasons—*Grey's Anatomy* referred to it as the penis fish. The eel-like fish follows a water source to its home in a host's orifice (you do the math), where it becomes impossible to remove without surgery due to its barblike spines.

• The fish parasite *Cymothoa exigua* attaches to the tongue of the spotted rose snapper and steals the tongue's blood supply. When the snapper's tongue eventually atrophies and falls off, the parasite attaches itself in the tongue's place, effectively becoming the fish's tongue, where it shares meals with its host.

• When it comes time for the wasp *Ampulex compressa* to lay her eggs, she finds a cockroach to act as host. But instead of simply laying her eggs in the unfortunate roach, she first lands on his back and inserts a specialized stinger into the roach's brain, which she then uses to steer the roach—under its own power—back to her burrow, where the zombie roach sits placidly as the wasp larvae gobble his living innards.

THREE APPLICATIONS OF GAME THEORY

1. In 1957, Anthony Downs used game theory to show how and why political candidates will converge toward the ideology of the median voter.

2. In 1994, game theorists hired by the FCC designed an auction for the electromagnetic spectrum, earning $42 billion from telecommunications companies bidding on slices of the pie.

3. In biology, game theory has been used to explain the evolution and stability of 1:1 sex ratios as well as the mobbing behavior of many prey animals attacking a larger predator.

FIVE SECRET SOCIETIES YOU CAN JOIN

ANCIENT ORDER OF THE ROSICRUCIANS

The AOR is the American offshoot of the Rosicrucian Order. The society's founding, seventeenth-century manifestos describe the journey of a heroic, mystic pilgrim, Christian Rosenkreuz (existence disputed by the unenlightened), who supposedly studied in the Middle East and brought back to Germany a full can of pseudo-mystic whoopass, which he proceeded to open.

The modern AOR describes itself as "an Aquarian Age mystery school in the Western Tradition," which translates into an organization that is one third hippie, one third druid, and one third Dungeons & Dragons. If you enjoy a good neopagan ritual aimed at communing with the universal idea of love, the Rosicrucians might be right for you. Download their membership application at www.rosenkreuzer-orden.org.

FREEMASONS

The Freemasons are a completely transparent and benign fraternal organization committed to morality and belief in an unspecified supreme being, with no freaky, secretive methods of controlling world leaders or major financial markets. At least this is what they would have you believe, thus lulling you, dear uninitiated, into a complacent sheep-state in which you will be unable to resist the inevitable Freemason uprising.

Unless, of course, you join them. Start as an Entered Apprentice and learn the secret handshake. No kidding—there really is a secret handshake.

OPUS DEI

Today, there are more than three thousand Opus Dei members in the United States, very few of whom are albino psychopaths. In fact, Opus Dei chapters have partnered successfully with many inner-city charity programs, promoting an agenda of education and spiritual guidance. As a "personal prelature" of the Catholic Church, the jurisdiction of Opus Dei's bishop isn't defined to a geographic area; rather, his influence and authority extend to all prelature members, wherever they live or hide.

Note: Opus Dei has nothing to do with Dan Brown or *The Da Vinci Code,* though needless to say, the bestselling book has been quite a recruiting tool.

SOVEREIGN MILITARY ORDER OF THE TEMPLE OF JERUSALEM

You might have heard the SMOTJ called by another name: the Knights Templar. And how cool is this—you, too, can become a knight. Get the ball rolling by sending a résumé and letter of introduction to Membership@smotj.org.

The Knights Templar were officially sanctioned by the Catholic Church in the aftermath of the First Crusade, to protect European pilgrims in the Holy Land. Today, the Templar's traditional weapon, the sword, has lost an *s,* becoming the *word,* and modern Knights Templar concern themselves more with antiquarian research and lobbying for the preservation of ancient sites in or near Jerusalem than with lopping off infidel heads (special bonus if said preserved sites can be linked explicitly or implicitly with an Indiana Jones movie).

ORDO TEMPLI ORIENTIS

When you picture a secret society, you likely picture something similar to the Ordo Templi Orientis, which includes complex initiation rites, occult rituals, and loose belief in a somewhat abstruse religious concept. In 1904, Aleister Crowley, known to followers as the Great Beast, codified the order's beliefs in his *Book of the Law*, the guiding principle of which is "Do what thou wilt shall be the whole of the law."

To join, first practice freeing yourself from inhibition. Then go to oto-usa.org.

HOW TO ASK FOR THE RESTROOM IN TWELVE LANGUAGES

FRENCH	*Où sont les toilettes?* (Oo son ley twalet)
SPANISH	*¿Dónde está el baño?* (Dondey estah el banyo)
GERMAN	*Wo ist das Badezimmer?* (Voh eest dahs bahdeyzimmer)
DUTCH	*Waar is de badkamers?* (Vor ees de bahdkahmers)
ITALIAN	*Dov'é il bagno?* (Dovey eel banyo)
PORTUGUESE	*Onde está o restroom?* (Ondey estah o restroom)
INDONESIAN	*Di mana toilet?* (Dee mana toylet)
RUSSIAN	*Gdye zdyes' tualet?* (Gdye zdyes twalet)
NORWEGIAN	*Hvor er badet?* (For air bahdey)
JAPANESE	*Toire wa dóko deska?* (Twarey was doko deskah)
HEBREW	*Eifo ha-sheirutim?* (Ayfo hasharootim)
HAWAIIAN	*Aia I hea ka lumi ho'opaupilikia?* (Aya I heyah kah loomee ho'opowpeeleekeya)

CONSTELLATIONS OF THE NORTHERN HEMISPHERE IN SUMMER

FIVE CLASSIC THOUGHT EXPERIMENTS YOU CAN DO WITHOUT GETTING OUT OF BED

Throughout history, scientists, philosophers, and Ph.D. students lacking funding for actual research have turned to the thought experiment in hopes of discovering something publishable, thereby retaining tenure and/or attracting the admiration of comely undergraduates. The best thought experiments throw light into dark corners of the universe and also provide other scientists, philosophers, and destitute Ph.D. students a way to kill time while waiting for the bus.

MAXWELL'S DEMON

The second law of thermodynamics states that a system will never spontaneously move toward a higher degree of order. It takes energy to increase order.

But imagine you had a box filled with molecules, vibrating away at various speeds and creating by their interaction a constant temperature inside the box. Now stick a divider down the middle of the box, splitting it into two chambers. In this divider is a tiny door operated by a demon. The demon opens and closes the door, allowing faster (hotter) particles to bounce naturally into the right chamber and slower (cooler) particles to bounce into the left chamber. Over time, the order of the system is increased—the right chamber gets hotter and the left chamber gets cooler. Remember, the demon has added or subtracted nothing from the system, only opened and closed a door, thus allowing particles to pass through on their natural paths.

Does this violate the second law of thermodynamics?

SHIP OF THESEUS

The Greek historian Plutarch described the following dilemma: "The ship wherein Theseus and the youth of Athens returned was preserved by the Athenians down even to the time of Demetrius Phalereus, for they took away the old planks as they decayed, putting in new and stronger timber in their place." By the time of Demetrius Phalereus, which was about a thousand years after Theseus's return from Crete, so many planks and timbers had been replaced that none of his ship's original wood remained.

The question is, was it still Theseus's ship? More generally, what creates identity? If all the molecules of a thing (or person) are identical to the molecules of another thing (or person) are the two the same? If they are different, what makes them so? If a person were teleported by a machine that disintegrated their molecules and then reassembled them in an exact copy, would it be the same person?

SCHRÖDINGER'S CAT

In 1949, the physicists Erwin Schrödinger and Albert Einstein got together to chat about reality. This led to a number of discoveries, among them the first law of physicist-assisted entropy, which states that whenever two physicists get together to chat about reality, the total amount of reality (R) in the universe is decreased in direct proportion to the combined IQ of said physicists. The FLOPAE was a product mostly of Schrödinger's Cat, a thought experiment in which the feline in question was eventually pronounced both alive and dead at the same time (according to quantum physics . . .).

First, imagine a cat in a box. You can't see in and the cat can't see out. What the cat *can* see is a rock, a Geiger counter, and a vial of poison. Now, the rock is slightly radioactive, with an exactly fifty-fifty chance of emitting a subatomic particle in the course of an hour. If the rock emits a particle, the Geiger counter will flip a switch that breaks the vial of poison, killing the cat. (Note to PETA: *thought* experiment.)

At the end of the hour, from the point of view of an observer outside the box, is the cat alive or dead? Maybe both at the same time? Has this event generated one world in which the cat is alive and another world in which the cat is dead?

Physicist Stephen Hawking said, "When I hear of Schrödinger's Cat, I reach for my gun."

THE CHINESE ROOM

Most proponents of strong artificial intelligence consider John Searle a naysayer. Searle, contrary to every AI-geek's dream, asserts that no matter how much code we write, a computer will never gain sentient understanding. He illustrates his claim with the following example:

Suppose a computer could be programmed to speak Chinese well enough that a Chinese speaker could ask the computer a question and it could respond correctly and idiomatically. The Chinese speaker would not know whether he or she was conversing with a human or a computer, and thus the computer can be said to have humanlike understanding, right?

Wrong, according to Searle.

He imagined himself sitting inside the computer, performing the very computerlike function of accepting the input of Chinese characters and then using a system of rules (millions of cross-indexed file cabinets, in his example) to decode these symbols and choose an appropriate response. He could do this for years and years, eventually becoming proficient enough to offer responses correct and idiomatic enough to converse with a native Chinese speaker. Still, he would never actually learn how to speak Chinese.

There are many counter-arguments, including the idea that, while Searle himself, sitting inside the computer, doesn't understand Chinese, the system as a whole—Searle, the input system, the filing cabinets, and the output system—does.

What do you think?

ACHILLES AND THE TORTOISE: ZENO'S PARADOX

Here's a classic, pulled straight from the humanities course you took senior year in high school:

Achilles and a tortoise have a race. Achilles, being much the faster, allows the tortoise a hundred-yard head start. Of course, because Achilles allowed the turtle to begin ahead of him, it takes time for Achilles to reach the tortoise's starting point. However, the turtle is no longer there; it has continued, and Achilles must again catch up. Every time Achilles reaches a point the turtle has passed, the turtle has used the time to travel farther ahead. Always having to make up some distance, however small, Achilles will never catch the tortoise!

Right?

SIX CHESS OPENINGS WITH COOL NAMES

Chess is as much art as game. Played at the highest level, it is as much intuition as information.

Played at a much lower level, it is about looking cool at coffee shops. Integral to this goal is being able raise an eyebrow at your opponent (who hopefully is wearing a turtleneck while smoking clove cigarettes), and challenge him or her in a voice audible at neighboring tables to counter your Nimzo-Indian Defense. (If you're *really* cool, you'll explain that the proper spelling is "defence.") In the boards below, white plays the named defense.

NIMZO-INDIAN

GIUOCO PIANO

ALBIN COUNTER GAMBIT

HEDGEHOG DEFENSE

BENKO GAMBIT

TARRASCH DEFENSE

THE chess champion (and proponent of Russian democracy) Garry Kasparov used the Grünfeld defense in his World Championship matches against Anatoly Karpov in 1986, 1987, and 1990. Kasparov won all three matches. If you want to be as cool as Garry Kasparov, you will use the Grünfeld defense too.

ASIMOV'S THREE LAWS OF ROBOTICS

1. A robot may not injure a human being or, through inaction, allow a human being to come to harm.

2. A robot must obey orders given to it by human beings except where such orders would conflict with the First Law.

3. A robot must protect its own existence as long as such protection does not conflict with the First or Second Law.

THE THREE BASIC PRINCIPLES OF ECONOMICS

SUPPLY AND DEMAND

The phrase "supply and demand" was first used by James Denham-Steuart in his 1767 work *Inquiry into the Principles of Political Economy*. Little has changed since then—supply and demand still explains that only if people want something will it be supplied and that it will be supplied in quantity commensurate with how much people want. Inefficiency results when supply does not meet demand. If supply exceeds demand, the excess good can be wasted (or sold for an inefficiently low price); if demand exceeds supply, consumers' needs go unfulfilled and money goes unspent (and eBay reselling flourishes).

PRICE

Price balances supply and demand. High demand (or low supply) equals a high price: only people with serious levels of demand will be willing to pay enough. Low demand (high supply) means low price—also known as the theory of big-box stores.

"You get what you pay for" is proved false by the idea of price. More apt is "you pay the price the market dictates, even if what you get is a piece of junk." Your goal as a geeky spendthrift is to avoid popular, scarce junk, while finding unpopular, common treasures.

MARGINALISM

Like the first two ideas, marginalism is another teeter-totter concept that balances markets for consumer and producer.

Consumer: when cost exceeds what something is worth to you, you stop buying it. Producer: when production cost exceeds the amount you can sell something for, you stop producing it. The proverbial profit to be found near the margin refers to the goal of producers to set a price that is near, but just below what people will pay, thus squeezing every red cent out of the consumer.

FIVE LATIN PHRASES TO SHOUT WHILE RIDING INTO BATTLE

Aut vincere aut mori!
To conquer or die!

Per aspera ad astra!
Through difficulties to the stars!

Aut viam inveniam aut faciam!
I'll either find a way or make one!

Fortes fortuna iuvat!
Fortune favors the brave!

Qui audet adipiscitur!
He who dares, wins!

A SAM LOYD PICTURE PUZZLE

Trace and then cut out the six pieces below. Rearrange them to make the best possible representation of a running horse.

The Pony Puzzle

SIX BAR BETS YOU CAN WIN

1. HOUSE OF STRAWS

Use six straws to create the classic house shape (a rectangular body with two straws forming the roof, all lying flat on the table). Bet that you can make four equal triangles by moving only three straws. Try it! To all but the most creatively freethinking, this is impossible. The trick is to go 3-D—pick up the three straws that make the bottom and sides of the rectangle and replace them so that one end of each straw is rooted in a corner of the triangle with all three moved straws touching above the center of the original triangle, like a tent or teepee—four equal triangles, each the size of the original roof.

2. PAPER MATCH

It is surprising how infrequently this bet's simple trick is discovered. Bet that you can throw a paper match into the air and make it land on its narrow side. This sounds impossible, and it is—until you bend the match!

3. TWO GLASSES I

Submerge two identical glasses in water and place them opening-together, so that when you take them out of the water and set them on the bar it looks as if any bump would separate the glasses, spilling the water out of the top glass. Bet that you can put a dime into the bottom glass without spilling a drop. Impossible, right? Wrong—surface tension makes this very possible. Gently tap the top glass until the glasses separate just enough to slip a dime through the exposed gap into the bottom glass.

4. TRUE MATH GENIUS

This trick will bring a smile to the face of even the most hardened math geek. First, lay matches on a table to form the equation I + II + III = IIII (crossed matches make the plus signs and parallel matches make the equals sign). Challenge your opponent to make this statement true by moving only one match. The trick is to pick up one match from the II, and lay it across the middle match in the III, making the full equation read: I + I + I + I = IIII.

THE phrase *per aspera ad astra* is the official motto of the South African Air Force, the city of Gouda in the Netherlands, Kansas, the Royal Air Force, and Pall Mall cigarettes.

Or move a match from II to IIII, making I + I + III = IIIII.

5. TWO GLASSES II

This time, use shot glasses—fill one with colorful liquor and the other with water. Bet that you can make the liquids in the two glasses trade places without using any additional receptacles including your mouth or other glasses. Here's the trick: cover the liquor shot glass with a driver's license or other plastic card and upend it, stacking it face-together with the water shot glass, which sits upright on a table. Gently remove the card—the heavier liquid will flow into the bottom glass, displacing the lighter water into the top glass.

6. BOTTLE CAP T

Arrange six bottle caps on the bar in the shape of a T, with four caps vertically and the remaining two caps on either side of the uppermost cap. Bet that by moving only one cap, you can create two lines of four. Like the first bar bet, the trick is thinking three-dimensionally—take the lowest cap and put it on top of the highest, middle cap. Both the horizontal and the vertical line now contain four caps!

Feynman's Waitress/ Water Glass Trick

Always the joker, the physicist Richard Feynman described leaving a two-nickel tip (generous at the time) with each nickel in an overturned glass full of water (he placed a card over each glass's top, turned over the cup, and then slowly removed the card). After spilling the first glass, how do you think Feynman's regular waitress retrieved the second nickel? In fact, she spilled the second glass, too, then cleaned up the mess and gave Feynman the stink-eye from then on. However, she *should have* gently slid the glass to the table edge and drained the water into a bowl before retrieving the tip (perhaps then deciding which bodily fluid would best augment Feynman's subsequent dinner orders).

FIVE UNSOLVED PROBLEMS IN MATHEMATICS

1. THE PERFECT CUBOID

A perfect cuboid is one in which the lengths of all edges are integers, the face diagonals are integers, and the body diagonal is also an integer. No example of a perfect cuboid has yet been found, but no one has proven that it can't exist.

2. LYCHREL NUMBERS

Most numbers eventually form a palindrome when the digits are reversed and then added, for example $56 + 65 = 121$ and $57 + 75 = 132 + 231 = 363$. Numbers that don't (for example, 196 and 879) are Lychrel Numbers. The question: do these numbers really never form palindromes? Can you prove it?

3. ODD, WEIRD NUMBERS

Odd, weird mathematicians have been proven to exist, but odd, weird numbers have not. A weird number is one in which the sum of its divisors is more than the number itself and no combination of its divisors adds up to the number (70: $1 + 2 + 5 + 7 + 14 + 35 = 74$). There are *even* weird numbers aplenty (836, 4030, 5830, etc.), but mathematicians are still searching for the first odd one.

4. GOLBACH'S CONJECTURE

In 1742 the mathematician Christian Golbach hypothesized that every even integer greater than two can be expressed as the sum of two prime numbers (12 = 5 + 7, 14 = 3 + 11, etc.). To date, no one has proven him wrong . . . or right.

5. HILBERT'S SIXTEENTH PROBLEM

German mathematician David Hilbert's sixteenth problem involves the search for the upper bound of the number of limit cycles in polynomial vector fields. Understanding the previous sentence is the first step toward solving the problem.

THREE MULTIPLICATION TRICKS YOU CAN DO IN YOUR HEAD

MULTIPLY UP TO 20 × 20

1. For example, take 17 × 13.

2. Place the larger number on top, in your head.

3. Imagine a box, encompassing the 17 and the 3.

4. Add these to make 20.

5. Add a zero to this, to make it 200.

IF the pure quest for mathematical knowledge doesn't make you spring to the chalkboard, what about a million bucks? That's the reward offered by the Clay Mathematics Institute for solving any of the Millennium Prize problems: P versus NP, the Hodge conjecture, the Poincaré conjecture, the Reimann hypothesis, the Yang-Mills existence of mass gap, the Navier-Stokes existence of smoothness (mathematical, not social), and the Birch and Swinnerton-Dyer conjecture. In fact, most people consider Grigori Perelman's solution to the Poincaré adequate, but so far Perelman hasn't pursued the million bucks.

6. Multiply the 7 and the 3 to get 21.

7. Add this to 200 to get the answer: 221.

MULTIPLY ANY TWO-DIGIT NUMBER BY 11

1. For example, take 79.

2. Add a space between the two digits, making 7 9

3. Add 7 and 9 to get 16.

4. Put 16 into the space (remember to carry the tens digit!).

5. The answer is 869.

MULTIPLY BY 9 ON YOUR FINGERS

1. Lay your spread fingers on a table in front of you.

2. To multiply by 4, fold down the fourth finger from the left.

3. Now read your fingers: There are three to the left of the fold and six to the right—this makes 36.

GET RICH (NOT SO) QUICK: COMPOUND INTEREST CALCULATOR

Compound interest grows exponentially, like little boy and girl bunnies that have vastly increasing numbers of bunnies in successive generations (because their twenty bunny children each have twenty children, etc.). How quickly does your money grow? If you simply stick a chunk of change in ye olde money market fund that compounds continuously and earns 6.5 percent a year, you can use the following equation: $P = Ce^{rt}$. P is the future value, C is the initial deposit, e is the very cool transcendental number approximately equal to 2.718, r is the interest rate as a decimal, and t is the number of years it sits. In this scenario, it takes about fifty years for an initial investment of $40,000 to reach a million dollars.

If, instead, you add a constant amount—say $7 a day—the equation gets a bit trickier: $P = C(1 - r)^n + A[(1 + r)^{n+1} - (1 + r)/r]$. To the variables of the previous equation, this adds A for the amount you add per period (your $7) and n for the number of periods (in our example, the number of days). It takes about fifty years of $7-per-day investments to reach a million dollars.

A SAM LOYD ALGEBRA PUZZLE

SAM LOYD'S
PUZZLING SCALES

SINCE THE SCALES NOW BALANCE

AND BALANCE WHEN ARRANGED THIS WAY

THEN HOW MANY MARBLES WILL IT REQUIRE
TO BALANCE WITH THAT TOP?

THREE REAL-WORLD PROBLEMS YOU CAN SOLVE WITH THE PYTHAGOREAN THEOREM ($A^2 + B^2 = C^2$)

1. If a baseball diamond is ninety feet per side, how far does the catcher have to throw the ball to nail a base runner trying to steal second?

2. You're building a ramp from your garage into the back of your truck. The truck is eight feet from the garage and the bed is forty-two inches high. How long should the ramp be?

3. The base of the eight-foot ladder you are using to paint your house needs to be three feet away from the wall to keep you from tipping over. How high will the ladder reach?

THE QUOTABLE YODA

Aristotle, Confucius, Lao-tzu, Nietzsche . . . screw 'em. Geeks know that true knowledge flows from the Force, as channeled by Yoda. The only entity that even comes close is Yogi Berra. (The similarities in name and physical appearance can't be a coincidence.)

• Do or do not . . . there is no try.

• Fear is the path to the dark side. Fear leads to anger. Anger leads to hate. Hate leads to suffering.

• Size matters not. Look at me. Judge me by my size, do you?

• Named must your fear be before banish it, you can.

• Ohhh, great warrior! Wars not make one great!

• Around the survivors, a perimeter create!

NINE AUSTRALIAN ANIMALS MOST PEOPLE THINK ARE FAKE

Echidna

Platypus

Bandicoot

Bilby

Cuscus

Cuttlefish

Tree kangaroo

Numbat

Dasyure

HOW TO BOX-STEP

While it is possible for members of society at large to twist, waltz, foxtrot, and even hump arhythmically while flashing a whiteman's overbite and still eke out a semblance of cool, nothing defines geek like the box-step. Learn it, love it, live it.

It goes a little something like this:

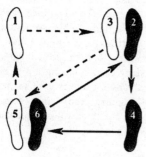

The box-step

FOUR RULES OF LOGIC

1. CHAIN RULE

If A leads to B and B leads to C, then A leads to C. For example, if Tom drinks a triple-shot mochaccino, he will short-circuit his pacemaker. If Tom short-circuits his pacemaker, he will be late for work. Thus, if Tom drinks a triple-shot mochaccino, he will be late for work.

2. CONTRAPOSITIVE (NOTE: NOTHING TO DO WITH BIRTH CONTROL).

If A then B can be rewritten as *if not B, then not A*. For example, if Tom is at work on time, then he has kept himself to a single-shot mochaccino. If Tom has *not* kept himself to a single-shot mochaccino, then Tom will *not* be at work on time.

3. DISJUNCTIVE ADDITION

If any statement is true, we may use the OR operator to add to it another statement, whether the other one is true or false. For example, for Tom, triple-shot espresso drinks are rather psychoactive. Thus, for Tom, triple-shot espresso drinks are

MOST experts believe Australia's unique animals resulted from unholy experiments performed by evil British scientists exported to the early penal colony in the late eighteenth century. For example, the platypus is the combination of a duck and a beaver, and the koala (not pictured) resulted from the coupling of a common raccoon with Danny DeVito.

rather psychoactive OR this morning he has chosen to wear a tutu for unrelated reasons.

4. *MODUS PONENS* (SETTING DOWN A RULE)

In an IF/THEN statement in which the IF is present, the THEN is also present. For example, if Tom drinks triple-shot mochaccinos every morning for the next two weeks, then he will gain an understanding of the sacred/divine heretofore experienced by only the Dalai Lama and Ken Kesey.

HOW TO COUNT CARDS: THE MIT BLACKJACK TEAM

Generally, because a dealer has to keep hitting until he reaches 17, a deck (or multiple decks in a "shoe") that retains its high cards is dangerous for the dealer, as higher cards increase the chances of the dealer going bust. Additionally, a deck retaining its high cards is more likely to offer the score of 21—a blackjack—which pays 1.5 to 1, or odds that favor the bettor.

By the early 1990s—the heyday of the MIT Blackjack Team—this knowledge was old hat; casinos were on the lookout for players drastically adjusting their betting strategy to take advantage of hot decks recognized by counting cards, i.e., playing minimums, then suddenly adjusting bets significantly higher as the shoe got hot. Thus the innovation of the MIT Blackjack Team was not necessarily in counting cards, but in devising a method to maximize their profits without getting caught.

Here's how it worked:

A spotter sat at a table, consistently playing the minimum while counting high and low cards. If the shoe happened to get hot, the spotter continued to play minimums but secretly signaled a "gorilla" who would arrive to bet big and take advantage of the favorable odds. While sometimes the gorillas lost their massive bets, the 2 percent advantage offered by card counting led to big payoffs over time (as well as massive amenity comps the casinos offered the high-rolling gorillas, which the team shared).

HOW TO READ A CHINESE ABACUS

1. Beads pushed toward the centerline are in use.

2. "Earth" beads from below the centerline count for one each; "Heaven" beads from above the centerline count for five each.

3. Each rod (column) is a digit. Thus the number in the picture above is 68170000.

HOW LONG YOU CAN SLEEP ON YOUR ARM WITHOUT LOSING IT

It's two in the morning, and you wake to find that someone has grafted a zombie arm to your left shoulder. You command it to move—no response. You poke it with your right hand—no response. You throw it against the wall—no response. Don't worry: It's extremely unlikely it will remain zombified forever. However, medical literature disagrees as to exactly *how* unlikely. The current guidelines for tourniquet use suggest a one-hour maximum for restricted blood flow to upper extremities and a two-hour maximum for lower extremities, but also admit that the onset and degree of tissue death (necrosis) varies according to patient age and physical condition. Past these thresholds, restricted blood flow can result in nerve damage. (The tingling you feel is your nerves' way of expressing angst—a call to roll over before they get really pissed.) After four hours without blood flow, wet gangrene and the decomposition of tissue due to stagnant blood trapped in extremities can begin. Generally, your arm will not fall off due to gangrene (as might a finger or a toe); rather, if you allow the infection to progress (the timing of which varies widely), you will be forced to have the arm amputated rather than allow the infection to become systemic.

The short answer: It's not good to restrict blood flow for more than about an hour and a half; it's very, very bad to restrict flow for more than four hours.

THE HIGHEST-SCORING WORDS IN SCRABBLE

If you're serious about Scrabble, you know legal words depend on which dictionary you use. (If you're that serious about Scrabble, there is no question you have made a wise purchase with this book. . . .) Official American tournament rules allow words from both the *Official Scrabble Players Dictionary* (OSPD) and *Merriam-Webster's Collegiate Dictionary* (MWCD). These rules make MUZJIKS and POPQUIZ the highest-scoring opening plays at 128 points each, with OXAZEPAM, BEZIQUES, CAZIQUES, MEZQUITS, and MEZQUITE sharing the honors for highest-scoring words in game play at 392 points (across two triple-word scores, with a high-scoring tile on the double-letter score).

However, beware the rogue British dictionary. With a nod toward the continued need for British pedantic dominance, *Chambers Official Scrabble Words* (OSW) includes the word QUIZZIFY, which, despite requiring a blank tile for one of the Zs, roundly thumps anything in American English.

HOW TO BREW YOUR OWN BEER

THE EQUIPMENT

1. A very large boiling pot
2. One large (10-gallon) plastic bucket with lid
3. About six feet of vinyl tubing
4. A hose clamp to fit vinyl tubing

THE INGREDIENTS

1. Malt extract: 40 oz
2. Brewer's yeast: 1 tsp
3. White sugar: 6 cups
4. Water: distilled or sanitized is best; tap will work

THE BREWING PROCESS

1. Sanitize all equipment using household bleach at 1 tbsp/gallon. This is *very* important.
2. Boil 2 gallons of water.
3. Add malt extract and boil uncovered for 20 minutes.
4. Add sugar.
5. Pour mixture into large plastic bucket.
6. Add 2.5–3 gallons of water.
7. Add yeast and stir well.
8. Cap lightly and let sit for 6–10 days.
9. Sample—if sweet, continue fermenting.
10. Bottle: Use hose and clamp to siphon liquid into glass or two-liter bottles. For best results, add a bit of sugar to the bottom of bottles. Don't disturb sediment in large plastic bucket. Cap bottles and let sit for another week (minimum).
11. Drink. Consider predosing victims and self with Pepcid, Immodium, and Advil.

THREE SPELLING RULES YOU LEARNED AND THEN QUICKLY FORGOT

1. I before E, except after C or when it sounds like A, as in *neighbor* or *weigh*.

2. When adding a suffix or verb ending to a word that ends with an E (e.g., *confuse*), drop the E if the suffix or verb ending starts with a vowel (making *confusing*, not *confuseing*).

3. When adding a suffix or verb ending to a word that ends with a Y, if the letter before the Y is a consonant, change the Y to an I (e.g., *geeky, geekiest*); if the letter before the Y is a vowel, keep the Y (e.g., *employ, employable*).

THE TINKERTOY COMPUTER

The term *computer* was first used by Sir Thomas Browne in 1646 A.D., or 329 B.B. (Before Bill) according to the Gatesian calendar. Coincidentally (perhaps?), the year zero of the Gatesian calendar, or 1975 A.D., corresponds to Daniel Hillis's and Brian Silverman's sophomore year at MIT. And it was during this year the two had the retro idea of constructing a nonelectronic computer—specifically, one made of Tinkertoys. Four years later, after a somewhat disappointing version 1.0, the pair started work on what was to become the Great Tinkertoy Computer, which plays a mean game of tic-tac-toe and is now housed at the Mid-America Science Museum.

Here's how it works:

Stored in a forty-eight-row matrix of Tinkertoy "memory spindles" is every possible combi-

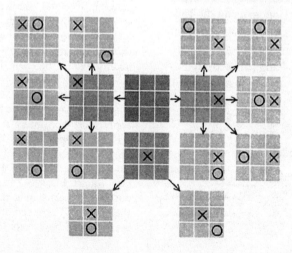

nation of Xs and Os in the game of tic-tac-toe. Based on the current board configuration (as input by a human operator), the computer scrolls through its library of possibilities, and then chooses the best next move. A diagram of the machine's top row is shown on the previous page, which describes all possible responses to a game's first move (all other combinations are actually rotations of the configurations shown). The crux is in the mechanics—Hillis and Silver-man's machine uses a gravity fed "read head," which falls down the front of the machine until coming to rest at the game's current X/O configuration, thus tripping an "output duck" (no kidding, it's a wooden duck), which swings down to point at a number signifying the computer's next move. An operator then inputs the human response to this move, raises the read head, and the Tinkertoy computer is again off and running. Note: you can't beat the robot. It will win.

IN 1998, Cornell University lecturer Michael Coleman and Andy Ruina, director of the Cornell Biomechanics/Robotics lab, took another small step forward in Tinkertoy science, using the toys to construct a robot that mimics the mechanics of walking (the schematics of which are below).

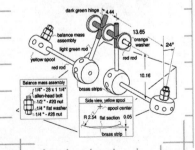

THINGS THAT WILL MAKE YOUR BRAIN HURT I: EINSTEIN'S SPECIAL RELATIVITY

Newton's apple fell from the tree and, after thumping the scientist on the head, fell benignly to the ground. If the same apple fell toward Einstein (and happened to have a little added atomic oomph), it could, according to special relativity, become infinitely massive, flattening not only the unfortunate Einstein as he sat bodhisattvalike beneath the tree, but also Earth itself.

This doesn't mean Newton was wrong, only that his theories apply more accurately to things traveling at speeds that don't approach the speed of light (from slow-moving atomic particles to city transit buses). The crucial postulate of Einstein's theory is the idea that the speed of light is measured to be *exactly the same* no matter the motion of the observer. If you think about it, this is a little weird: usually speed *does* depend on the motion of the observer. If you are driving down the highway, you will measure the relative speed of a bicyclist very differently than would a kid sitting at a roadside lemonade stand. Don't worry—unless you, the bicyclist, or the kid is traveling near the speed of light, you can leave your intuitive understanding of this situation intact.

With the speed of light remaining constant ($c = 3 \times 10^8$ m/s), other terms in equations that include c must—sometimes counterintuitively—be variable. For example, Einstein's now-accepted interpretation of the Lorentz transformation proves that time is variable, meaning that if a very, very fast spaceship returned to Earth, the clocks on the ship would lag behind the time shown on Big Ben. Special relativity also relates mass and energy as variables ($E = mc^2$), which explains nuclear power and explosions. Because c is a huge constant—especially c *squared*—there's a whole lot of energy trapped in a little bit of mass. When scientists found a way to liberate this energy, things went boom.

PATENT YOUR INVENTION IN SIX EASY STEPS (!)

1. Make sure you own the idea. Are you a professor or student? Did your job inspire this idea? Better hope your million-dollar widget has nothing to do with your university or employer. Check with your institution's higher-ups before proceeding. If your idea is any good, they will certainly get involved at some point.

2. Make sure the idea is unique. It would be a shame to invest time and money only to later find that, in fact, the mechanical backscratcher already exists. Search the U.S. Patent and Trade Office (www.uspto.gov) and Delphion (www.delphion.com). Later, you will likely hire a patent attorney to formalize this search for you.

3. Document your idea in writing. First write a description of your idea and then, throughout the process, keep all correspondence, illustrations, pictures, etc. Keep sales receipts or anything else that documents your progress. If you like, file these documents with the U.S. Patent and Trade Office under their Disclosure Document Program. Otherwise, hide your invention as if it were a CIA list of covert operatives.

4. "Reduce to practice." In order to get a patent, your invention has to work. Build and test your idea or otherwise prove it will work (maybe in a lab setting).

5. If you haven't hired a patent attorney, do it now. He or she will determine, once and for all, whether your idea is new and unique or whether it's already floating around out there in the ether.

6. Finally, file for a patent (www.uspto.gov). The application includes three parts: a written description of the invention, an illustration, and a rather hefty filing fee.

THE WORLD'S BEST CORNFIELD AND HEDGE MAZES

The evolution of the life-size maze neatly parallels the widely held stereotype of the interplay of cultural knowledge between Europe and the United States. Specifically, most hedge mazes—and certainly the oldest—are European; Americans imported the idea, enlarged and mass produced it in the form of a patchwork of cornfield mazes, invented and refined the method of turning a buck on the idea (tourism!), and exported the retooled (and popularized) life-size maze back to Europe, especially the United Kingdom, where the maize maze craze now supports a thriving industry of designers and practitioners.

Here is a list of the world's best mazes:

HAMPTON COURT PALACE, SURREY, UK

This is the oldest known hedge maze, designed and planted by the royal gardeners of King William III of England between 1689 and 1695. While it is historically significant, it covers only a scant half acre—a good stop for the history buff, not the thrill seeker.

COOL PUMPKIN PATCH AND CORN MAZE, DIXON, CALIFORNIA

At 40 acres of gut-busting fun, fun, fun, Dixon's cornfield maze was listed in the 2007 Guinness Book of World Records as the world's largest. (Just off I-80! Now with a video on YouTube!)

PEACE MAZE, CASTLEWELLAN FOREST PARK, COUNTY DOWN, NORTHERN IRELAND

The world's largest permanent hedge maze takes up 2.7 acres and uses more than 6,000 yew trees. Integral in the design and planting were the efforts of more than four thousand schoolchildren. The construction of the maze followed 1998's Good Friday Agreement.

PINEAPPLE GARDEN MAZE, DOLE PLANTATION, HAWAII

A 1.7-mile trail through more than 11,400 colorful Hawaiian plants. In 2001, it was the world's biggest. At Dole, there is little in the way of aloha for residents of Dixon, California, who (as described above) eclipsed their record.

CASTLE RUURLO, NETHERLANDS

We can only assume the publicists of the maze at Castle Ruurlo had to work with the language a bit to maintain this maze's mystique. Thus, it is "the oldest, largest permanent hedge maze in Europe" meaning that in 1881, when it was planted, it was a big deal.

LONGLEAT HEDGE MAZE

This is the UK hedge maze at its best: almost 1.5 acres and 1.7 miles of trails through 16,000 English yews.

CHÂTEAU DE THOIRY, FRANCE

This is the largest hedge maze in France. The online description asks (in a thick French accent), "Will you be able to piece [sic] its mysteries?"

THE MAZE AT SCHÖNBRUNN, VIENNA, AUSTRIA

This maze was reconstructed in 1998 based, whenever possible, on the layout of an earlier incarnation of it, which existed from 1698 to 1740. With 1.7 miles of devious trails, be sure to wear athletic shoes and bring a lunch. The palace itself sees over 1.5 million visitors annually.

SEVEN MATERIALS-SCIENCE BLUNDERS THAT BECAME EVERYDAY PRODUCTS

Louis Pasteur said, "Fortune favors the prepared mind," and nowhere is this truer than the field of invention, in which today a team of materials scientists may stand around a vat of mysterious precipitate and tomorrow declare it the substance that will forever revolutionize the fart can.

SUPER GLUE

Contrary to popular belief, Super Glue was not originally used to seal cuts on the battlefield; that application came later. First, Harry Coover (who even in 1942 *must* have been teased for his name) stumbled onto the substance while trying to develop a clear plastic for use in gunsights.

VULCANIZED RUBBER

In 1839, Charles Goodyear spilled rubber, sulfur, and white lead onto a stove. Voilà: the hearty rubber instrumental in the development of automobile tires.

MAUVE

In 1856, a novice chemist named William Henry Perkins tried to synthesize quinine, instead (after much exploratory futzing) stumbling onto a color he named *mauve*. The synthetic dye industry was born.

SILLY PUTTY

In the early 1940s, the war effort required massive quantities of rubber. Scientists at General Electric thought it would be swell if they could synthesize it. Instead, Silly Putty was born. Oh, *applesauce*, as they say.

TEFLON

In 1938, while searching for a new type of Freon, the geekily onomatopoetic Roy Plunkett stumbled onto Teflon.

SCOTCHGARD

Working at 3M in 1953, a lab assistant spilled experimental rubber on Patsy Sherman's shoes. Despite scrubbing with soap and water, and then with alcohol, the gunk wouldn't come out. While said lab assistant did not help his chances of getting a date with the newly deshoed Sherman, Scotchgard was born.

SAFETY GLASS

In 1908, Jacques Brandenberger knocked a glass flask off his desk. Inside the flask was the evaporated film of a liquid plastic. Instead of shattering across the floor, the glass shards were held together by the film. The discovery proved hugely useful for World War I gas mask lenses and later for automobile windshields.

SERENDIPITOUS INVENTIONS OUTSIDE MATERIALS SCIENCE

Radar, polyethylene, the microwave oven, X-ray machines, Velcro, cellophane, Viagra, artificial sweeteners, rayon, potato chips, the popsicle, penicillin, Post-it notes, LSD.

GREAT MOMENTS IN PSEUDOSCIENCE

DEREK OGILVIE: BABY TELEPATHIST

Is your baby inconsolable? Do you live in Scotland? If so, Derek Ogilvie might be your answer. A failed bar owner, Ogilvie now promotes himself as a "professional medium and baby telepathist." He discovered his ability to commune with the incommunicable after a chat over tea with a recently departed next-door neighbor. According to his website, Mr. Ogilvie's favorite color is blue, and he would like to be an elephant in the next life.

A FLAT EARTH

"You can't orbit a flat earth," says Charles K. Johnson, president of the Flat Earth Research Society. "The Space Shuttle is a joke—and a very ludicrous joke." And, according to Johnson, at the South Pole lies an insurmountable wall of ice, ringing the disk-shaped world. You, too, can join the Flat Earth Society, but only after signing a promise never to defame it.

HUMANS FROM ALIENS

A long time ago in a galaxy not so far away, intelligent extraterrestrials visited a small, blue planet, the third from a G2V star later named the sun. Depending on whom you believe, the human population of this planet descended from these extraterrestrials, or said extraterrestrials thoroughly freaked out the existing protohumans to the point of being immortalized in cave paintings and such. Think this is straight kooksville? Carl Sagan gave it some brain space.

USELESS STATS OF FAMOUS PIRATES

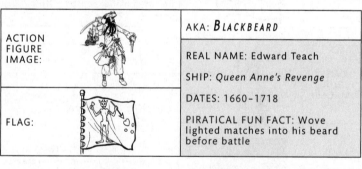

ACTION FIGURE IMAGE:		AKA: *BLACKBEARD*
		REAL NAME: Edward Teach
		SHIP: *Queen Anne's Revenge*
FLAG:		DATES: 1660–1718
		PIRATICAL FUN FACT: Wove lighted matches into his beard before battle

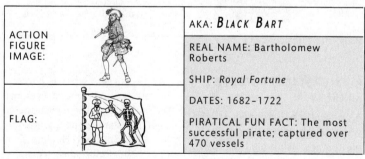

ACTION FIGURE IMAGE:		AKA: *BLACK BART*
		REAL NAME: Bartholomew Roberts
		SHIP: *Royal Fortune*
FLAG:		DATES: 1682–1722
		PIRATICAL FUN FACT: The most successful pirate; captured over 470 vessels

ACTION FIGURE IMAGE:	AKA: *NO AKA*
	REAL NAME: Mary Read
	SHIP: *The Treasure*
	DATES: 1690–1721
FLAG: None	PIRATICAL FUN FACT: Lived as a man until outed by fellow female pirate Anne Bonny

ACTION FIGURE IMAGE:	AKA: *CALICO JACK*
	REAL NAME: Jack Rackham
	SHIP: *The Treasure*
FLAG:	DATES: 1682–1720
	PIRATICAL FUN FACT: Employed both Mary Read and the equally infamous (and female) Anne Bonny, until executed with his crew in Jamaica

ACTION FIGURE IMAGE:	AKA: *NO AKA*
	REAL NAME: Jean Lafitte
	SHIP: *The Republican*
	DATES: 1776–1854
FLAG: A solid, blood-red flag	PIRATICAL FUN FACT: The 3,000 men of his "kingdom of Barataria" helped Andrew Jackson repel the British in the Battle of New Orleans

ALEX ORBITO'S PSYCHIC SURGERY

A patient lies stripped to the waist on an operating table. Orbito lunges, using his bare hands to rip a small hole in the patient's abdomen. There's little blood, but Orbito extracts what is surely a massive tumor. It works even better underneath the eleven-meter-high glass-and-stone pyramid of his Asia Spiritual Healing Center in the Philippines (currently closed due to termite damage). In

2005, Alex Orbito was arrested in Canada for fraud, but the case was dismissed. Orbito also cures blindness by extracting, cleaning, and reinserting eyeballs.

SYLVIA BROWNE SAYS:

In heaven, it is 78 degrees all the time, and you can build your house wherever you like, as long as it doesn't obstruct the view. The frequent *Larry King Live* and *Montel Williams* guest also has a string of forty churches across the United States, each of which preaches her doctrine of *Novus Spiritus* and pays Ms. Browne a licensing fee. Dumb like a fox?

PHRENOLOGY

No discussion of pseudoscience is complete without phrenology—the idea that skull bumps hold clues to a patient's personality and potential criminality.

THE BASICS OF EXTRATERRESTRIAL DETECTION

Most scientists agree that our best bet of discovering alien intelligence is "listening" to the sky, using the various dishes and dish arrays constructed for this purpose. One such listening system is Project Phoenix, which uses the massive radiotelescope at Arecibo, Puerto Rico, to scan the sky for intelligent, extraterrestrial radio signals. A new program

THINGS WE SHOOT AT ALIENS

We also broadcast signals *into* the sky, the most famous of which was the Arecibo broadcast of 1974. In this broadcast, we zapped a coded message toward star cluster M13, nearly 21,000 light years away. The message contained coded information about our solar system, DNA, and human physiology. We should expect a reply around the year 43,974 A.D. Interestingly, this is the same year in which current analysis predicts NASA will send a manned mission to Mars. Coincidence?

meant to update Phoenix is now under way: the Allen Telescope Array (thank you Paul Allen). The first 42 antennas went live on October 11, 2007. When completed, the ATA will consist of 350 six-meter dishes. It will be very, very cool.

A SAM LOYD PICTURE PUZZLE

Cut the board into the fewest number of pieces that will fit together to form a perfect square.

TEN SPORTS REQUIRING ALMOST NO PHYSICAL EXERTION

The crux of this question is the definition of the word *sport*. Does billiards count? How about golf? This list defines *sport* as something more than a game of skill— something requiring at least a minor physical component, that component being more than hand-eye coordination. Granted, this allows a somewhat blurry line, but what are you gonna do?

1. Casting: like fishing but without all the strenuous reeling in of struggling aquatic creatures.

2. Lawn bowling: like bowling but without the heavy ball and with tea instead of beer.

3. Skydiving: once you throw yourself out of the airplane, gravity will do the rest.

4. Sport stacking: the timed stacking and unstacking of empty plastic cups. (This is real.)

5. NASCAR: a popular NASCAR e-zine states, "The NASCAR driver's physical conditioning is very similar to athletes in other sports except different areas are built up." For an athlete who spends the sport's duration sitting on a rather unpadded seat, one can only imagine what these built-up areas must be.

6. Curling: like bocce, only much, much colder.

7. Skijoring: while cross-country skiing is one of the most physically demanding sports, in the refinement known as skijoring, competitors on skis strap themselves to a horse or a team of dogs, while enjoying the combined effects of too much alcohol and too little common sense.

8. Yachting: OK, you may need to operate a winch. But it's not like you're paddling.

9. High Speed Telegraphy: decoding Morse code can lead to carpal tunnel syndrome, implying a level of physical exertion and thus making this a valid sport per the listed rules.

10. Cricket: slower than baseball. Enough said.

FOUR OF HISTORY'S GREATEST HEISTS

THE BRINKS-MAT BULLION HEIST

At 6:30 on the morning of November 26, 1983, six men posing as security guards entered the Brinks-Mat warehouse near London's Heathrow Airport. After overpowering the real guards, dousing them with gasoline to generate loose tongues, and disabling the vault's advanced electronic security systems, the gang opened the vault door to find—instead of the cash they expected—over 26 million pounds sterling in gold bullion. The flexible thieves commandeered the vault's forklift to load their getaway van and, two hours later, made a clean escape.

Unfortunately, the heist's masterminds didn't necessarily deserve the "master" portion of their title. They were apprehended a couple weeks later inside a grand estate, paid for in cash and guarded by two Rottweilers responding to names *Brinks* and *Mat*.

THE GREAT TRAIN ROBBERY

On August 8, 1963, the Glasgow-to-London mail train met an unexpected red light and rolled to a stop. Just as the train's fireman discovered that the cables of the emergency call box had been cut, a gang of twelve men jumped from the ditch. Using nothing more deadly than fists and one quick whack with a crowbar, the gang overpowered everyone on the train and drove off with more than 2.5 million pounds in booty. Unfortunately, the gang had left fingerprints all over the nearby farmhouse they had purchased as a hideout, and soon the jig was—as they say—up. The aftermath of the robbery is almost as good as the crime itself, involving slick trial moves resulting in acquittal for one of the gang, anonymity of the remaining gang members, known only as numbers one, two, and three, and a jail escape followed by plastic surgery that allowed one member to stay hidden in Brazil until giving himself up in 2001.

ART thefts are all the rage. In addition to the *Mona Lisa*, the following paintings have been—at one time or another—jacked: Panels from the Ghent Altarpiece, three paintings by Georgia O'Keeffe, Vermeer's *The Concert*, Rembrandt's *The Storm on the Sea of Galilee*, Mather Brown's *Thomas Jefferson*, Edvard Munch's *The Scream*, *Madonna*, and *Blue Dress*, various works by Gainsborough, Brueghel, Renoir, Picasso, Monet, Cassatt, Pissarro, Henry Moore, and many others. Clocking in at four thefts since 1966, Rembrandt's *Jacob de Gheyn III* is the world's most stolen piece of art.

SIXTEEN ESOTERIC TEXT MESSAGE ABBREVIATIONS

TXT	MEANING
2G2BT	Too good to be true
^5	High five
AYSOS	Are you stupid or something?
BIBO	Beer in, beer out
CMAP	Cover my ass, partner
EBKAC	Error between keyboard and chair
GDR	Grinning, ducking, and running
IMAO	In my arrogant opinion
MTFBWU	May the Force be with you
MUAH	Multiple, unsuccessful attempts at humor
NIFOC	Naked in front of computer
SWMBO	She who must be obeyed
WISP	Winning is so pleasurable
YRYOCC	You are running your own cuckoo clock

THE *MONA LISA* THEFT

In 1911, Vincenzo Perugia hid in the Louvre after it closed, and then, in the middle of the night, walked off with the *Mona Lisa*. After a two-year search that included questioning Pablo Picasso and arresting one of Picasso's friends, who was innocent, the police still had no leads. That is, until Vincenzo got greedy. He was arrested after trying to sell the painting to a gallery in Florence. Vincenzo claimed that, as an Italian patriot, he had stolen the famous painting to return it to its rightful home in Italy.

BANCO CENTRAL BURGLARY: BRAZIL

Truckloads of soil frequently left the new landscaping company that was located near Brazil's Banco Central. Neighbors had no idea this supply of soil came from beneath the business itself—specifically from a 256-foot tunnel that stretched underneath two city blocks from the landscape company to the vault of the bank. On the weekend of August 6–7, 2005, burglars tunneled the last 3.6 feet, broke through steel-reinforced concrete, and carried off over $70 million in loot. A couple of the thieves have been caught, a few have turned up dead, but many remain at large.

TÊTE DE VEAU: A RECIPE FOR A TRULY DISTURBED FRENCH FOOD

The French have long been famous for their cuisine. This, despite serving cow tongue, camel's feet, and steak tartare cheval (raw horse meat). But who are we—living in the country of Rocky Mountain oysters and SPAM—to judge? Caution: Henry Harris, an English chef who serves tête de veau at his restaurant, Racine, in Knightsbridge, encourages aspirant chefs to "allow [tête de veau] to cool completely, otherwise it will explode."

INGREDIENTS	PROCEDURE
1. A calf's head, sliced along the central median plane; skin, hair, and fat removed	**1.** Secure head and vegetables in a cooking net.
2. Vegetables (various).	**2.** Poach on low heat for five hours or until inserted meat thermometer meets no resistance. For reasons that should be obvious, do not undercook.
3. Salt, pepper to taste.	**3.** Slice into thick pieces and top with portion of calf's brain and (optionally) a mustard-based sauce. Serve with broth.

TWO LIKELY OPTIONS FOR A SECOND EARTH

	GLIESE 581 C	*55 CANCRI F*
YEAR	13 days	260 days
COMPARABLE SIZE	1.5 times Earth	Saturn
CONSTELLATION	Libra	Cancer
DISTANCE	20.4 light-years	41 light-years
WATER	With a surface temperature estimated at between 0 and 40°C, this planet could hold liquid water	The planet itself is likely a gas giant, but as it lies within the "habitable zone," any moon could hold liquid
POTENTIAL FOR LIFE (ACCORDING TO PATRONS OF DARGAN'S IRISH PUB AND RESTAURANT, VENTURA, CA, 11/9/07)	Definite: Though residents of Gliese 581 c are likely a bit stockier than earthlings, as the planet's gravity is approximately 22 m/s² compared to Earth's 9.8 m/s²	Unlikely: Who would want to live on a gas giant? Though probable on orbiting moon.

THINGS THAT WILL MAKE YOUR BRAIN HURT II: EINSTEIN'S GENERAL RELATIVITY

Back to Newton: his apple fell due to the force of gravitational pull exerted by Earth (yes, the apple had a little gravitational pull, too, but not much because it wasn't a very big apple). Einstein wondered *what* exactly created this pull. Specifically, in the vacuum of space, what transmitted this pull in the absence of any "stuff" to convey the information of force? (Very basically, think of force like sound waves, needing to travel *through* something.)

So, instead of a sucking force, Einstein's theory of general rela-

tivity proposed that stars, planets, and very large apples warp the fabric of space-time, so that anything nearby rolls toward them like pennies in the big donation funnel that sits in the lobby of your local publicly funded science museum. (Picture it—this is actually a very close analogy.)

WHAT RICHARD FEYNMAN KNEW ABOUT SAFECRACKING

While as yet unproven, a promising theorem in particle physics states that physicists are people, too. (If you prick them, the theorem goes, they are likely to bleed, etc.) So far, the strongest support for this idea is the anecdotal evidence of Richard Feynman, a Nobel Prize–winning physicist who was almost certainly a person. Feynman's reputation for humanizing buffoonery included his ability to open supposedly secure safes—a skill he honed while working on the atom bomb at Los Alamos during World War II.

First, Feynman noticed that safe dials were not as precise as they might be. A combination might include the number 42, but Feynman found that the adjoining numbers 40, 41, 43, and 44 also worked. This narrowed the total possibilities from nearly 1,000,000 (100^3) to only 8,000 (20^3). With practice, Feynman found that he could try 400 combinations in thirty minutes, so even in the unlikely case of opening the safe on the last possible permutation, it could take a maximum of only ten hours. Still, who has ten hours to spare when also racing Nazi Germany into the atomic age?

If Feynman could define one of a combination's three numbers, then opening the lock could take him only a maximum of half an hour (20^2 combinations). To do this, when in a colleague's office with the safe open, Feynman would pretend to idly play with the lock. In fact, he found that a lock resets itself only after spinning past the first number in its combination. So Feynman would turn the combination lock, going one number further each time until the lock clicked shut, at which point

he would know he had found the combination's first number. Voilà—half an hour, tops.

In fact, it usually took much less time, as Feynman first tried psychologically likely numbers—the factory preset, birthdays, phone numbers, or, most common at Los Alamos, a snippet of the number pi.

THE CLASSES REQUIRED FOR MIT'S B.A. IN ELECTRICAL ENGINEERING AND COMPUTER SCIENCE

In addition to core classes in science, math, humanities, and open-ended electives, classes from the following lists are required. One can only assume that comprehending the class description is a prerequisite.

FOUR OF THE FOLLOWING:

6.002—**Circuits and Electronics:** Fundamentals of the lumped circuit abstraction.

6.003—**Signals and Systems:** Fundamentals of signal and system analysis.

6.004—**Computation Structures:** Introduces architecture of digital systems.

6.005—**Principles of Software Development:** Topics include key paradigms and design patterns, the role of interfaces and specification in achieving modularity and decoupling, reasoning about code using invariants, etc.

6.006—Introduction to Algorithms: Introduction to mathematical modeling of computational problems, etc.

6.007—Applied Electromagnetics: Photons and their interaction with matter in detectors, sources, optical fibers, and other devices and communication systems.

AND THREE OF THE FOLLOWING:

6.011—Introduction to Communication, Control, and Signal Processing: Input-output and state-space models of linear systems driven by deterministic and random signals, etc.

6.012—Microelectric Devices and Circuits: Microelectronic devices modeling, and basic microelectronic circuit analysis and design.

6.013—Electromagnetics and Applications: Electromagnetic phenomena are explored in modern applications.

6.021J—Quantitative Physiology: Principles of mass transport and electrical signal generation for biological membranes, cells, and tissues.

IN this picture, the Cassini space probe fires radio signals through a conceptualized matrix showing Einstein's general relativity. Researchers measured the time the signal took to travel from the space probe to Earth. It was delayed as predicted by general relativity—the path was warped and thus extended because of the sun's gravitational bending of space-time.

6.033—Computer System Engineering: Techniques for controlling complexity; strong modularity using client-server design, operating systems, etc.

6.034—Artificial Intelligence: Applications of rule chaining, heuristic search, constraint propagation, constrained search, inheritance, etc.

6.046—Design and Analysis of Algorithms: Topics include sorting; search trees, heaps, and hashing; divide-and-conquer; dynamic programming; greedy algorithms; amortized analysis; graph algorithms; and shortest paths.

FIVE CLASSIC MacGYVER HACKS

Episode 1.04—"The Gauntlet": To create a distraction, MacGyver ties firecrackers to the inside of a church bell, attaches a lit candle to the bell's clapper, and uses rope to hold the bell raised to the side. When another candle burns through the rope, the bell is released and the candle on the clapper swings to ignite the firecrackers.

Episode 2.01—"The Human Factor": To re-create the fingerprint of a person who recently used an electronic hand-scan machine, MacGyver coats the scanner with a thick layer of plaster dust. When he gently blows away the dust, some remains stuck to the previous operator's sweat print. MacGyver then presses the dust print with his jacket: hand-scan verified.

Episode 2.07—"The Road Not Taken": To evade jungle pursuers, MacGyver creates a time-release catapult. He bends four small trees to the ground and secures them using a thin vine. Then he uses his friend's rosary to concentrate sunlight, which slowly burns through the vine. When released, the trees spring up, throwing rocks.

Episode 3.10—"Blow Out": When MacGyver stumbles onto a robbery in progress at the local grocery store, he mixes tear gas from cayenne pepper, vinegar, and baking soda—all this inside a hot water bottle, which pressurizes like a balloon as the vinegar and baking soda react. When MacGyver punches a hole in the rubber water bottle, it spews pepper spray.

Episode 4.14—"Gold Rush": MacGyver listens to an old phonograph record by attaching a pin to the end of a paper cone and holding the pin gently against the record, which he rotates on a cylinder.

SIX PEOPLE WHOSE OBITUARIES WERE PUBLISHED BEFORE THEIR DEATHS

PERSON	PUBLISHED	DEATH	NOTES
Alice Cooper	November 1972: *Meloday Maker*	Pending	A concert review in the form of an obit fooled readers. Cooper responded, "I'm alive and drunk as usual."
Joe DiMaggio	January 1999: NBC news ticker	March 8, 1999	DiMaggio watched the report of his death scroll across the bottom of the NBC broadcast.
Bob Hope	June 5, 1998: AP website	July 27, 2003	After seeing the AP article, congressman Bob Stump announced Hope's death on the floor of the U.S. House of Representatives. "He's happily having his breakfast," responded Hope's daughter.
Abe Vigoda	1982: *People* magazine	Pending	Abe then posed for a photo, sitting up in a coffin while holding the offending *People* magazine. Vigoda's current status (dead/alive) can be found at abevigoda.com.
Rudyard Kipling	Unattributed magazine	January 18, 1936	Responded in a letter: "I've just read that I am dead. Don't forget to delete me from your list of subscribers."
Paul McCartney	1966: Call in to WKNR-FM in Detroit	Pending?	As proved by the many clues hidden in Beatles songs (played backward) Paul did, in fact, die in 1966 and was replaced by a look-alike, perhaps an android.

WWF STARS OF THE 1980S

If "geek" is one end of a socio-cultural spectrum, then certainly the other end is WWF. Why then is WWF (now WWE) so inherently fascinating to us geeks? Maybe it's the expression by wrestlers of the geek's repressed id; more likely, it has something to do with steroidal meatheads taking themselves oh-so-seriously while clad in neon Lycra skimpy enough to make even a Frenchman blush.

HULK HOGAN

Hulk's Three Demandments: training, say your prayers, eat your vitamins.

JUNKYARD DOG

JYD entered the ring to Queen's "Another One Bites the Dust," wearing a collar and chain, with THUMP printed on his wrestling trunks.

CAPTAIN LOU ALBANO

Albano appeared in Cyndi Lauper's "Girls Just Wanna Have Fun" video.

ANDRÉ THE GIANT

7'4", 540 lbs—film appearances included *Conan the Destroyer* and *The Princess Bride*.

WENDI RICHTER

After a supposed contract dispute with WWF owner Vince McMahon, Richter lost her women's title to the Fabulous Moolah on a too quick three count and never wrestled in the WWF again.

SUPERFLY JIMMY SNUKA

Introduced the high-fly style to professional wrestling.

HILLBILLY JIM

In 2005, Hillbilly Jim was hired to DJ country music and Southern rock on Sirius Satellite Radio in a program called *Hillbilly Jim's Moonshine Matinee*.

TITO SANTANA

Tito's finishing move was known variously as the flying forearm smash, the Mexican hammer, the flying burrito, and the flying jalapeño.

INTERNET POKER: BY THE NUMBERS

No matter what you read in the various published strategy guides and online chat rooms about pot odds, implied odds, reverse implied odds, and pot equity, there is no mathematically definite strategy for poker played in casinos. Because the best poker is unpredictable and in casinos you are likely to experience the best poker, all decisions are eventually somewhat intuitive. (Like the stock market, you can't figure out

ROWDY RODDY PIPER
In early *Piper's Pit* segments, Rowdy Roddy ended almost every interview with a brawl.

THE IRON SHEIK
Also a bodyguard for the Shah of Iran.

NIKOLAI VOLKOFF
Currently works as a code enforcement officer in Baltimore County, Maryland.

THE FABULOUS MOOLAH
In 1984, Moolah lost the women's world title she had held for almost 30 years to Wendy Richter.

BIG JOHN STUDD
BYOS: Big John Studd brought his own stretcher to the ring, usually for his opponents.

Dan Harrington. If you could, you could beat him. Note: you can't.)

However, online poker—for better or for worse—is different. The sheer volume of online players (and the relatively low investment of time and money needed to play online) means that Internet games tend to be fast and loose. Your opponents can't be trusted to fold when you bluff, and frequently—because your opponents are idiots—you can trust very little "information" gathered in the course of a hand.

Thus, the best strategy is to play tight, mathematically precise poker, while seeing as many hands per hour as possible in order to make this slow-'n'-steady strategy pay a decent hourly wage. A good, tight player will earn around $10 per every 100 hands of low-limit poker. In a casino that deals 30 hands per hour, this translates into $3.33 an hour. You would be better off working at Starbucks, where at least you get health benefits. But online poker sites frequently deal upwards of 60 hands per hour, immediately bumping the hourly wage of a solid, no-frills player up to $6. Now find a site that allows you to play multiple tables at once. If you're playing six fast tables simultaneously, you're seeing 360 hands per hour, and—if you can avoid going completely insane—you can make somewhere in the neighborhood of $36 an hour.

FINGER AMPUTATION DATA

A 2001 study by the National Center for Injury Prevention and Control (NCIPC) estimated that nearly 21,430 fingers are amputated annually due to nonoccupational injuries. This translates into almost exactly a mile of disembodied finger, laid end to end. The two populations most at risk for injuries that result in finger amputation are children below the age of four (slammed doors) and men between the ages of forty-five and sixty-five (power tools, specifically the table saw). The authors of the NCIPC study suggest teaching young children to open doors that have slammed on their finger(s) before attempting to remove any trapped body part in order to avoid ripping loose said body part(s).

THE BEST COLLECTIBLES FOR INVESTMENT PURPOSES

The value of a collectible is based mostly on rarity and appeal—it makes sense that if something is rare and people want it, it will cost a lot to get it (see "The Three Basic Principles of Economics," page 12). The question is, what creates appeal? If, in the case of collectibles, this is simply nostalgia, then what makes an original Star Wars action figure more nostalgic than, say, a 1984 Hot Wheels car? (OK, bad example. We all *know* that an original Star Wars action figure is worth more than its weight in diamonds.)

The tough news is that collectibles don't tend to return at rates comparable to a stock market index fund—that is, if you are buying collectibles that are already on the market. A collectible best-case scenario is to either stumble onto established items at below market value (that Honus Wagner card from your grandfather's boyhood time capsule) or find items whose value is not yet recognized (the garage sale table with the simply elegant, handhewn dovetail joints that bespeak its Shaker origins).

Generally, you can count on coins, stamps, and antiques to hold market value (due to established track records), while the value of sports cards, action figures, comic books, and other nostalgia can fluctuate wildly. As with any investment, pick your poison—high risk, high reward, or low risk, low reward.

NINE SHADOW PUPPETS YOU CAN MAKE WITH YOUR HANDS

Goose Prisoner

Deer

Grandpapa

Bunny

Bird in Flight

Goat

Dog Toby

Elephant

Pig

BEWARE, MLB HURLERS: TED WILLIAMS MAY BE BACK

The theory of human preservation via cryogenics states that if temperature is reduced quickly to that of liquid nitrogen (−196°F) or below, then water in human tissue doesn't have time to form the destructively sharp crystalline structure associated with traditional freezing. Instead, water effectively stops in place, in a state of suspended animation (others posit that this also requires suspended disbelief). Additionally, some cryogenic institutes replace a good portion of the brain's water with cryoprotectant liquids like those found in some Arctic animals.

While the reports of Walt Disney's cryopreservation are simple urban myth, it is actual 100 percent fact that when Ted Williams died in 2002, his head was removed and frozen. Potentially, when technology catches up with science fiction, the Splendid Splinter will return to unleash his 521 career home runs and .344 lifetime batting average on unsuspecting future pitchers. Note to pitchers: be on the lookout for Frankensteinesque stitches ringing the neck.

HOMOPHONES, HOMOPHENES, HOMOGRAPHS, HOMONYMS, AND HETERONYMS

Can you match the following definitions to the correct terms listed in this section's title?

• Words with identical spellings but different pronunciations and meanings. For example, *close* and *present* both have multiple pronunciations and meanings.

• Words that share spelling and pronunciation, but differ in meaning. For example, *stalk, bear,* and *left* all have multiple meanings.

• Words or phrases that look the same to lip readers. For example, *olive juice* and *I love you,* or *vacuum* and *fuck you.*

IN 2007, Paris Hilton bought shares in the Cryogenics Institute, hoping to preserve herself along with her pets, the Chihuahua Tinkerbell and the Yorkshire terrier Cinderella.

- Words pronounced the same, but differing in meaning. For example, *two* and *too*, or *know* and *no*.

- A type of homonym (the preceding phrase offers the chance for some old-school deductive reasoning) in which spelling is the same, pronunciation may or may not be the same, and meaning differs. For example, *bass, contract, incense,* and *wound* all have multiple pronunciations and meanings.

A DIAGRAM OF THE CAFFEINE MOLECULE

Oh sweet, sweet $C_8H_{10}N_4O_2$, you psychoactive little argonaut! Come, cross the blood-brain barrier, antagonize our adenosine receptors, and jack our dopamine!

A SAM LOYD LOGIC PUZZLE

On each signed section of track, there is space for only one car.
How will the trains pass?

GREAT MOMENTS IN MORK & MINDY

Episode 38: Mork becomes a cheerleader for the Denver Broncos.

Episode 47: Unless he can find someone to marry, Mork may be deported!

Episode 53: The Elder, an Orkan whose name is pronounced by blowing a raspberry, converts Mindy's attic into a typical Orkan home to help Mork regain his Orkan ways.

Episode 67: Mork learns the ways of love from a swinger named T.N.T. and turns into a party animal.

Episode 77: Mork gives birth to an egg from his navel. It hatches to reveal a fully grown man (because Orkans age backward): Jonathan Winters.

Episodes 91–93: Mork and Mindy meet the evil alien Kalink, who bombs their apartment. Hilarity ensues. Fin.

THE TOOLS OF THE WORLD'S LARGEST SWISS ARMY KNIFE

Two pounds, eleven ounces, 8.75 inches wide. Notice the telescopic pointer, laser pointer, and golf divot repair tool.

2.5" 60% serrated locking blade

Adjustable pliers with wire crimper and cutter

Spring-loaded, locking needle-nose pliers with wire cutter

Phillips-head screwdriver bit 1

Flat-head screwdriver bit, 0.6 mm × 4.0 mm

Double-cut wood saw with ruler (in./cm)

Removable 4 mm curved Allen wrench with Phillips-head screwdriver

Universal wrench

Metal saw, metal file

Cupped cigar cutter with double-honed edges

Snap shackle

Mineral crystal magnifier with precision screwdriver

Flashlight

Micro tool adapter

Fine fork for watch-spring bars

Round needle file

Multipurpose screwdriver

Phillips-head screwdriver
bit 2

2.5" clip-point blade

Patented locking screwdriver,
cap lifter, can opener

Micro scraper, curved

Screwdriver bit, 1.2 mm

Removable screwdriver bit
holder

Reamer/awl

Toothpick

Key ring

Double-cut wood saw

Nail file, nail cleaner

Removable screwdriver bit
adapter

Flat-head screwdriver bit,
1.0 mm × 6.5 mm

Bike chain rivet setter,
removable 5 mm Allen
wrench, screwdriver for
slotted and Phillips-head
screws

Removable 10 mm hexagonal
key

Laser pointer with 300 ft.
range

4 mm Allen wrench

12/20-gauge choke-tube
tool

Telescopic pointer

2.4" springless scissors with
serrated, self-sharpening
design

Fish scaler, hook disgorger,
line guide

Micro scraper, straight

Pin punch, 1.2 mm

Removable tool holder with
expandable receptacle

Flat Phillips-head screwdriver

Phillips-head screwdriver
bit 0

Self-centering gunsight
screwdriver

Can opener

Golf club face cleaner

Golf shoe spike wrench

Special tool holder

Screwdriver bit, 0.8 mm

Magnetized recessed bit
holder

Patented locking screwdriver,
cap lifter, wire stripper

Tweezers

Extension tool

Corkscrew

2.5″ blade for official World
Scout Knife

Flat-head screwdriver bit,
0.5 mm × 3.5 mm

Magnetized recessed bit
holder

Removable tool for adjusting
bike spokes, 10 mm
hexagonal key for nuts

Patented locking Phillips-
head screwdriver

1.65″ clip-point utility blade

2.5″ blade

Watch case-back opening
tool

Compass, straight edge, ruler
(in./cm)

Shortix laboratory key

Micro tool holder

Pin punch, 0.8 mm

Removable tool holder

Flat-head screwdriver bit,
0.5 mm × 3.5 mm

Flat-head screwdriver bit,
0.6 mm × 4.0 mm

Phillips-head screwdriver

2.4″ round-tip blade

Golf divot repair tool

Phillips-head screwdriver bit,
1.5mm

Mineral crystal magnifier,
fork for watch spring bars,
small ruler

Tire tread gauge

Chisel-point reamer

Fiber optic tool holder

Fine metal file with precision
screwdriver

GUITAR TABLATURE FOR THE OPENING OF AEROSMITH'S "WALK THIS WAY"

Why are there so precious few hard rock anthems covered by 80s rap groups? Really, there should be more. The following guitar tablature describes one of the easiest and most recognizable riffs ever written.

```
|----------------------|----------------------|----------------------|
|----------------------|----------------------|----------------------|
|----------------------|----------------7-----|----------------------|
|----------------------|------7------7-----7-----|----------------------|
|----------------------|----------------------|----------------------|
| - 5 - 6 - 7 - - - 5 - 6 - 7 - - - O - - - x - x - | - 5 - 6 - 7 - 5 - 6 -
7 - 5 P O - O - ( x ) - | - 5 - 6 - 7 - - - - - 5 - 6 - 7 - - - - - O - - - |
```

```
|--------------------5\8-|
|--------------------5\8-|
|--------------------6\9-|
|------------------7\10-|
|------7------7----7\10-|
|-5–6-7—-5-6-7--5\8-|
```

SIX UNQUESTIONABLY TRUE CONSPIRACIES

1. Few people know what David Icke knows. Diana, princess of Wales, knew. Paul McCartney, too. The Bush family, the British Royals, and Kris Kristofferson found out the hard way. What David Icke knows is this: Most world leaders and some 80s pop stars have, in fact, been replaced by reptilian humanoids that require periodic ingestion of human blood to maintain their appearance.

2. The Denver Airport is bigger than it really needs to be and is suspiciously removed from the city itself. Throughout, there are strange Masonic symbols. Conclusion: it's the Western base of the New World Order and the tip of the iceberg of a massive underground base and city.

3. Six steps to a vast electrogenic Armageddon: 1. Replace precious metals with paper currency. 2. Replace paper currency with credit cards. 3. Replace cards with Internet commerce.

4. Consolidate banks by merger. 5. Implement worldwide identity card. 6. Cut the power. Sit back and watch the world overcome by chaos. (Brought to you by the New World Order or, potentially, by their reptilian overlords.)

4. In addition to its pastoral setting, Montauk, New York, is known as the site of a 2004 *Sports Illustrated* swimsuit shoot—Veronika Varekova made the cover. Less known are the area's experiments with teleportation, extraterrestrials, psychological warfare, time travel, and quantum stealth technology.

5. Beware the barcode of the beast. Yes, that's right, along with your caffeine cola and *Cosmo,* pick up a little deftly disguised 666 at the grocery store.

6. Fossil fuel, wind, water, solar, nuclear . . . Vril. Unfortunately, you can't use Vril. Only the matriarchal, socialist, utopian superior beings who live under, for example, Mount Shasta can use Vril. Sucks to be you.

HIGHLIGHTS OF EARLY MATHEMATICS EDUCATION

This one goes out to all those little geeks out there.

Pre-kindergarten: Develop understanding of shapes and whole numbers, including . . . counting!

Kindergarten: Learn to compare and order objects.

Grade 1: Addition and subtraction.

Grade 2: Long addition and subtraction, counting by tens.

Grade 3: Multiplication and division, basic fractions, and geometric ideas, including congruence and symmetry.

Grade 4: Fluency in multiplication and division, fractions and decimals, and the area of shapes.

Grade 5: Long multiplication and division, adding and subtracting fractions and decimals, and 3-D shapes.

Grade 6: Multiplying and dividing fractions and decimals, solving and writing word problems.

Grade 7: Ratio and percent problems, such as discounts, interest, and taxes. Volume and surface area. Manipulating negative integers.

Grade 8: Basic algebra (linear equations). Geometry using distance and angle. Basics of data sets (mean, median, range, average).

SYMBOLISM OF THE REVERSE SIDE OF THE ONE-DOLLAR BILL

• The separated top of the pyramid shows the unfinished United States.

• The shadow cast by the pyramid represents the undiscovered lands to the west.

• The rising sun represents the new nation.

• The eye may or may not represent the Illuminati secret society.

• The free-standing shield represents the country's ability to stand on its own.

• An eagle looks toward an olive branch but also holds arrows—looking toward peace but ready for war.

• The number 13 symbolizes the original colonies and is represented by the stars above the eagle, steps on the pyramid, letters in ANNUIT COEPTIS, letters in E PLURIBUS UNUM, vertical bars on the shield, horizontal stripes at the top of the shield, leaves on the olive branch, berries on the olive branch, arrows, hats, and the combined symbols of 1776 and its Roman numeral (MDCCLXXVI).

THE QUOTABLE HE-MAN AND THE MASTERS OF THE UNIVERSE

SKELETOR: Tell me about the loneliness of good, He-Man. Is it equal to the loneliness of evil?

MAN-AT-ARMS: Never think while you're hungry.

EVIL-LYN: Outnumbered? Outclassed is more like it.

MAN-AT-ARMS: That's very interesting, but silly.

SORCERESS: Men who crave power look back over the mistakes of their lives. Pile them all together and call it destiny.

HE-MAN: By the power of Grayskull! I have the power!

HOW TO HAVE SEX ON SECOND LIFE

1. Buy genitalia

2. Buy desired "scripted" devices (clothes, bed, toys, etc.). These devices will animate your character's actions for the desired use (may have to click "pose ball").

3. Find private area or sex club. Many free orgy rooms exist, or pay to play in a private sex room.

4. Either hire an escort (500–1,500 Linden Dollars or $2–$6 per session) or hit on an avatar by chatting, Skype, or phone.

5. Let the good times roll.

SUDOKU STRATEGY

If you've ever solved a Sudoku puzzle, you've used these strategies, but you might not have known their names. Check the later list entries for advanced strategies, guaranteed to crack even that *diabolical New York Times* Will Shortz nightmare.

1. Squeezing: using two of the same number in related blocks to infer the necessary placement of the same number in the third block.

THE original cast of *He-Man* included the voice of Dolph Lundgren as the title hero and Courtney Cox as Julie Winston. Frank Langella, winner of three Tony Awards, provided the voice of Skeletor. Note: Despite popular misconception, He-Man has been governor of neither Minnesota nor California.

2. Cross-hatching: using solved numbers to rule out both vertical and horizontal options, leaving only one possible space for a given number.

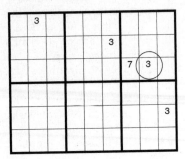

3. Three or fewer: when squeezing and cross-hatching are played out, look for boxes, rows, or columns with three or fewer options. Mark these options in pencil.

589	6	589
589	2	4
7	3	1

4. Continue to cross-hatch: Look for ways to eliminate numbers from your three-or-fewer lists.

89	6	89	5	
589	2	4		
7	3	1		

5. Spotting the lone number: if (as in the example from number 4) your pencil marks leave only one available option for a number, you have solved this number.

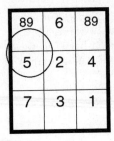

6. Advanced cross-hatching: expand your mind. Can you correctly place a 3 in the upper-right box in the example below?

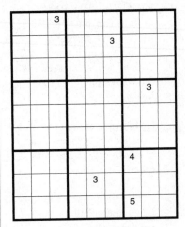

MORAL LESSONS BROUGHT TO YOU BY THE MONSTERS OF *THE ODYSSEY*

Calypso: the lonely nymph who waylays Odysseus for eight years on her island of Ogygia. Though the beautiful Calypso offers ease and even immortality, she is in fact selfish, caring only to alleviate her own loneliness. Watch out for self-serving kindness.

Cyclops: Polyphemus, the Cyclops, traps Odysseus and his crew in his cave and eats six men before Odysseus gets him drunk, blinds him with a wooden stake, and escapes with his remaining crew by hiding under sheep. Polyphemus, with his one eye, represents a person with only one point of view. Beware: if you are monofocused and that monofocus fails, you are SOL, just like Polyphemus.

Circe: the nymph whose palace on the vowel-heavy isle of Aeaea is defiled by Odysseus's men. Circe turns the greedy men into pigs. (And then back to men when Odysseus threatens her.) Circe is rather blameless in this exchange, but from the crew's actions on the island, we should learn not to be greedy pigs.

The Sirens: if Odysseus had not been chained to his ship's mast, surely he would have jumped overboard toward the Sirens' song describing his heroics in the Trojan War. Keeping with Homer's track record of rather misogynistic morality (nymphs, Sirens, etc., all equal bad news), we should learn from the Sirens not to be overly in love with our past.

The Lotus Eaters: the gentle hippies of the *Odyssey*. The moral: don't do drugs. Also, beware distraction of any type.

Scylla: as Odysseus sails past, Scylla reaches from her cave to pluck away six of his men—one for each of Scylla's six heads. Scylla represents sudden tragedy, with which we should learn to deal as well as Odysseus.

Charybdis: the whirlpool monster that sucks in O's ship (though Odysseus clings heroically to a branch until Charybdis closes and the danger is passed). Like the gravitational pull of a black hole, at Charybdis's outskirts, you might not know you are caught in a deadly current. Beware of getting sucked slowly into things that plan to eat you.

CAFFEINE LEVELS IN DESIGNER COFFEE

A 2004 study commissioned by the *Wall Street Journal* found that coffee purchased in designer houses such as Starbucks and Seattle's Best has, on average, 56 percent more caffeine than similar coffee purchased at 7-Eleven, and 29 percent more caffeine than coffee from Dunkin' Donuts. The *Journal* also found that people purchased coffee to avoid an irritable no-coffee state rather than for perceived positive effects, leading some to question whether said designer coffee houses are involved in a massive addiction and mind-control conspiracy aimed at world domination by said companies' top geeks. Note: in terms of bang for your buck, drip coffee reigns supreme.

DRINK	CAFFEINE (MG)	OUNCES AS TESTED	OCTANE (MG/OZ)
Drip Coffee	145	8	18.13
Brewed Decaf	5.6	8	0.70
Espresso	77	1.5	51.33
Bottled Frappuccino	90	9.5	9.47
Tall Cappuccino	75	12	6.25
Tall Mocha	95	12	7.92
Tall Latte	75	12	6.25
Grande Americano	225	16	14.06
Grande Caramel Macchiato	150	16	9.37

A SAM LOYD PICTURE PUZZLE

Cut this picture of a dog's head into two equal shapes.

THREE STEPS TO SUCCESSFUL EXORCISM

There are many mediums in which evil spirits may reside (most notably dwellings, persons, and computers), each requiring its own specific rite of exorcism. The steps enumerated below deal specifically with human exorcism, or ridding the body of an undesired spirit/demon possession, in the Roman Catholic tradition.

Note: before performing an exorcism, evaluate the subject's potential for violence (with the strength and malignity of the possession in mind), and restrain accordingly, usually with ropes, straps, or duct tape.

Note II: The following ritual may or may not work with computers, depending on operating system and waterproofing.

1. Priest is dressed in cassock, surplice, and purple stole.

2. Trace sign of cross over self, person possessed, and all present. Sprinkle all with holy water.

3. Recitation by priest and response by those present of the Rite of Exorcism, including the following highlights:

• *I cast you out, unclean spirit, along with every satanic power of the enemy, every specter from hell, and all your fell companions!*

ACCORDING

to Father Gabriele Amorth, the Vatican's go-to guy for exorcism and honorary president for life of the International Association of Exorcists, a curse can originate from "maledictions by close relatives, a habit of blaspheming, membership in the Freemasonry, spiritic or magic practices, and so on." If you feel that you are or may be possessed by a malignant spirit, you should immediately employ the following steps (a Roman Catholic *stop, drop, and roll*):

1. Immediately reject any and all types of unnatural insights.

2. Avoid drugs, alcohol, illicit sex, and pornography.

3. Terminate associations with Freemasonry, Eastern religions, and the Harry Potter series.

4. Install the newest version of Catholic Firewall.

- *I adjure you, ancient serpent, by the judge of the living and the dead, by your creator, by the creator of the whole universe, by Him who has the power to consign you to hell, to depart forthwith in fear, along with your savage minions, from this servant of God!*

- *Therefore I adjure you, profligate dragon, in the name of the spotless Lamb, who has trodden down the asp and the basilisk, and overcome the lion and the dragon, to depart this man!*

IN 2002, former United States Attorney General John Ashcroft said, "There are only two things necessary in life—WD-40 and duct tape . . . WD-40 for things that don't move that should, and duct tape for things that do move but shouldn't." In 2005, the Henkel company sold enough Duck brand duct tape to wrap around Earth twenty times.

- *Begone now! Begone, seducer! Your place is in solitude; your abode is in the nest of serpents; get down and crawl with them!*

NOTABLE EMERGENCY USES OF DUCT TAPE

- At the Salt Lake City Olympics, snowboarder Chris Klug used duct tape to repair a broken binding and went on to win a bronze medal in the parallel giant slalom.

- In duct tape occlusion therapy, a square of the tape is worn over a plantar wart until the wart disappears.

- In NASA's famous Apollo 13 incident, the astronauts used duct tape to connect square carbon dioxide filters to the lunar module's round receptacles.

- In 1942, the U.S. Army used "duck tape" to seal cases of ammunition against rain and humidity.

- NASA astronauts aboard Apollo 17 used duct tape to attach extra-long wheel covers to a lunar rover, reducing the amount of lunar dust the rover kicked up.

- In 2003, the Department of Homeland Security advised Americans to stock up on duct tape and plastic sheeting for use in sealing homes after a potential biological or chemical attack.

• In April 2000, Gemini Wink found himself lost in a Florida swamp and instead of spending the night on the ground, he climbed a tree and duct-taped himself to the branches.

THE GREAT MYTH OF THE METRIC SYSTEM

Pierre-François-André Méchain and Jean-Baptiste-Joseph Delambre—in addition to their names implying equally indecisive parents—spent the years 1791–1799 measuring the length of Earth's arc between Dunkirk, France, and Barcelona, Spain. They endured the hardships you would expect of late-eighteenth-century travel, including imprisonment by skeptical townspeople. By measuring this arc, the pair hoped to calculate the distance from the North Pole to the equator, allowing them to standardize the meter as one ten-millionth of this span.

It was a noble goal: relating all lengths to this meter would define all distances based on their ratio to Earth—a natural system of measurement!

Unfortunately, they blew the calculations. Messrs. Méchain and Delambre forgot to adjust for oblateness—Earth is not a perfect sphere, as they assumed in their calculations; it's flattened at the poles. And the planet isn't uni-

form; it's lumpy. So each meridian is, in fact, a different length.

Other metric measurements are based on the flawed meter. The liter is defined as a cube with sides of 0.1 meter, and the kilogram as the mass of a liter of water at maximum density. Thus, while the metric system sucks much less than the system of English units, it is still based on human rather than natural definition.

THE SCOUTING HIERARCHY

CUB SCOUTS
• Bobcat
• Tiger Cub
• Wolf
• Bear
• Webelos
• Arrow of Light

BOY SCOUTS

Phase I

• Scout
• Tenderfoot
• Second Class
• First Class

Phase II

• Star
• Life
• Eagle

GREAT MOMENTS IN PRE-1980 KUNG FU MOVIES

Year	Film	Star	Great Moment
1965	Temple of the Red Lotus	Jimmy Wang Yu	Wu, the movie's hero but a shameful fighter, gets his ass kicked in turn by every female member of Dragon House, including the clan's grandmother.
1970	The Chinese Boxer	Jimmy Wang Yu	Employing the deadly Iron Palm in a conveyor belt of bring-it-on ass kickings, a young hero takes revenge on the Japanese fighters who killed his friends.
1973	Enter the Dragon	Bruce Lee	"When the opponent expands, I contract. When he contracts, I expand. And when there is an opportunity, I do not hit. It hits all by itself." [shows fist]
1976	Executioners from Shaolin	Kuan Tai Chen	In the opening scene, the evil priest Pai Mei (later seen in Tarantino's Kill Bill), uses kung fu techniques to retract his privates into his groin.
1978	The Five Deadly Venoms	Kuo Chui, Lu Feng, Lo Mang, Sun Chien, Wei Pei	The Centipede strikes with a hundred arms and legs; the Snake uses precise finger control (picture it); the Scorpion kills with a single kick; the Lizard walks on walls; the Toad is nearly impervious to attack.
1978	Drunken Master	Jackie Chan	In the first true example of kung fu comedy, Chan employs the fighting style of the Eight Drunken Immortals to defeat the assassin Thunderleg, who has been contracted to kill his father.

A BIT OF CARD-BASED MATHEMATICAL FLIMFLAMMERY

While your co-geeks may out this as a simple math trick, most people unable to recite pi past the decimal point will be amazed. It also has the advantage of requiring almost no physical, sleight-of-hand expertise.

1. Set the deck—from the top down, it should read 2, 3, 4, 5, 6, 7, 8, 9, A, A, A, A (the numbers in any suit and all four aces).

2. Shuffle, being sure not to affect the top twelve cards (yes, this is a cheap trick).

3. Ask an audience member to pick and state a number between ten and nineteen.

4. Taking one at a time from the top of the deck, count that many cards into a face-down pile on the table.

5. Ask your dupe to add the two digits of his/her number and state the sum.

6. From your small pile, count that many cards back onto the top of your larger deck (throughout you will reverse and reinstate the original order—don't lose it!).

7. The next card in your small pile is the first ace. Turn it face up and leave it out.

8. Place the remaining cards in your small pile back atop the deck.

9. Fake another shuffle and repeat steps 3 to 8 two more times (finding two more aces).

10. To finish, ask your dupe to think of a number between one and nine, and then have him/her count that number of cards off the top of the deck, turning the last card face up. If he/she picked the number nine, the card turned over will be the ace.

11. If he/she did not turn over the ace (i.e., didn't pick the number nine), then have him/her count additional cards from the deck, the number of additional cards matching the number on the card they overturned (i.e., if your dupe turned over a three, have him/her count off three more cards). The face-up card counts as the first! The last card dealt is the final ace.

THE CLASSIC LOGIC PROBLEM

The vast majority of geeks will be familiar with the technique for solving logic problems from their early experiences with *Games* magazine. If you are a little rusty—and/or if you are getting ready for the logic section of the GRE—check out the example on the next page (chart given: place X's in the spaces that are ruled out, and O's in the answers).

PROBLEM

Tom, Fred, Bill, Andy, and Carl are all aging athletes and each is the worse for wear. Can you match each former star to his sport and injury?

CLUES

1. Tom played soccer, so his arms still work perfectly, unlike the baseballer, who has a torn rotator cuff.

2. Strangely, the fellow who used to curl was sidelined due to multiple concussions while the footballer hurt his hip.

3. Despite living in Minneapolis, Andy has always hated curling (as does Bill), which is for the best because Andy's bum wrist would limit his involvement anyway.

4. Carl hurt something below the waist playing one of the big-three American sports.

		Injuries					Sports			
		Knee	Shoulder	Hip	Wrist	Concussions	Football	Basketball	Baseball	Soccer	Curling
Guys	Tom										
	Fred										
	Bill										
	Andy										
	Carl										
Sports	Football										
	Basketball										
	Baseball										
	Soccer										
	Curling										

THE RULES OF PIG LATIN

1. If a word starts with a consonant, move the consonant (or consonant cluster) to the end of the word and add *ay*. For example, *pig* becomes *igpay,* and *brain* becomes *ainbray.*

2. If a word begins with a vowel or silent consonant, just add "way" to the end. For example, *Intel* becomes *Intelway,* and *anime* becomes *animeway.*

FIVE COOL CONSTANTS FROM THE WORLD OF PHYSICS

c	VALUE: 3×10^8 m/s
SPEED OF LIGHT	MISCELLANY: In fourteenth-century notes in the margin of an Indian Rig Veda is written, "O Sun, you who traverse 2,202 *yojanas* in half a *nimesa*"—a fairly accurate estimate of light speed almost 300 years before Western, scientific measurement

n_A	VALUE: 6×10^{23} per mole
AVOGADRO'S NUMBER	MISCELLANY: A's number allows us to count things—most commonly atoms or molecules—and thus to compare, convert, and describe them. For example, a mole of oxygen atoms weighs about 16 grams, while a mole of hydrogen weighs one gram, making the mass of one mole of H_2O about 18 grams. (Bill Murray: "To kill, you must know your enemy, and in this case my enemy is a varmint.")

h	VALUE: 6.6×10^{-34} J·s
PLANCK'S CONSTANT	MISCELLANY: Quantifies the energy emitted by photons per Joule second using the equation $E = hV$ (with V being frequency). Implications for wave-particle duality, electromagnetic radiation, and other quantum wackiness.

g	VALUE: 9.8 m/s^2
ACCELERATION DUE TO EARTH'S GRAVITY	MISCELLANY: Yields all sort of cool Newtonian stuff, including $F = mg$ (Force, mass, g), $v^2 = 2gh$ (velocity, g, height), $E_p = mgh$ (Potential energy, mass, g, height). It also describes what happens when you climb trees and then drop water balloons onto unsuspecting passers-by.

e	VALUE: 1.6×10^{-19} C
ELEMENTARY CHARGE	MISCELLANY: The charge of a single proton. In 1909 Millikan and Fletcher suspended charged oil drops in an electric field of known charge, thus calculating e.

FOUR GREEK MYTHS IN EXACTLY 200 WORDS

CUPID AND PSYCHE:

Cupid is sent by the jealous Venus to curse Psyche, but instead falls in love with her. They snog, with one condition: Psyche can never light the lamp to discover Cupid's true identity. Oops, she blows it and loses Cupid. To get him back, Psyche has to please Venus. With supernatural help, Psyche succeeds and scores both Cupid and immortality.

PROMETHEUS AND PANDORA:

Prometheus tricks Zeus into accepting a subpar offering from mankind. Zeus punishes mankind by withholding fire, but Prometheus steals it. Zeus further punishes mankind by sending the first woman, and also chains Prometheus to a rock where every day an eagle eats his liver. Zeus 2, Prometheus 0.

ORPHEUS AND EURYDICE:

The two were married, but Eurydice dies of snakebite. Orpheus journeys to the underworld, where his music softens Hades' heart, who allows Orpheus to take Eurydice back to the living—*as long as he doesn't look back before reaching the surface.* He does. She dies.

DAEDALUS AND ICARUS:

King Minos imprisons Daedalus. To escape, Daedalus makes wings of wax and feathers for himself and his young son, Icarus. Icarus flies too close to the sun, softening the wax, falls into the sea, and drowns.

THE 10 MOST VALUABLE COMIC BOOKS

Without intrinsic value (such as being made out of a valuable raw material) or the backing of a major governmental reserve (perhaps the *Marvel* defined in relation to the dollar), technically a comic book is worth what you can sell it for. Meaning that the whims of eBay dictate comic book value. As of this book's printing, generally held Internet wisdom estimates the following comic book prices:

1. Action Comics 1 (1938)—$1,560,000: first appearance of Superman

2. Detective Comics 27 (1939)—$1,470,000: first appearance of Batman

3. Superman 1 (1939)—$702,000: first comic devoted to Superman

4. Detective Comics 1 (1937)—$654,000: Slam Bradley vs. Ching Lung

5. All-American Comics 16 (1940)—$486,000: first appearance of Green Lantern

6. Marvel Comics 1 (1939)—$461,000: Human Torch vs. Namor the Sub-Mariner

7. Batman 1 (1940)—$337,000: first comic devoted to Batman

8. Flash Comics 1 (1940)—$323,000: limited printing

9. More Fun Comics 52 (1940)—$312,000: first appearance of the Spectre

10. New Fun Comics 1 (1935)—$299,000: first publication with all-original content

THE QUOTABLE CHE GUEVARA

Ernesto Guevara de la Serna—Che—is cool. Why, exactly, he is so cool is hard to pinpoint. Certainly the whole *Motorcycle Diaries* thing has the ring of a mad, idealistic, South American *On the Road,* and you gotta like the combination of scraggly-ass sideburns, a cigar, and a submachine gun, but really—is Castro's "supreme prosecutor" a role model? Popular opinion doesn't care. Like Bruce Lee, JFK, and Yoda, Che—through the hazy filter of popular memory—can do no wrong. Besides, we like the shirts.

"I know you are here to kill me. Shoot, coward, you are only going to kill a man."

"If Christ himself stood in my way, I, like Nietzsche, would not hesitate to squish him like a worm."

"Cruel leaders are replaced only to have new leaders turn cruel."

"Better to die standing than to live on your knees."

"It's a sad thing not to have friends, but it is even sadder not to have enemies."

FIVE BRILLIANT RUSSIAN NOVELISTS YOU'VE NEVER HEARD OF

Vasily Zhukovski (1783–1852): The illegitimate son of a landowner and a Turkish slave, Zhukovski is known as the father of Russian romantic literature. He was Pushkin before Pushkin was Pushkin. (The preceding is, to date, the only published example of a seven-word sentence that uses the word "Pushkin" three times.)

Mikhail Artsybashev (1878–1927): As might be expected from his surname, Artsybashev was an artist first and a novelist second. The protagonist of his little-known masterpiece, *Sanin* (1907), roams the countryside seducing innocent country girls (proto-Nabokov? proto-Kerouac?).

Nikolai Semyonovich Leskov (1831–1895): Considered by many to be the most Russian of all Russian writers (something to do with divested family land, work as a clerk in the bureaucracy, battles with the church, and other assorted suffering). Among his many little-known works is *The Tale of Cross-eyed Lefty from Tula and the Steel Flea* (1881).

Vsevolod Vyacheslavovich Ivanov* (1895–1963): After running away to be a circus clown, Vsevolod joined the Red Army, fighting in Siberia during the Civil War. Accordingly, many characters in his stories are very, very cold.

Konstantin Paustovsky (1892–1968): In 1965, Paustovsky was nominated for the Nobel Prize in literature. Admit it—you haven't heard of him! Much of his work describes wandering the Soviet countryside, where he worked odd jobs ranging from fisherman to law professor to boiler fabricator.

*Name implies potential vampirism.

GREAT CARS IN 007 FILMS

MOVIE	CAR	GADGETS
Goldfinger	1964 Aston Martin DB5	Oil slick, passenger ejection seat, machine guns, hubcap knives, and revolving license plates
Tomorrow Never Dies	1997 BMW 750iL	Cell phone–operated remote control of missiles, chain cutter, flash grenades, and tear gas
The Spy Who Loved Me	1975 Lotus Esprit	Transforms into a missile-equipped submarine
The Living Daylights	1985 Aston Martin Volante	Laser-beam hubcaps, jet propulsion, missiles (of course), and a self-destruct button
The World Is Not Enough	1999 BMW Z8	Only the requisite missiles, but damn is that a nice looking car!
Die Another Day	2002 Aston Martin Vanquish	In addition to the expected weapons, sports spiked tires and the ability to become invisible (no kidding)

HOW TO MAKE AND USE A QUILL PEN

There is nothing—*nothing*—like a love letter written in calligraphic quill pen to get a geek off the couch in the garage. (Note: the calligraphic love letter requires the ability to manipulate a non-keyboard writing utensil and expertise in a nonprogramming language—both skills lost to many geeks. Therefore, instead of actually *writing* with a quill, consider laying it on parchment stamped with a red wax heart somewhere she will see it, to imply romantic intent.) For those requiring a functional quill pen for romantic, reenactment, or role-playing use, follow these directions:

1. Purchase or pluck goose or turkey feather (craft store, online, or drive toward low light density and look for "coop").

2. Buy or gather enough sand to fill a baking dish and heat it in oven at 375 degrees until hot throughout. Remove from oven.

3. To temper quills, place them tip down in hot sand until sand cools.

4. Cut off tip, diagonally. If you're feeling ambitious,

further shape nib to look like the tip of a fountain pen.

5. Purchase and use ink made for dip pens.

POLTI'S 36 DRAMATIC SITUATIONS

Think all good ideas have already been written? Georges Polti would agree (if he hadn't died in the early twentieth century). His book *36 Dramatic Situations*—in print since 1917—continues to help screenwriters from Hollywood to Bollywood to Nollywood meet deadlines. With the thirty-six situations listed below, you, too, can plot a blockbuster.

FIVE USEFUL PHRASES IN KLINGON

Klingon is the official language of the Klingon people and the first language of Shakespeare (via time travel; see remark by High Chancellor Gorkon in the documentary *Star Trek VI: The Undiscovered Country*—"Shakespeare is best read in the original Klingon"). Just as the Inuit language includes many words for snow, so too does Klingon include many ways to describe weaponry and warfare, as well as many curses. (In fact the Athabaskan language family that encompasses Inuit is phonetically the closest terrestrial approximation to Klingon.)

Supplication	Deliverance	Crime pursued by vengeance
Vengeance taken for kin upon kin	Pursuit	Disaster
Falling prey to cruelty/misfortune	Revolt	Daring enterprise
Abduction	The enigma	Obtaining
Enmity of kin	Rivalry of kin	Murderous adultery
Madness	Fatal imprudence	Involuntary crimes of love
Slaying of kin unrecognized	Self-sacrifice for an ideal	Self-sacrifice for kin
All sacrificed for passion	Necessity of sacrificing loved ones	Rivalry of superior vs. inferior
Adultery	Crimes of love	Discovery and dishonor of a loved one
Obstacles to love	An enemy loved	Ambition
Conflict with a god	Mistaken jealousy	Erroneous judgment
Remorse	Recovery of a loved one	Loss of a loved one

In general, extreme use of glottal stops and starts best approximates the pronunciation of native speakers.

Everyone encounters Tribbles occasionally.
Rot yittmey ghom Hoch.

Do I *need* to sleep on the floor?
rauDaqj IQongn ISq''a'?

Where is the bathroom?
nuqDaq 'oH puchpa''e'?

Today is a good day to die.
Heghlu 'meH QaQ jajvam.

Your mother has a smooth forehead!
Hab SoSlI' Quch!

TEN SOMEWHAT ARCANE DIAGRAMS OF PULLEY SYSTEMS

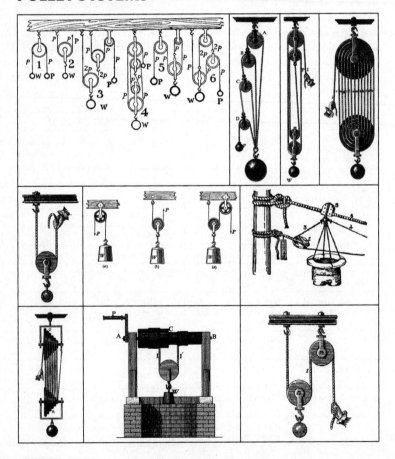

WINE VARIETALS: GET SNOOTY QUICK

RED WINES	
Cabernet Sauvignon	The Elizabeth Taylor of red wines, cab sauv is known for depth of flavor and ability to age well. Many cabs have undertones of cherry and currant. Can overpower yuppies.
Syrah	The only grape to rival the cab's reputation for big, complex wines, though different in its spices of berry, plum, and smoke.
Merlot	Merlot is the safe wine—the go-to dinner-party gift. Typically with herb flavors, it is softer than a cab or syrah.
Petite Sirah	A bastard California grape not to be confused with the parent grape of similar name. Most often blended with Zinfandel to tone down a zin's "jammy" flavor.
Pinot Noir	The "heartbreak grape," pinots require very specific growing conditions and a late harvest that can be threatened by frost. Pinot noir is light to medium, and delicate but still complex. A subtle wine.
Zinfandel	Can range from light- to full-bodied and usually includes berry or spice flavors. An ingredient in the popular blush wine White Zinfandel, which might as well be a wine cooler.
Sangiovese	The grape behind Chianti and thus very good with liver and fava beans. A smooth texture topped with spice, raspberry, and licorice.

WHITE WINES	
Chardonnay	Usually oak aged, chardonnay ranges from clean and crisp to rich and complex. Most experts respect chardonnay most among white wines.
Chenin Blanc	A slightly sweet white, usually with floral undertones. Can range from dry to off dry.
Sauvignon Blanc	Usually with grassy, herbal flavors. Best served with fish or shellfish.
Gewürztraminer	A spicy, sweet wine best served with Asian food or pork.
Pinot Blanc	The poor man's chardonnay.
Pinot Grigio	Low acidity and high perfume make this a wine that any man should be embarrassed to be seen purchasing.
Riesling	Similar to gewürztraminer, Riesling is a light, white, summer wine, but can still range widely from crisp and dry to full-bodied and sweet.

THE BASICS OF GEOCACHING

If fly-fishing is a good excuse to stand in a river at sunrise, then the GPS-dependent sport of geocaching is a good excuse to wander everything from city streets to country roads to backcountry trails to your neighbor's backyard. Geocaching also connects with the primal side of geeks who never quite stopped seeing themselves as Jim Hawkins searching for buried gold. To geocache, first purchase a GPS unit (and learn to use it). Then, go online to find the coordinates of caches in your area (www.geocaching.com). When you find a cache, sign the logbook. If you take something out of a cache, replace it with something of like value. Most caches include items remarkably similar to a historical collection of every white-elephant gift you have ever received at an office party.

CONVERSION: CELSIUS TO FAHRENHEIT TO KELVIN

In 1724, when Daniel Gabriel Fahrenheit proposed his temperature scale, the lowest temperature he could consistently replicate was that of water mixed with ice and salt. This became zero on his scale. By 1742, many people realized that the Fahrenheit scale was rather arbitrary and nonintuitive. These people included the astronomer Anders Celsius, who proposed an alternative, with zero being water's freezing point and 100 being the boiling point. (In fact, Celsius initially had these exactly switched, with 0°C being boiling and 100°C freezing.) The Kelvin scale, most useful to scientists and people living north of Minneapolis, moves zero another 273 Celsius degrees lower, to the temperature known as *absolute zero*. At absolute zero (0°K), matter, which Einstein showed to be another form of energy, would cease to exist (mull that one— which law of thermodynamics would it contradict?).

Below are equations for conversion.

$$\text{Celsius} = {}^{5}/_{9} (\text{Fahrenheit} - 32)$$

$$\text{Fahrenheit} = {}^{9}/_{5} (\text{Celsius} - 32)$$

$$\text{Kelvin} = \text{Celsius} + 273$$

THE botanist Carl Linnaeus was the first scientist to use the Celsius scale, known then as centigrade. He swapped the temperatures of Celsius's original scale, making freezing 0°C and boiling 100°C.

A SAM LOYD LOGIC PUZZLE

The boys in this class were asked to say their names and were photographed just as they started to pronounce the first letters. Their names are Oom, Alden, Eastman, Alfred, Arthur, Luke, Fletcher, Matthew, Theodore, Richard, Shermer, and Hisswald. Match the names to the correct boys.

A Lip-Reading Puzzle —BY— SAM LOYD.

HOW TO MAKE A LASER

There are many types of lasers, very few of which focus enough energy to destroy a planet the size of Alderaan. Basically, a laser squeezes energy into a defined visible wavelength (i.e., red or green), concentrating this energy into a low-divergence beam. The three primary parts of a laser are an initial energy source (pump source), a medium that, when excited, spits out photons of defined wavelength (gain medium), and a way to jack the power of these photons (optical resonator). In most lasers—like the helium-neon laser shown on the next page— electrical energy (pump source) passes through a tube of gas (gain medium). This energy is trapped between two mirrors, one that reflects all the light and one that reflects most of the light. Thus, the energy bounces back and forth in the gas, exciting photons, before finally leaking out through the semi-transparent mirror and totally annihilating anything in its path (or providing a nifty way to highlight areas of a PowerPoint presentation).

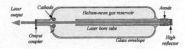

SPEED READING MADE EASY

Sorry: there is necessarily a trade-off between reading speed and comprehension—the faster you read, the less you will understand. Even by practicing the techniques herein described, it's unlikely you will reach the same level as Howard Stephen Berg, the self-proclaimed world's fastest reader (whose book-slinging website opens with "Dear Friend, Today marks the turning point of your life!!!"). On *Live with Regis and Kathie Lee*, Berg memorized the two-hundred-page book *Going to the Movies* and scored 100 percent on a comprehension test given by the author. Berg claims to read twenty-five thousand words per minute.

APPLICATIONS of laser technology range from barcode readers to industrial cutting to guiding military munitions. There would be no CD or DVD players without lasers, which reflect off a disc's LP-like system of minuscule bumps. And how would anyone survive his or her teen years without the edifying experience of late-night Laser Zeppelin at the local planetarium? (Rock on!) We all know what happens to the spy with the red dot on his chest (or to Bill Duke playing Sergeant Mac Eliot in *Predator* when three red dots appear on his forehead). On the less destructive side, laser technology corrects vision, whitens teeth, removes moles and tattoos, and is instrumental in many new surgical techniques. Lasers can even drive nuclear reactions by blasting a pellet of deuterium-tritium from all angles at once, thus compressing it, heating it, and leading to *inertial confinement fusion.**

*Note: high Death Star potential.

SPEED READING STRATEGIES

• Define your information goals before reading: What do you need? What don't you need? By preplanning what you are looking for, you can separate the wheat from the chaff (and could have avoided reading the preceding sentence).

• Practice visualizing larger chunks of text. In first grade, your chunks were letters, later they were words, now these chunks may be clauses or sentences. Aim for paragraph-size visual chunks.

• Use your finger to guide your eyes in an even, rhythmic flow across the page.

• Do away with sounds. Try not to subvocalize, or listen to the word in your mind. Go straight from letters to meaning.

• Reduce rereading (skip-back). Practice tracking through material only once.

• Periodically test your speed using one of the many online speed-reading tests.

THE 10 ALL-TIME GEEKIEST WRITERS

10. Orson Scott Card—His books *Ender's Game* and its sequel, *Speaker for the Dead,* are required reading on any geek list. Card is especially notable as one of the few sci-fi authors to have attended BYU and served as a missionary for the Church of Jesus Christ of Latter-Day Saints.

9. Arthur C. Clark—Clark was knighted and nominated for a Nobel Prize for his work on satellite communication systems. We know him as the author of *2001: A Space Odyssey* (as well as *Rendezvous with Rama* and *The Fountains of Paradise*).

8. Joe Haldeman—Teaches writing at MIT. Enough said, though it's also worthwhile to note his B.A. in astronomy and his novels *The Forever War* and its follow-up, *Forever Peace.*

7. Neal Stephenson—Stephenson wrote the seminal virtual-reality book *Snow Crash,* along with what is perhaps the geekiest novel of all time: *Cryptonomicon* (1999). He also writes about nanotechnology and pop-sci, and in 2008 published a space-opera (*Anathem*).

6. Robert A. Heinlein—*Stranger in a Strange Land, Starship Troopers.* With Asimov and Clark, considered one of the Big Three sci-fi writers.

5. Frank Herbert—*Dune* is the bestselling sci-fi novel of all time.

4. Isaac Asimov—You know his books (*Foundation* and *I, Robot*), but did you know he was also the longtime vice president of Mensa International?

3. Anne McCaffrey—Perhaps the first (and certainly the most read) author to posit kicking ass while sitting atop a dragon. Massively prolific.

2. J. R. R. Tolkien—An obscure author of limited imagination; author of a few little-read novels.

1. Ursula K. Le Guin—As of this writing, there are 580 Amazon entries listing Le Guin as author. Seriously. She's written sci-fi, sociology, poetry, translations from French, kids' books, young adult, and pretty much anything else you can think of (including the *Earthsea* novels and the *Hainish Cycle*). Though, what lands her in first place on this list is her very, very cool name.

ARE YOU FAT? DETERMINING BODY DENSITY THROUGH HYDROSTATIC WEIGHING

Fat floats and muscle sinks, so by comparing your underwater weight to your dry weight you can accurately determine your body composition.

1. Weigh yourself. Write down the number. Don't cheat.

2. Place a scale on the bottom of a hot tub or pool.

3. Stand or sit on the scale. If needed, use a weight belt to make yourself sink, and then subtract the weight from your total.

4. Submerge yourself completely. Blow the air out of your lungs. Holding air will make you seem fatter, so blow it all out.

SOMEWHAT ABSTRACT EMOTICONS

(:3= I am the walrus	>:] Evil smile	:*) Blushing	----<--{@ A rose	*<|:{> Santa
(. Y .) Breasts	d-_-b Listening to music	\m/[>.<]\m/ Rocking out to music	=^_^= Blushing	d-(^_^)-b Thumbs up
T_T Crying eyes	><((((°> Fishy	m(__)m Bowing	:-L Zombie	O<:O) Clown

5. Read your underwater weight. Write it down. Don't cheat.

6. Plug your numbers into the following equation: DryWeight / (DryWeight / WetWeight) = BodyDensity

7. Convert body density to percentage of body fat using the following equation: %BodyFat = (495 / BodyDensity) − 450

In the United States, women average 22–25 percent body fat, while men average 15–19 percent. The ideal range is 20–21 percent and 8–14 percent for women and men, respectively, with over 30 percent for women and 25 percent for men considered obese.

THE FINGER CALCULATOR TRICK

Have trouble multiplying the numbers six through ten? Looking for an abstruse way to accomplish this task that is likely much more difficult than passing yourself off as a third-grade student for the couple of weeks needed to relearn basic multiplication skills? Read on, dear geek, read on. . . .

1. Assign the following numbers to your fingers: thumb = 10, index finger = 9, the bird = 8, ring finger = 7, pinky = 6.

2. Place your hands palm up in front of you, as if you were a Rockbiter wondering why your powerful hands failed to keep the world of Fantasia from slipping into the Nothing.

3. Choose a problem using the numbers 6 through 10, for example, 8 × 9.

4. Touch the fingers that represent these numbers (i.e., middle finger left hand, index finger right hand).

5. Count your touching fingers as ten each (i.e., 10 for left middle and 10 for right index).

6. Count any fingers below those touching as ten each (i.e., left ring and pinky; right middle, index, and pinky).

7. Multiply fingers above those touching (i.e., two times one from left thumb and index times right thumb).

8. Add the numbers from steps 5–7 (i.e., 20 + 50 + 2). This is your answer.

CHINESE NAMES OF POPULAR TAKE-OUT FOODS

Imagine you were magically transplanted from your cubicle, bedroom, dorm room, laboratory, or favorite comic store to the heart of mainland China. How would you survive? What would you eat?

Likewise, imagine what would happen if your local source of Chinese take-out changed to non-English-speaking management. Again, how would you survive?

Just in case, consider photocopying the chart below and carrying it with you at all times.

ANGLICIZED NAME	CHINESE CHARACTERS	APPROXIMATE TRANSLITERATION
Orange Chicken	陳皮鵪	Chen pi ji
General Tso's Chicken	左宗堂	Zuo zong tang ji
Kung Pao Chicken	宮保　丁	Gong bao ji ding
Moo Goo Gai Pan	菟　片	Moo goo gai pan
Sweet and Sour Pork	肉	Tang cu liji
Chow Mein	炒面	Chow mein
Wonton Soup	馄饨	Wantan
Crab Rangoon	蟹角	Xie Jiao
Potstickers	子	Jiaozi

33 SONGS YOU CAN PLAY ON GUITAR WITH ONLY THE FOLLOWING THREE CHORDS

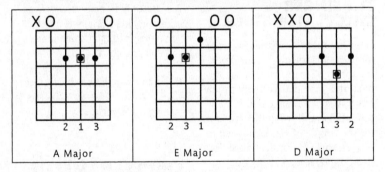

A Major　　　E Major　　　D Major

Practice the three chords above and then use your ear to figure out any of the following songs:

"O Susanna"

"Happy Birthday"

"Home on the Range"

"Twinkle, Twinkle, Little Star"

"You Are My Sunshine"

"Old MacDonald"

"Puff, the Magic Dragon"

"This Land Is Your Land"

"She'll Be Coming 'Round the Mountain"

"Blowin' in the Wind"

"John Henry"

"For What It's Worth"

"Feelin' Alright"

"Margaritaville"

"If Not for You"

"I Shot the Sheriff"

"Tangled Up in Blue"

"Sittin' on the Dock of the Bay"

"Heart of Gold"

"Wild World"

"Barbara Ann"

"Get Back"

"Love Me Do"

"Twist and Shout"

"Give Me One Reason"

"Lay Down Sally"

"All Along the Watchtower"

"Candle in the Wind"

"Not Fade Away"

"Sweet Home Chicago"

"Lively Up Yourself"

"Hound Dog"

"The First Cut Is the Deepest"

THREE TWO-PLAYER PAPER-AND-PENCIL GAMES

REVERSI RULES	
	1. Start with a graph-paper game board of any size.
	2. One player is X's and the other is O's (write lightly in pencil).
	3. Start with the position shown.
	4. Take turns placing your symbol. On each turn, you *must* trap an opponent's symbol between yours (horizontally, vertically, or diagonally), which you then flip to your symbol. (If you cannot trap at least one of your opponent's symbols, you lose your turn.)
	5. Once all squares are used, the player with the most symbols wins.

BOXES RULES

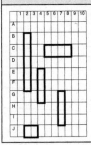

1. Start with a matrix of dots, as shown.

2. Take turns drawing a line horizontally or vertically between dots.

3. Your goal is to make closed squares. If you close a square mark it as your own (place an X or an O in that box).

4. If you close a square, move again.

5. Once all squares are closed, the player with the most symbols wins.

BATTLESHIP RULES

1. You need four boards like the one shown, two for each player.

2. Draw your five ships on one board (as shown).

3. Take turns shooting, by naming grid spaces (e.g., E-3). The opponent calls a hit or a miss. Mark your shots on your blank grid and your opponent's shots on your ship grid.

4. Continue until one player sinks all the other's ships.

CLASSIC EYE-BENDERS FROM THE WORLD OF GESTALT PSYCHOLOGY

Gestalt psychology considers the brain a holistic machine, the effect of which is greater than the sum of its parts. For example, different centers of the brain might be responsible for processing light signals, flipping through the mental Rolodex to match these light patterns with something we have seen before, recalling words to describe this picture, and sorting the sociocultural data that implies the scene might be of interest to others, but the sum of these functions is our ability to say, "Look! Two dogs humping!"

Key to Gestalt psychology is the study of the brain's process of visual cognition, specifically the brain's ability (and desire) to imply form from the seemingly formless using the strategies of *emergence, reification, multistability,* and *invariance* (examples shown here).

To test the limits of your brain's ability to create form using the rules of Gestalt psychology, try staring at a wall of faux painting until images emerge (or, for a more traditional example, at clouds). Some claim an auditory equivalent, such as listening to white noise machines until they hear words (or, for a more traditional example, to Beatles records played backward).

Multistability is the ability to see multiple stable visual interpretations in a picture.

Emergence describes your brain's ability and tendency to impose form on the formless.

Invariance is the brain's ability to recognize a shape despite rotation, translation, and scale.

Reification is the brain's ability to imply or generate shape from incomplete visual information.

GREAT THINKERS WHO HAVE MET TRAGICOMICALLY GRUESOME ENDS

Tycho Brahe was a sixteenth-century Danish astronomer, astrologer, and alchemist, most famous as the mentor of Johannes Kepler. In 1566, after a rousing night of drinking, Tycho lost a good part of his nose in a duel. Tycho was also patron to a clairvoyant dwarf and kept a tame moose, the latter of which died after consuming an enormous quantity of beer and falling down the stairs. Popular wisdom holds that Tycho Brahe died from an infection caused by a severely strained bladder, gained while trying to avoid leaving the table in the middle of a formal banquet. Other accounts hold that Kepler murdered Tycho with a mercury draught.

In 1626, the philosopher and essayist Sir Francis Bacon was trying to prove that freezing preserves food. His experiments included stuffing a chicken with snow. Not long after said experiment, he died of hypothermia.

In 1687, composers commonly conducted their music by banging a staff on the floor of the podium. In a fit of musical exuberance, composer Jean-Baptiste Lully accidentally pierced his foot and later died of gangrene.

Hypatia of Alexandria is considered the first important woman in mathematics. After being accused of heresy, she was killed in 415 by a Christian mob wielding sharpened seashells, using them to peel the flesh from her body. Her remains were then burned. Some say this marked the official end of Greco-Roman civilization.

The Greek philosopher Chrysippus is known as the second founder of Stoicism. His death in 207 B.C. is widely believed to have been the result of intense laughter sustained after feeding his donkey a significant quantity of wine and then watching it try to eat a fig.

Grigori Rasputin was adviser to Nicholas II of Russia, offering political counsel, mystic predictions, and faith healing. After being stabbed in a failed assassination attempt, Rasputin's intestines were sewn into his body. The next assassination attempt was more serious. First, Rasputin was given a massive dose of cyanide (he was largely unaffected); next, he was shot (again, largely unaffected, he managed to strangle his shooter to death); additional assassins arrived, shooting Rasputin three more times, clubbing him, wrapping him in a sheet and throwing him through a hole in an ice-covered river. The cause of death was hypothermia.

IMPORTANT LINKS FOR USE WITH THE SIX DEGREES OF KEVIN BACON

MOVIE	COSTARS
A FEW GOOD MEN	Tom Cruise, Jack Nicholson, Demi Moore, Kiefer Sutherland, Kevin Pollak, James Marshall
FLATLINERS	Kiefer Sutherland, Julia Roberts, William Baldwin, Oliver Platt, Benjamin Mouton
JFK	Kevin Costner, Tommy Lee Jones, Gary Oldman, Jack Lemmon, Laurie Metcalf, Sissy Spacek, Joe Pesci, John Candy, Walter Matthau, Donald Sutherland
DINER	Steve Guttenberg, Mickey Rourke, Tim Daly, Ellen Barkin, Paul Reiser
SLEEPERS	Billy Crudup, Robert De Niro, Vittorio Gassman, Minnie Driver, Dustin Hoffman, Ron Eldard, Jason Patric, Brad Pitt
OCEAN'S ELEVEN	(After linking through *Sleepers* with Pitt) George Clooney, Bernie Mac, Elliot Gould, Carl Reiner, Matt Damon, Andy Garcia, Julia Roberts
FOOTLOOSE	Lori Singer, John Lithgow, Dianne Wiest, Chris Penn, Sarah Jessica Parker, John Laughlin
APOLLO 13	Tom Hanks, Bill Paxton, Gary Sinise, Ed Harris, Kathleen Quinlan

AI AND THE END OF HUMAN RELEVANCE

In 1989, the Russian chess champion Garry Kasparov easily defeated the computer Deep Thought (name drawn from the Douglas Adams book). In 1997, Deep Blue kicked his ass, spawning accusations of cheating (which IBM denied). In a million-dollar rematch in 2003, Kasparov fought Deep Junior to a draw.

If, as Marcel Duchamp said, chess has "all the beauty of art and more," do Kasparov's break-even results mean that computers have drawn abreast of human creation, soon to overtake our brain's ability to interpret, create, and learn?

Researchers and developers of Artificial Intelligence say yes—yes, it does. Soon, they say, humans will be at best slaves and more likely relegated to distant, digitally archived memory (for better or for worse).

Since 1950, when Alan Turing (see "Turing Machine," page 205) posed the question Can computers think? the race has been on to make human beings obsolete. The real question, according to most AI researchers, is not whether computers can replicate human intelligence closely enough to be

USING data from the Internet Movie Database (www.imdb.com), Patrick Reynolds at the University of Virginia Department of Computer Science has computed the ideal Hollywood "centers" for use with the game six degrees of separation. According to Reynolds at oracleofbacon.org, Mr. Bacon is, in fact, only the 1,049th-best actor to use as the connecting center of your movie trivia universe (with a Bacon number of 2.946 steps). Contrast this with Robert De Niro's number of 2.758 (28th best center), Sean Connery's number of 2.730 (13th best center), and the top four centers Donald Sutherland (2.701), Dennis Hopper (2.698), Christopher Lee (2.684), and the king of them all, Rod Steiger, with a minuscule 2.679 (due mostly to the 146 movie appearances listed in his IMDb history).

PERHAPS more disturbing than the idea of being able to program computers to accomplish nearly anything better than humans is the idea that we won't need to program computers at all—they will soon be perfectly capable of learning to outperform us on their own. DARPA is currently investing heavily in Bootstrapped Learning (BL), or the idea of electronic systems that learn from human instructors without the need for programming (i.e., Robo X sits in the back of your child's kindergarten classroom, later attends lectures at MIT, and finally creates its own generation of improved, studious robots).

indistinguishable from it (already, in many situations, it can) but whether quacking like a duck is the same as *being* a duck—is the exact replication of intelligence actually intelligence? (For more, see the Chinese Room argument in the Thought Experiment described on page 10.)

The tools of AI are hugely complex, drawing not only on the idea that more and faster 1's and 0's are good, but also on mathematics, economics, probability theory, psychology, genetics (and natural selection), advanced concepts of neural networks, and many, many other seriously abstruse technical and scientific concepts. However, the general problems of AI are fairly well defined, breaking the overall goal of "intelligence" into the following eight subtasks: deduction/reasoning/problem-solving, knowledge representation, planning, learning, language processing, perception, motion, and social intelligence.

The combination of these tasks would result in Strong AI, or general intelligence. Like astro- and quantum physicists working toward a Unified Theory from the angle of their individual specialties, many AI researchers concentrate on one of the aforementioned problem areas, hoping to solve their tentacle, for later combination with other tentacles to create the full octopus; others consider Strong AI itself a necessary step toward solving any component, citing the interconnectedness of tasks.

No matter the approach, the accelerating pace of AI successes will soon necessitate sending a small pod of humans in search of another planet, and upon discovery, destroying all remnants of technology that traveled with them, in hopes of restarting and thus prolonging the human race.

THANKSGIVING DINNER IN 30 MINUTES OR LESS

1. TURKEY

Buy a cook-in-the-bag turkey breast roast. Turn on the oven. Throw it in. If your guests or house pets don't see you carve it, they will never know your dinner never gobbled (or, more precisely, that it is the unholy conglomeration of many separate gobblers).

2. MASHED POTATOES

Buy instant. Just add boiling water and enough butter and cream cheese to mask the slightly musty taste.

3. GRAVY

In the can.

4. CRANBERRY SAUCE

In the can. Be sure to actually place in dish and mash until the dog-food-esque shape is unrecognizable.

5. STUFFING

Stove Top. Consider adding craisins.

6. BUTTERMILK ROLLS

In the can. Look for Pillsbury or other similar rolls. Plop on baking sheet and set the timer.

7. PUMPKIN PIE

Because pumpkin pie freezes so well, buying the Cadillac frozen model is almost indistinguishable from the real thing.

SUGGESTIONS/ REFINEMENTS

• If you start the evening with a bottle or three of good wine, by the time you serve dinner, your guests will be predisposed to expect quality and will be inebriated enough to overlook telltale signs of corner-cutting.

• Consider making one of the above dishes from scratch. Then, regale your guests with stories of the painstaking creation. They will assume you slaved over the other dishes, as well.

• Use your best dishes and silverware (or rent place settings from a party shop). Again, heighten guests' expectations of quality.

• Be sure to dispose of all boxes and cans before guests' arrival.

APOLYTON UNIVERSITY: B.A. IN BS OR NEW-WAVE IT DEGREE?

The online game Civilization III is tricky to master. Do you beat competing civilizations into submission with your military? Do you conquer with diplomacy? Do you emphasize culture and learning? Each goal requires a different strategy, and winning strategies are highly specialized and precise. In fact, learning to play the game optimally can be as intricate and time-consuming as a college course.

Enter Apolyton University, the Web's premier Civ3 learning site, where you can take courses titled "The glory of culture" or "Give peace a chance" (or other, less pacifistic classes). Quality control is provided by deans functioning under the intellectual umbrella of the university president.

There are two situations that make Apolyton especially cool:

1. The goal of Apolyton University is to transform newbies into game users capable of assisting with later Civilization development. In fact, Dr. Kurt Squire, writing in the journal *Interact* (vol. 31, no. 10–11) described a lull in Apolyton's courses when many deans were hired to consult on Civilization IV. In other words, AU not only teaches game skills, but offers technical training with real-world value—the completion of AU courses leads to jobs.

2. Due to Civ3's inclusion of historically accurate civilization details (and the accompanying *Civilopedia*, which includes hundreds of pages of information on civilizations' technologies, geography, and militaries), the game is, in fact, useful in existing history education classrooms. Middle-school teachers have a tough time getting kids to read textbooks—not so (for better or for worse) with video games.

TWELVE HARRY POTTER SPELLS FOR USE IN DUELING

Accio: summons an object to hand.

Confringo: the blasting charm.

Confundus: causes the target to become confused.

Engorgio: causes target, or specific part of target, to grow (countercharm: reducio).

Evanesco: makes target disappear.

Expelliarmus: this disarmament spell is Potter's signature charm.

Impedimenta: slows target's progress toward the caster.

Incarcerus: ties target with ropes.

Incendio: produces fire.

Protego: the shield charm causes minor jinxes to rebound.

Reparo: repairs broken or damaged objects.

Stupefy: a red jet of light blasts the target into unconsciousness.

THE SIMPLEST ELECTRIC MOTOR

In 1986, the band Tesla recorded their debut album, *Mechanical Resonance,* which included the classic track "Modern Day Cowboy," alongside catchy arena anthems such as "EZ Come EZ Go." While their album title accurately describes the physical process that led to the collapse of the Tacoma Narrows Bridge in 1940, it has little connection to the Serbian-American inventor Nicola Tesla. However, the name of the band itself resuscitated the inventor's street cred. Apparently, discovering the rotating magnetic field principle, thereby fathering the electric motor and thus indirectly jump-starting the second industrial revolution, doesn't necessarily generate groupies among semimodern American teenagers. (The scientist Michael Faraday also advanced the field of electromagnetism, but his name has, to date, failed to inspire adoption by a post-Zeppelin pseudoglam band.)

The electric motor uses two magnets: one fixed permanent magnet and one electromagnet that spins within this fixed field. As you would expect, the rotating magnet would like to come to rest with its north pole pointing at the fixed magnet's south, and its south pole pointing at the fixed magnet's north (remember, opposites attract). Here's the trick: As soon as the relevant poles align, the rotating electromagnet flips its electrical field and thus reverses its magnetic poles (thank you, Tesla). All of a sudden, like poles are aligned and the rotating magnet must keep spinning in order to stick its south end toward the fixed magnet's north. And, just as this happens, the rotating magnet again flips fields, and—ride a painted pony, let the spinning wheel spin.

PATTERNS IN THE PERIODIC TABLE OF THE ELEMENTS

As any chemist knows, the periodic table is so much more than

THE PERIODIC TABLE OF THE ELEMENTS

1 H Hydrogen 1.00794								
3 Li Lithium 6.941	4 Be Beryllium 9.012182							
11 Na Sodium 22.989770	12 Mg Magnesium 24.3050							
19 K Potassium 39.0983	20 Ca Calcium 40.078	21 Sc Scandium 44.955910	22 Ti Titanium 47.867	23 V Vanadium 50.9415	24 Cr Chromium 51.9961	25 Mn Manganese 54.938049	26 Fe Iron 55.845	27 Co Cobalt 58.933200
37 Rb Rubidium 85.4678	38 Sr Strontium 87.62	39 Y Yttrium 88.90585	40 Zr Zirconium 91.224	41 Nb Niobium 92.90638	42 Mo Molybdenum 95.94	43 Tc Technetium (98)	44 Ru Ruthenium 101.07	45 Rh Rhodium 102.90550
55 Cs Cesium 132.90545	56 Ba Barium 137.327	57 La Lanthanum 138.9055	72 Hf Hafnium 178.49	73 Ta Tantalum 180.9479	74 W Tungsten 183.84	75 Re Rhenium 186.207	76 Os Osmium 190.23	77 Ir Iridium 192.217
87 Fr Francium (223)	88 Ra Radium (226)	89 Ac Actinium (227)	104 Rf Rutherfordium (261)	105 Db Dubnium (262)	106 Sg Seaborgium (263)	107 Bh Bohrium (262)	108 Hs Hassium (265)	109 Mt Meitnerium (266)

58 Ce Cerium 140.116	59 Pr Praseodymium 140.90765	60 Nd Neodymium 144.24	61 Pm Promethium (145)	62 Sm Samarium 150.36
90 Th Thorium 232.0381	91 Pa Protactinium 231.03588	92 U Uranium 238.0289	93 Np Neptunium (237)	94 Pu Plutonium (244)

a list. In fact, the table's progenitor, Dmitri Mendeleev, added the word "periodic" to describe the recurring trends of his carefully arranged elements.

Read left to right, top to bottom, the elements are organized by increasing atomic weight (the number of protons, which defines the element). Each row is known as a *period,* and subsequent rows represent shells of electrons. For example, helium has only one shell of electrons orbiting around its two protons (with two negatively charged electrons in this shell balancing the protons' positive charge). Gold (Au) has 79 electrons organized into six shells to balance its 79 protons. Elements in columns are known as *groups,* with these groups determining many characteristics, including reactivity (because elements in groups have the same number of electrons in their outermost or *valence* shell, which is the shell governing atomic interactions).

								2 **He** Helium 4.003
			5 **B** Boron 10.811	6 **C** Carbon 12.0107	7 **N** Nitrogen 14.00674	8 **O** Oxygen 15.9994	9 **F** Fluorine 18.9984032	10 **Ne** Neon 20.1797
			13 **Al** Aluminum 26.981538	14 **Si** Silicon 28.0855	15 **P** Phosphorus 30.973761	16 **S** Sulfur 32.066	17 **Cl** Chlorine 35.4527	18 **Ar** Argon 39.948
28 **Ni** Nickel 58.6934	29 **Cu** Copper 63.546	30 **Zn** Zinc 65.39	31 **Ga** Gallium 69.723	32 **Ge** Germanium 72.61	33 **As** Arsenic 74.92160	34 **Se** Selenium 78.96	35 **Br** Bromine 79.904	36 **Kr** Krypton 83.80
46 **Pd** Palladium 106.42	47 **Ag** Silver 107.8682	48 **Cd** Cadmium 112.411	49 **In** Indium 114.818	50 **Sn** Tin 118.710	51 **Sb** Antimony 121.760	52 **Te** Tellurium 127.60	53 **I** Iodine 126.90447	54 **Xe** Xenon 131.29
78 **Pt** Platinum 195.078	79 **Au** Gold 196.96655	80 **Hg** Mercury 200.59	81 **Tl** Thallium 204.3833	82 **Pb** Lead 207.2	83 **Bi** Bismuth 208.98038	84 **Po** Polonium (209)	85 **At** Astatine (210)	86 **Rn** Radon (222)
110 (269)	111 (272)	112 (277)	113	114				

63 **Eu** Europium 151.964	64 **Gd** Gadolinium 157.25	65 **Tb** Terbium 158.92534	66 **Dy** Dysprosium 162.50	67 **Ho** Holmium 164.93032	68 **Er** Erbium 167.26	69 **Tm** Thulium 168.93421	70 **Yb** Ytterbium 173.04	71 **Lu** Lutetium 174.967
95 **Am** Americium (243)	96 **Cm** Curium (247)	97 **Bk** Berkelium (247)	98 **Cf** Californium (251)	99 **Es** Einsteinium (252)	100 **Fm** Fermium (257)	101 **Md** Mendelevium (258)	102 **No** Nobelium (259)	103 **Lr** Lawrencium (262)

Elements like to have full valence shells. The rightmost column (group 18) has naturally full valence shells—these "noble gases" don't need to take, give, or share electrons to get what they want and thus have very low reactivity. Conversely, the halogens in group 17 need to pick up only one electron to be happy (in the quantum sense) and are thus very friendly when given the chance to react with, for example, hydrogen (to make hydrofluoric, hydrochloric, hydrobromic, and hydroiodic acids). In the leftmost group, hydrogen tends to grab a shared electron in hopes of filling its two-electron valence shell (becoming like helium). Lithium,

sodium, potassium, and the others in group 1 tend to ditch an electron, thus clearing out this last valence shell and becoming positively charge ions (because their protons now overpower their electrons). This is why the elements of group 1 react so readily with the elements of group 17, which have followed similar strategy in sucking in an additional electron to fill their valence shells, thereby become negatively charged ions (thus table salt—NaCl). This is also why potassium reacts so violently with water, ripping into H_2O to make KHO with a whole bunch of extra heat and hydrogen, which tend to go boom.

A SAM LOYD MATHEMATICS PUZZLE

How close can the young archer come to scoring a total of 100, using as many arrows as she pleases?

A BIT OF PSEUDO-INCOMPREHEN-SIBILIA FROM A PAPER MY FRIEND WROTE

"The rift tips will only propagate in this manner if the strength to tensile fracture of the adjacent lithosphere is small relative to the strength of the frozen rift. If, on the other hand, the adjacent lithosphere is too strong to be fractured by rift tip propagation, deformation and faulting will remain localized on the rift centre."

Richard F. Katz and Eberhard Bodenschatz, "Taking Wax for a Spin: Microplates in an Analog Model of Plate Tectonics." *Europhysics News* Sept.–Oct. 2005, 155–58.

DRAGONS IN MYTH

Many researchers point to the similarities between dragon myths of widely disparate ancient cultures as proof of one of the following three theories: pre-Columbian contact between ancient cultures, the dragon's actual existence across said cultures, or the existence of an Atlantean nexus of learning, enlightenment, and mythical beasts, long since reclaimed by the sea. Other, less open-minded scientists blame the dragon on humans' collective unconscious fear of snakes, lions, and birds of prey, or on the exaggeration of real-life models such as monitor lizards and dino-saur bones. Still other researchers point to the rather loose definition of *dragon*, which allows any fairly scaly beast larger than a horse to claim the title, thus augmenting the distribution.

In the Phillipines, the sea-dwelling Bakunawa eats the sun or moon during eclipses; in Japan, the snakelike Ryu grants wishes (à la *Neverending Story*); Fafnir, an Old Norse *lindworm*, killed his father for want of gold; Smok Wawelski used to maraud around the Polish countryside causing the general badness you would expect of a dragon; the Hungarian Sárkány loses power as it loses heads; and beware Quetzalcoatl, the Mesoamerican dragon that is due to make another appearance in 2012, when it will destroy and thus re-create the world.

SECURITIES SAVINGS ACCOUNTS: IRA VS. 401(K)

IRA		401(κ)	
DESCRIPTION	Both ROTH and traditional IRAs offer tax incentives to invest in retirement.	**DESCRIPTION**	An employer-sponsored retirement account, typically using money withheld from your paycheck, which is invested in a diversified stock or bond account, where it grows tax-free until you retire.
WHO FOR?	Employees looking to augment 401(k) savings or anyone without a 401(k).	**WHO FOR?**	Employees looking long term.
COMMENTS	Due to differences in withdrawal penalties, ROTH is generally better for younger people, while a traditional IRA is better for older. After your 401(k), this is the next step. Contribute as much as possible every year.	**COMMENTS**	Some employers match to a certain level. If so (and in most situations even if not), this should be your primary retirement savings account. Put in the max possible every year.

VS. MUTUAL OR INDEX FUND VS. BONDS

MUTUAL OR INDEX FUND	
DESCRIPTION	A highly diversified stock portfolio in which your risk is minimized by spreading money across many companies (with your type of fund determining risk and reward).
WHO FOR?	Investors looking for a hands-off way to grow money over the midrange.
COMMENTS	Most investors consider index funds an attractive balance between safety and returns. Best results are in the 10+ year range.

BONDS	
DESCRIPTION	When you buy a bond, you become the bank, lending money with the expectation of being paid back with interest at a set future date (maturity date).
WHO FOR?	Long-term investors looking for low risk.
COMMENTS	Bonds occupy a middle ground between no-risk bank accounts and riskier stocks, with payback commensurate with risk. Bonds are a good place for a nest egg that doesn't need to grow much.

HACKING 101

"Bingo," sniffed acne-prone seventeen-year-old computer whiz Harvey Schlep. "We're in." Harvey proceeded to divert Microsoft's 2020 profits into an offshore account in the Caymans, spam the whereabouts and results of the U.S. government's extraterrestrial interrogation program all over cyberspace, and remotely activate and stream all in-computer webcams of female MySpace users between the ages of sixteen and twenty-four.

This is every hacker's dream. The reality is a bit grittier.

Basically, to be an Internet hacker, you need to be smarter and more creative than the person doing the initial programming. And this programming draws on the massive combined expertise of security companies under the umbrellas of huge companies like Microsoft, Google, and the U.S. government. Generally speaking, the combined wisdom of these institutions trumps your measly Linux/C++ expertise. However, like Neo, you might be different. You, like Chuck Yeager, might have the right stuff.

The crux of hacking is (of course) finding a way into a remote computer. This can be through the front door, using the target's password (gained by phishing for it, intercepting it in transit, or other less high-tech techniques, such as trash sifting and/or getting the target extremely inebriated and then asking for it), or it can be through the back door, i.e., circumventing a system's security. In the latter case, you can depend on your target to download, install, or otherwise place a rigged application on the system, thus accidentally compromising it himself (using a Trojan horse, virus, or worm), or you can try to force your way into the target's system (for example, using a vulnerability scanner to scroll through known security weaknesses).

But the true art to hacking lies in the ability to recognize and exploit *unknown* security weaknesses. To do this, you will need to know how to program. In fact, you will need to know how to program very, very well. It takes years of expertise and, like the aforementioned Neo, the ability to see through thousands of lines of code into the Matrix itself, where there may or may not be holes.

FOUR CLASSIC TYPES OF RAT MAZE

THE CLASSIC RAT MAZE

A mouse/rat starts at an entrance and makes its way through the expected twists, turns, dead ends, and splits until reaching a reward at the maze's end. Researchers measure speed and accuracy of subsequent passes to determine a rat's learning.

THE RADIAL ARM MAZE

A rat sits at the hub of tunnels that radiate like spokes away from it. Often food pellets are placed at the far end of each tunnel and researchers watch the rat to see if it remembers which tunnels it has already visited.

THE MORRIS WATER MAZE

In a tub of opaque water sit two small platforms, submerged only far enough to be invisible. A rat starts on one platform and researchers evaluate the rat's ability to swim to the other platform.

T MAZE AND Y MAZE

A rat travels along a corridor and then two paths diverge (frequently in a yellow wood). The rat chooses between these identical options.

THE PREDICTIVE POWERS OF THE IOWA ELECTRONIC MARKETS

Contango! That's what you could be yelling if you buy low and sell high in the futures market! (All in the comfort of your own home!)

Basically, when you buy a "future" you are agreeing to buy stuff at a given price at a later date. If, for example, you buy futures in oil at a price of $89 per barrel, you have locked in this price for a future date, and if at that future date the actual price has followed the upward-sloping curve known as "contango" and is higher than $89, you win. (The

opposite of contango is backwardation, which is not nearly as much fun to yell.) Here's how this works in the Iowa Electronic Markets (IEM):

You could have bought futures on the 2008 presidential election, choosing to be paid a dollar if the Dems won or a dollar if the Reps won. Based on current buyers and sellers, the price of these one-dollar futures varied. For example, when this market opened in 2006, Democratic and Republican shares sold for nearly 50¢ apiece (reflecting buyers' fifty-fifty view of who would win). In 2007, after the Democrats cleaned up in the midterm elections, you could have bought a future payable on a 2008 Republican win for 31¢, but it would have cost you nearly 90¢ for a Democratic future.

How, exactly, this differs from Internet gambling is anyone's guess.

However, in addition to lining the winners' pockets, the IEM has a surprising function: it predicts things. If, on election eve, the IEM shares for Democrats are selling higher than the shares for Republicans, there is a very, very good chance the Democrats are going to win (in fact, the IEM is consistently more accurate than professional polling data). And the IEM predicts more than just political races. In 2007, you could have bought futures on predicted *Beowulf* profits, on Microsoft's price level, or on the returns of the computer industry.

Most observers credit the IEM's predictive accuracy to its

ability to disentangle what people *want* from what people *expect,* thus measuring not only the wisdom of a crowd, but the wisdom of a crowd that has been forced to put its money where its mouth is. For example, you may be a committed Green Party voter, and on election eve you might wax poetic to a pollster about your candidate's chances, but would you *really* put a hundred dollars on Ralph Nader?

MANGA, ANIME, AND THE GRAPHIC NOVEL

The term *manga* was used in Japan as early as 1798 and refers simply to a comic strip (literally, "whimsical pictures"). Like any country's artwork, Japanese manga evolved an endemic set of artistic and stylistic values, notably influenced by kung fu, sci-fi, and robotics. When comic books hit TV and movie screens, manga's moving version became known as *anime.* Anime's hits in the United States include *Pokemon* and *Dragonball Z.*

For the most part, modern graphic novels skip the niceties of anime's kids series, instead connecting with the dark, fantastical side of manga. The modern graphic novel is effectively a thick comic book, usually with a complex story line and highly stylized black-and-white illustrations. While comic book publishers such as DC and Marvel were the first to embrace the genre, mainstream book publishers have jumped aboard, and some graphic novels have sold in excess of a hundred thousand copies.

THE LESS-KNOWN FICTION OF J. R. R. TOLKIEN

Unless you've recently arrived through a wormhole from some related but not wholly identical world, you know about *The Lord of the Rings.* It's likely you even know about the book's predecessor, *The Hobbit.* If you are an armchair Tolkien geek, you've heard of the *Silmarillion,* and if you are starting to stand out of said armchair, you've actually read it. But what about Tolkien's other works? The following list omits nonfiction and all works incomplete at the time of the author's death in 1973.

- 1945—*Leaf by Niggle*

- 1949—*Farmer Giles of Ham*

- 1953—*The Homecoming of Beorhtnoth Beorhthelm's Son*

- 1962—*The Adventures of Tom Bombadil*

- 1967—*Smith of Wootton Major*

THE FOUR LAWS OF THERMODYNAMICS

Zeroth: If two thermodynamic systems are in thermal equilibrium with a third, they are also in thermal equilibrium with each other.

First: Energy can be converted from one form to another, but it cannot be created or destroyed. (The total amount of energy and matter in the universe is constant.)

Second: The total entropy of a system tends to increase over time (especially if one is parent to toddlers).

Third: Nothing can reach absolute zero, the state of zero entropy at which all molecular motion ceases. If one did reach absolute zero, it would result in all life as you know it stopping instantaneously and every molecule in your body exploding at the speed of light and/or in the destruction of Gozer the Gozerian.

ROBOGAMES AND OTHER ROBOTICS COMPETITIONS

Every year since its inauguration in 2004, very serious geeks have gathered at the RoboGames in San Francisco, nominally to test

WHEN J. R. R. Tolkien died in 1973, he left behind a huge number of partial and unfinished manuscripts, spawning an entire academic field of Tolkienology, many of whose practitioners seem to have difficulty dissociating Middle-earth from English and Norse history and vice versa. Most notably, the author's son Christopher Tolkien jumped into the field, editing much of the senior Tolkien's work. Between 1983 and 1996, Christopher Tolkien published a twelve-part history of Middle-earth, aptly titled *The History of Middle-earth*.

their robots' skills in Olympic-themed events such as the septathalon, weightlifting, and the marathon, but in actuality to see if their robot can kick others robots' asses in various combat genres and weight classes. For example, in 2007 in the 340-pound weight class, the Canadian robot Ziggy thrashed the American robots The Judge and Vladiator to claim the gold medal.

Other, less overtly destructive robotics competitions include the following:

• International Aerial Robotics Competition: fully autonomous robots compete to complete simulated real-world tasks, such as searching a disaster scene, remote surveillance, and hazardous waste location and identification.

• DARPA Ground Challenge: Driverless cars compete to navigate a course in the shortest time possible. In 2007, the prize was $2 million.

• RoboCup: The stated goal of RoboCup is to create a team of autonomous humanoid robots that, by 2050, can beat the most recent human World Cup champions (playing by FIFA rules and without the use of other long-promised technologies such as jetpacks, laser guns, or the flying car).

FUN QUOTES FROM THE WORLD'S TOP DICTATORS

I would not vote for the mayor. It's not just because he didn't invite me to dinner, but because on my way into town from the airport there were such enormous potholes.

—Fidel Castro while visiting New York City under Rudy Giuliani

On the last day when I was speaking before the assembly, one of our group told me that when I started to say "In the name of God the almighty and merciful," he saw a light around me, and I was placed inside this aura. I felt it myself.

—Mahmoud Ahmadinejad after speaking to the United Nations General Assembly

The devil came here yesterday and it smells of sulfur still today.

—Hugo Chavez, speaking of George W. Bush to the United Nations General Assembly

Our party must continue to strike fear into the heart of the white man, our real enemy.

—Robert Mugabe in a December, 2000, speech to ZANU-PF congress

COOL INVENTIONS OF THE ANCIENT CHINESE

The wheelbarrow allowed one person to accomplish the work of many, dramatically speeding up construction projects from the 1st century B.C. onward.

When combined with the compass, the rudder helped the ancient Chinese to explore the world, including, by 1000 A.D., India, North Africa, Persia, and the Mediterranean.

The ancient Chinese used the compass to navigate when out of sight of land.

The ancient Chinese invented paper, which was popular from around 100 B.C. until early in the 21st century.

Gunpowder allowed the ancient Chinese to blow stuff up, notably each other.

Paper money has value only because "the man" says so, thus requiring confidence in a powerful and stable political system. Also, if you are trapped in a snowstorm, paper money can be used to start a fire.

NASA'S CENTENNIAL CHALLENGES

If you're looking for an easy way to make your first million, look elsewhere. These challenges stump NASA rocket scientists. However, if you're looking for a good way to while away an engineering Ph.D. or for a fun basement project that will teach your kids the value of process-based rather than results-based inquiry, read on. These NASA challenges are meant to spur private-sector interest in solving the vexing problems of space colonization.

MOON REGOLITH OXYGEN EXTRACTION CHALLENGE— $1 MILLION

Hands-down, this prize has the coolest nickname: MoonRox. To win this "first to demonstrate" prize, you have to extract breathable oxygen from lunar regolith— the dust and broken rock covering the moon's surface.

REGOLITH EXCAVATION CHALLENGE—$750,000

Of course, in order to use moon regolith, one must first gather it. This sounds easy, but lunar regolith—mostly in the form of a glassy, jagged, frozen, four-foot-thick blanket—is an especially feisty substance. To win this head-to-head challenge, your team must excavate and deliver more regolith than other teams in a thirty-minute period.

PERSONAL AIR VEHICLE CHALLENGE—$300,000

Still looking for that flying car or jetpack? So are the entrants of this competition.

BEAM POWER CHALLENGE— $900,000

Even NASA has gone wireless. In this challenge, design teams beam power from a ground-based transmitter to a receiver on a "car" that must use this power to climb a tether (see Tether Challenge) to a height of fifty meters.

TETHER CHALLENGE— $900,000

In conjunction with the Beam Power Challenge, the Tether Challenge hopes to promote space elevator technology, specifically, a system by which people or materials could climb up a superstrong tether, leaving Earth's atmosphere. Though, to win this competition all you have to do is to create a tether that is at least 50 percent stronger than last year's winner.

ASTRONAUT GLOVE CHALLENGE—$400,000

This is a yearly head-to-head competition during which teams test their gloves in a variety of challenges, mostly focusing on dexterity, flexibility, durability, sensitivity, and effective contraception.

LUNAR LANDER CHALLENGE—$2 MILLION

This prize hopes to spur development of a craft that could ferry people and supplies from lunar orbit to lunar surface. To win, your craft has to take off vertically, fly for a set period of time, land, launch again, and return to its starting point.

THE PREDICTIONS OF NOSTRADAMUS

No more sifting through unsanitary goat knuckles, searching for abstractions in tea leaves, shaking the Mattel Magic 8 Ball, listening to *Yellow Submarine* backward, or trudging India's highlands in search of infamously reclusive gurus—instead, look no further for answers than *Les Propheties*, the 1555 work of Michel de Nostradame. Basically, Notradamus assumed that planetary alignment influenced world events. He correlated celestial configurations to concurrent events, and then calculated when the planets would again reach this alignment, predicting that, at that time, similar events would occur—this enhanced by trance-aided pseudoscholarly interpretation of existing sources, including Savonarola, Joachim de Fiore, the Bible, and Egyptian hieroglyphics, the last of which had not yet been interpreted but were widely understood to be cool in a magically arcane sort of way.

Though some naysayers point to "retroactive clairvoyance" (i.e., the interpretive clarity of hindsight), it is generally understood by readers of the *Celestine Prophecy* and frequent posters to the news pages of National UFO Reporting Center that Nostradamus successfully predicted the death of Henry II of France, the great fire of London, the French Revolution, the rise of Napoleon (and Hitler), the exile of Franco, the works of Louis Pasteur and Charles De Gaulle, and the Kennedy assassination (and perhaps the terrorist attacks of September 11, as well). For example, he writes of Henry II's death:

*The young lion will overcome the
    older one
On the field of combat in a single
    battle
He will pierce his eyes through a
    golden cage
Two wounds made one, then he
    dies a cruel death.*

Henry II was killed in a jousting accident when a splinter from his younger opponent's lance snuck through the visor of his golden helmet, piercing his left eye and exiting his ear. Henry suffered for days before finally succumbing. Both jousters used shields embossed with lions. Spooky, huh?

Unfortunately, Nostradamus also predicts massive earthquakes, World War III, and the rapidly approaching end of the world, so, generally speaking, very soon it will suck to be us.

THE TRAGIC CASE OF LEE SEUNG SEOP

On August 5, 2005, a twenty-eight-year-old South Korean man, Lee Seung Seop, died of exhaustion and dehydration-induced heart failure after sitting at an Internet café for fifty consecutive hours while playing the game StarCraft.

MALE/FEMALE RATIO AND BAND TRIVIA FROM AMERICA'S TOP UNIVERSITIES

School	% Female Students	University Band Trivia
Princeton	46	At the end of each year, the Princeton band goes to White Castle, where the member who consumes the most Slyders is named king of the castle.
Harvard	49	The Harvard band's eight-foot-diameter bass drum is known as Bertha.
Yale	49	At the annual Yale-Harvard game, Yale uses überprops such as the 2007 stegosaurus named Bessie to destroy John Harvard in effigy.
Stanford	48	The Stanford band is likely the most controversial (read "tastelessly entertaining") of all university bands, having at various times lampooned polygamy, Catholicism, and O. J. Simpson, and transformed an anagram formation NEUT for *tune* into NCUT for something else.
Penn	50	After the third quarter of every Penn game, the band plays *Drink a Highball* and fans throw toast onto the field (how droll!).
Cal Tech	28	There is currently no Caltech marching band. This hasn't stopped Caltech from pranking other bands.
MIT	44	Every year the MIT band sacrifices SPAM in hopes of generating heavenly influence for a better football season. So far this has either validated atheism or shown that God hates SPAM.
Duke	48	You can likely guess the acronym of the Duke University Marching Band.
Columbia	51	The CUMB performs at 11:59 P.M. on the night before every Organic Chemistry final.
Chicago	50	The University of Chicago has a marching band and a football team. Really they do.
Dartmouth	51	Motto: "The Band Always Wins."
Cornell	49	During every home game, an "aardvarker," usually suspended from a railing or ladder, warbles shrilly while shaking his or her arms.

FOUR PRETTY CONVINCING UFO SIGHTINGS

CHICAGO O'HARE INCIDENT

At 4:30 P.M. on November 7, 2006, United Airlines ramp employees were pushing back flight 446 bound for Charlotte, North Carolina. In their accounts of what followed, said employees denied huffing jet fuel. An unlit, saucer-shaped craft hovered over gate C-17 for nearly two minutes, during which time the ramp employees called pilots, supervisors, and other UA employees—nearly a dozen in all—who then watched the mysterious craft rocket up through the clouds. The FAA at first denied anything out of the ordinary, but after a *Chicago Tribune* reporter filed a Freedom of Information Act request, the FAA had to admit that yes, they had received official reports, and no, they had no plans to investigate further. The story was reported on CNN, MSNBC, Fox News, and NPR.

MEXICAN UFO INCIDENT

On March 5, 2004, a Mexican Air Force Merlin C-26A was scanning the skies of Campeche state for drug-smuggling airplanes. The plane's dome-mounted IR system recorded at least eleven very hot spheres traveling irregularly. The plane pursued. The plane's commander described chasing the lights, which disappeared only when the plane stopped chasing (playful aliens?). Video footage is available online.

HEIGHT 611 UFO INCIDENT

In Dalnegorsk, as in most of the USSR on the night of January 20, 1986, it was really fricking cold. That night, a red ball of fire cruised through Dalnegorsk at about 15 m/s and a height of about 700 m. The ball hovered and finally landed on Mount Izvestkovaya, also known as Height 611. The next day, investigators found a burned landing zone of about two meters square, lead deposits, and a "black film" covering much of the mountaintop.

THE CASH-LANDRUM INCIDENT

On the night of December 29, 1980, Betty Cash and Vickie Landrum were driving home from dinner in Cash's Oldsmobile Cutlass. Little did they know they were about to be (nearly) melted into flesh puddles by a diamond-shaped UFO blazing from its underside like a massive gas broiler ("That's Jesus," said Vickie Landrum at the time. "He won't hurt us.") Soon after, they claim, the UFO was surrounded by at least twenty-three army helicopters, which escorted it away. Both women later required hospitalization for radiation poisoning, which they blamed on the government and for which they have subsequently sued.

STARTING PAY BY COLLEGE MAJOR

More proof that geeks rule the earth—the Top 10:

1. Chemical Engineering—$55,900

2. Computer Engineering—$54,877

3. Electrical/Electronics/ Communications Engineering—$52,899

4. Mechanical Engineering—$50,672

5. Computer Science—$50,046

6. Accounting—$45,723

7. Economics/Finance/ Banking—$45,191

8. Civil Engineering—$44,999

9. Business Administration/ Management—$39,850

10. Marketing/Marketing Management/Marketing Research—$36,260

Other Popular Majors:

Music—$35,610

English—$31,169

Biology—$29,750

Elementary Education—$27,317

Journalism—$27,646

Psychology—$25,032

THE MYSTERIOUS NUMBER PHI

What do Greek architecture, the seashell, and the proportions of the human body have to do with the Fibonacci sequence (. . . 3, 5, 8, 13, 21, etc.)? Each yields the number phi, or approximately 1.618. The Fibonacci connection is fairly obvious: Just divide any number in the sequence by its predecessor and you end up with an approximation of phi. In Greek architecture, phi defines the proportions of temple base to height, length to width of frieze panels, and columns to overall height; in many seashells, phi defines the ratio of one curl to the next; in the human body, it is the ratio of your thumb to your first finger, below your belly button to above it, and the width of your shoulders to your torso (among many others). Da Vinci applied the "golden rectangle" of phi proportions to the human face (as seen in the drawing on page 107). Phi is also the ratio of length to width of a credit card. Mathematically, phi is defined by the line segments a and b in which $a + b$ is to a as a is to b. Is the prevalence of phi ratios a massive evolutionary and aesthetic coincidence? Maybe.

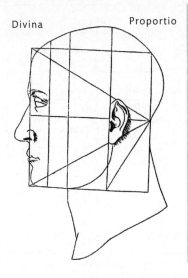

Divina   Proportio

THE 121 CURRENT BOY SCOUT MERIT BADGES FROM MOST TO LEAST GEEKY

After exploring the list below, use the rankings to compute your Boy Scout Geek Ranking (BSGR): Subtract the numbers of your merit badges from 121 and then add all your scores. Any BSGR greater than 500 implies high danger of becoming a Rotarian in middle age.

1. Bugling	2. Traffic Safety	3. Basketry	4. Genealogy
5. Reptile and Amphibian Study	6. Composite Materials	7. Nuclear Science	8. Emergency Preparedness
9. Theater	10. Stamp Collecting	11. Coin Collecting	12. Dentistry
13. Computers	14. Fire Safety	15. Insect Study	16. Textile
17. Crime Prevention	18. Space Exploration	19. Astronomy	20. Bird Study
21. Electronics	22. Chemistry	23. Communications	24. Electricity
25. Safety	26. Energy	27. Engineering Entrepreneurship	28. Surveying
29. Pioneering	30. Fingerprinting	31. Radio	32. Weather
33. Journalism	34. Collections	35. Cinematography	36. Pottery
37. Leatherwork	38. Model Design and Building	39. Pulp and Paper	40. Mammal Study
41. Citizenship in the Community	42. Law	43. Music	44. Metalwork

45. Oceanography	46. Orienteering	47. Scholarship	48. Geology
49. Cooking	50. Architecture	51. Railroading	52. Environmental Science
53. Graphic Arts	54. Gardening	55. Public Health	56. Archery
57. Wood Carving	58. Aviation	59. American Business	60. Fish and Wildlife Management
61. American Heritage	62. American Cultures	63. Animal Science	64. Archaeology
65. Art	66. Citizenship in the Nation	67. Citizenship in the World	68. Drafting
69. First Aid	70. Fly Fishing	71. Forestry	72. Landscape Architecture
73. Medicine	74. Nature	75. American Labor	76. Painting
77. Photography	78. Plant Science	79. Public Speaking	80. Sculpture
81. Soil and Water Conservation	82. Veterinary Medicine	83. Indian Lore	84. Salesmanship
85. Family Life	86. Wilderness	87. Skating	88. Survival
89. Hiking	90. Backpacking	91. Pets	92. Lifesaving
93. Camping	94. Canoeing	95. Disabilities Awareness	96. Dog Care
97. Reading	98. Rowing	99. Rifle Shooting	100. Swimming
101. Shotgun Shooting	102. Small-Boat Sailing	103. Cycling	104. Golf
105. Fishing	106. Woodwork	107. Climbing	108. Home Repairs
109. Horsemanship	110. Personal Management	111. Motorboating	112. Farm Mechanics
113. Water Skiing	114. Auto Mechanics	115. Athletics	116. Personal Fitness
117. Snow Sports	118. Sports	119. Whitewater	120. Plumbing
121. Truck Transportation			

THE NINE TAXONS USED TO CLASSIFY ALL LIVING THINGS

By the early eighteenth century, the Swedish botanist Carl Linnaeus realized the field of biology needed a precise system to classify living things. (Pre-Linnaeus conversation: Biologist I says, "The *little* green bug?" Biologist II replies, "No, the *really* little green bug." Biologist I says, "The one with the legs?" Biologist II replies, "No, the one with the wings, dumbass." Biologist I coldcocks Biologist II, setting back aphid research by years.) In Linnaeus's system, an organism is described to increasing degrees of specificity by naming its kingdom, phylum, class, infraclass, order, suborder, family, genus, and species. For example, the California sea slug is classified as Animalia Mollusca, Gastropoda, Orthogastropoda Heterobranchia, Opistobrachia, Anaspidea, Aplysiidae, Aplysia californica. The bettong (see "Nine Australian Animals That Most People Think Are Fake," page 20) is: Animalia, Chordata, Mammalia, Marsupialia, Diprotodontia, Macropodiformes, Potoroidae Caloprymnus potorous.

(see "Nine Australian Animals That Most People Think Are Fake," page 20)

A SAM LOYD PICTURE PUZZLE

Can you find the star in the jumbled shapes below?

THE LOST STAR.

FIVE VERY GOOD PLACES TO EAT PIE (THE DESSERT)

DUTCH MOTHER'S RESTAURANT—LYNDEN, WA

If your budget doesn't allow a trip to Holland, Dutch Mother's Restaurant in Lynden, Washington, is an acceptable alternative. In fact, the pie here is so good that some have claimed out-of-body experiences. (Perhaps secret ingredients flown straight from Amsterdam?) Try the raspberry.

KITCHENETTE— NEW YORK, NY

It's hard to maintain the air of disaffected Weltschmerz required of Greenwich Village in this down-home diner, complete with pies you wish your grandma had made.

THE CRAZY MOUNTAIN INN—MARTINSDALE, MT

Do not snap your fingers at the waitress, or you risk being shot by six-gun-wielding locals. Despite the location (central Nowhere), once you go Crazy, you'll never go back.

NOON MARK DINER— KEENE VALLEY, NY

The pies bake early and thus at about 7:00 A.M. a line of hikers, anglers, climbers, and other hoary-faced roustabouts forms outside the door, drawn from their tents by the smell of berry pies.

BLUE OWL RESTAURANT AND BAKERY— KIMMSWICK, MO

Is quantity quality? You won't go away hungry from the Blue Owl. Try the caramel apple pecan pie (Rachael Ray recommends it too!).

ESSENTIAL EQUATIONS: DETERMINING THE ALCOHOL CONTENT OF HOME BREW

Ah sweet, sweet yeast feces! As though turning lead to gold, these blessed little alchemist martyrs transform unexciting sugar into thrilling alcohol, finally dying in their own waste (thereby making the Super Bowl what it is today, and making Oktoberfests possible across the world). But how potent is your homemade potable? (If you got that reference, it's time for a *Jeopardy!* holiday.) Rather than depending on your friends' recollections of your depravity and then calculating alcohol content based on your behavior, try one of the equations below.

WITH HYDROMETER

$$\%ABW = 76.08 \times \left(\frac{OG - FG}{1.7575 - OG}\right)$$

OG = specific gravity of wort at 60°F (before adding yeast)
FG = specific gravity after fermentation
%ABW = percentage of alcohol by weight

$$\%ABV = ABW \times \left(\frac{FG}{.794}\right)$$

%ABV = percentage of alcohol by volume

WITHOUT HYDROMETER

$$MAX\%ABV = \frac{11.39 \, (F + .8M)}{W - .5}$$

S = weight of sugar in kg
M = weight of malt extract in kg
W = volume of wort in gallons

MAX%ABV is the potential percentage of alcohol by volume, assuming you allow all sugar to ferment.

HEIGHT/WEIGHT CHART

Despite helping to develop superior finger-eye coordination and leading to overuse injuries that allow you to sue major electronics companies, playing Halo III for every available waking hour has not yet been demonstrated to help one achieve healthy body mass index (BMI, not to be confused with the recording company of same initials, home of, among others, Hannah Montana and Willie Nelson). The chart below is the malicious handiwork of the United States Department of Health and Human Services, but what do they know?

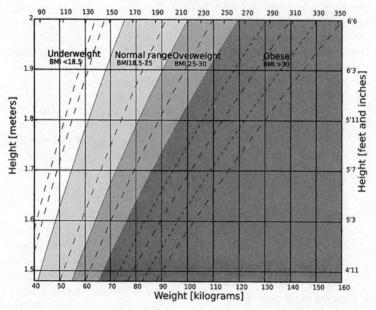

A FILM-CANISTER CANNON NEARLY GUARANTEED TO REMOVE EYEBROWS AND/OR BLOW OFF FINGERS

Do you ever feel like annihilating the world in a massive nuclear flash? If so, perhaps it's time to start seeing a therapist. Or better yet, vent your barely repressed rage through somewhat less destructive forms of pyromania, like this nifty cannon, capable of blasting a film canister (*film*, n.: a thin, translucent strip of cellulose coated with emulsion sensitive to light, used until the early twenty-first century in cameras) nearly thirty feet in the air—and the accompanying blast of flame does away with the need for costly electrolysis!

DIRECTIONS:

1. Remove igniter from fireplace lighter or other electronic lighter.

2. Solder or otherwise attach a short copper wire to each igniter element.

3. Push wire ends through slits in loose top of film canister so the exposed ends are close but not touching (an electrical charge should jump from one to the other). Secure.

4. Spray one hit of Binaca or a short blast of hair spray into film canister and quickly close the wire-rigged lid.

5. Place film canister lid-down on the ground (or mount the whole contraption).

6. Press igniter element button.

7. Seek medical attention.

COMMON PROGRAMMING LANGUAGES

JAVA

Java is the Man, in the big-brother-is-watching sense of the word, the juggernaut that threatens to homogenize the programming world—or would be, if it weren't for programmers' inherent skepticism of the Man and the compounding realization that Java lacks features. Still, if for some reason you happen to have time to learn only one programming language, Java is one of your best (and fairly simple) options.

C

While primarily used for system programming (coding operating systems), C can also be used for applications. Unfortunately, C can be a bit unwieldy for the amateur programmer. That is, it can be hard to get what you want and easy to get what you don't, but this also results in minimal constraints.

VISUAL BASIC

Are you late to jump on the Linux train or still unimpressed by Mac gadgetry? Still doggedly running Windows? If so, Visual Basic might be for you. Keep your eyes peeled for VisualBasic.net, up soon. Maybe the update will solve the memory management issues. For now, Visual Basic is one of the big four (with Java, C++, and C). It's known for quick and easy use.

PHP

Born of the web, PHP is used mainly for server-side scripting (by Golem-like hackers starting to lose inessential body functions, like speech and hearing, while accentuating finger length and gluteal padding). With your PHP account, you can take over the world but might have difficulty writing traditional applications to manage it.

C++

C++ is another likely choice "if you're going to learn only one language." It is flexible, portable, efficient, and perhaps a bit more intuitive than others. Though beware of C++'s flexibility—it allows cool stuff but also allows you to make mistakes.

PYTHON

Python is less controlled by the Man and depends rather on the Python community for develop-ment (Python is to Java as GIMP is to Photoshop). However, this isn't to minimize the role of Guido van Rossum, Python's founder and continuing principal architect, known to Pythonists as Benevolent Dictator for Life. Py-thon is the principal coding lan-guage of YouTube and lotsa other Web 2.0 stuff.

FORTRAN

Developed by IBM in the 1950s, Fortran is still used sporadically by somewhat crusty scientists and engineers. Fortran was no-table for its useful update to the classic 8 × 8 grid Star Trek game, originally programmed in BASIC.

FOR examples of programming languages, visit 99-bottles-of-beer. net, whose database includes programs that generate the bottles-of-beer lyrics in (as of this writing) 1,145 languages, including Beatnik, Turing Machine, and Cow.

FAMOUS SWORDS OF HISTORY, MYTH, AND LEGEND

SWORD OF GOUJIAN

The inscription on the blade reads, "Made for the personal use of the King of Yue," which narrows its possible dates of manufacture to between 510 B.C. and 334 B.C. The Sword of Goujian spent more than two thousand years underwater and, upon its discovery in 1965, still had a sharp edge and lacked any significant tarnish. The bulk of the blade is copper, while the edges are tin. The composite construction creates a flexible sword that resists shattering, while still allowing hard edges that retain sharpness. In other words, this is a seriously kick-ass historical sword.

ZULFIQAR

In the Battle of the Trench, the Islamic leader Ali used the sword Zulfiqar to cut the powerful and heavily armored Amr ibn Abdawud and his shield cleanly in half. Thus the sword's name is widely interpreted to mean "cleaver of the spine." This sword is especially important to Shiite Muslims.

EXCALIBUR

If you have read this far in this book, you already know about Excalibur. Still, no list of swords would be complete without it. Also in the category of great Medieval swords are Charlemagne's blade, Joyeuse, and Lancelot's sword, Arondight.

HONJO MASAMUNE

The great Japanese swordsmith Masamune Okazaki made a number of legendary swords, mostly katanas, between 1288 and 1328. His masterpiece is the Honjo Masamune, which was worn by a succession of shoguns and is generally held to be the finest katana ever made. It was lost in the aftermath of World War II. Other famous Masamune swords include the Fudo, Hocho, Kotegiri, and a katana known as Helmet Breaker.

CHANDRAHAS: MOON BLADE

The ten-headed Ravana is the antagonist of the Hindu *Ramayana*, and Chandrahas—also known as the Moon Blade—is his weapon. Notably, Ravana uses Chandrahas to kill the benevolent vulture demigod Jatayu while Ravana is fleeing Lord Rama with the kidnapped Sita in tow.

THE THREE MOST COMPREHENSIBLE IRRATIONAL NUMBERS

1. When a circle's diameter is 1, its circumference is pi (π) or approximately 3.14159265358979.

As such, it is also the ratio of any circle's circumference to its diameter. Pi is an irrational number (a nonrepeating, infinite decimal) and has contributed to many a mathematician's descent into irrationality. If you find patterns in pi, you will be a god among mortals.

2. Second only to pi in most mathematicians' pantheon of irrational numbers is the number e, approximately equal to 2.7182818284. The natural logarithm ($e^{\ln(x)} = x$) is applicable to problems ranging from compound interest to probability theory to asymptotics to derangements (see mathematicians' descent into irrationality as described above). Very generally, e describes exponential decay and growth in the natural world.

3. Pythagoras knew the length of the hypotenuse of a right triangle with sides 1 and 1 was the square root of 2, or approximately 1.41421. In fact, by 1800 B.C., the Babylonians had the square root of two nailed to about six decimal places. This isn't surprising, as the number is a virtual necessity for anyone hoping to build a structure with a square base.

NICKTOONS AND CARTOON NETWORK SHOWS THAT ARE PERHAPS BEST APPRECIATED BY ADULTS

I AM WEASEL

This is one of the only shows on this list that doesn't depend on nostalgia for inclusion. Simply put, *I Am Weasel* rocks. Like Stephen Colbert, *I Am Weasel* got its start as a segment on another,

better known show, namely *Cow and Chicken* (also on Cartoon Network and also very good). We can only hope the warped mind of David Feiss continues to offer quirky gems.

SUPER FRIENDS

Superman, Batman, Robin, Wonder Woman, and Aquaman "fight injustice, right that which is wrong, and serve all mankind." And their slogan is grammatically correct, too.

REN & STIMPY

One of the first post-*Bullwinkle* shows to be truly twisted. While it's old enough to have lost some of its shock-value cachet, no geek's quote library is complete without the R&S references. (Ren: "What EEZ it, man?" Powdered Toast Man: "Quick, man! Cling tenaciously to my buttocks!" Ren: "Psst, hey Guido. It's all so clear to me now. I'm the keeper of the cheese and you're the lemon merchant, you get it? And he knows it. That's why he's gonna kill us. So we got to beat it, ya, before he lets loose the marmosets on us.") For a conceptually related spin-off, check out the show *CatDog*.

SPACE GHOST

A precursor of today's dark superheroes as well as tech-themed manga spin-offs, the classic *Space Ghost* episodes still retain their counterculture mystique, which was in direct opposition to the cheery boy-and-girl scouts of *Justice League* and *Super Friends*.

TOM & JERRY

Like your revenge served bloody? The original is only a small step more pacifistic than the *Simpsons* parody *Itchy and Scratchy*.

SECRET SQUIRREL

Mel Blanc's voice (Daffy Duck, Barney Rubble, Bugs Bunny, Yosemite Sam, etc.) resonates deeply in the psyche of most modern geeks, and Blanc's Secret Squirrel is no exception. It's impossible not to love the 007 squirrel and Morocco Mole, his fez-wearing sidekick. Inspector Gadget, eat your heart out.

CALCULATING MONTHLY MORTGAGE PAYMENTS AND FUTURE INVESTMENT WORTH

Exploring monthly payments on a loan is as easy as searching "mortgage calculator" and picking one of the many returned links. But what does this magic equation do? What, really, does it mean?

Calculating a monthly mortgage payment uses the same mechanics as discovering what your investments might be worth in the future, only, in the case of a mortgage, you are *paying* interest in exchange for immediate use of a large sum of money, and in the case of an investment, you are *earning* interest in exchange for allowing institutions to use your money. Below is a simple equation to determine how much your investment will be worth in the future:

$$FutureValue = PresentValue$$

$$(1 + i)^n$$

where i is the interest rate expressed as a decimal (5% = .05) and n is the number of periods (usually years).

Below is the equation used by online calculators to determine your monthly payments (M_p) based on loan amount (L), term in months (T), and yearly interest rate (I) in decimal format.

$$M_p = L\,[I / 12\,(1 + I / 12)^T] /$$

$$[(1 + I / 12)^T - 1]$$

DECIMAL, BINARY, AND HEXADECIMAL

We have ten fingers and ten toes (or, most of us do. Exceptions include the noted alpinist Reinhold Messner, who has only three toes and seven fingers. Luckily, this leaves him with ten total digits and thus Messner presumably has few inherent, morphological difficulties with the decimal system). Because of our built-in base-10 bias and the fascism of our system of mathematics education, we humans have come to view the decimal system as the only logical way to count. We count to nine, and then as we raise our second thumb, we stick a placeholder in the next column to the left.

But computers don't conform to the evolution of human bone structure. They can only count to two. (Technically, they can only count to one, starting at zero.) This is binary. To count in binary, use your first two fingers—every time you would raise the second finger, add another *one* in a column to the left. Here are binary representations of decimal numbers: 1 = 1, 2 = 10, 3 = 11, 4 = 100, 5 = 101, 6 = 110, 7 = 111, 8 = 1000, 9 = 1001. In practice, computers are a bit more sophisticated than coding in unadorned binary numbers. Instead, characters are assigned specific codes within an 8-bit system (for example in the standard language of ISO 8859-1, the character R is coded with the pattern 01010010). Because there are eight places of two choices each, there are 256 possible combinations and thus 256 possible character codes. (The ASCII code uses 7 bits and thus offers 128 possible characters.)

If binary is decimal truncated, hexadecimal is decimal expanded, adding the "digits" a, b, c, d, e, and f to the numbers 0–9 to create a base-16 system. As you have probably guessed, to count in hexadecimal, every time you reach sixteen, add a placeholder in a column to the left. Here are hexadecimal representations of binary numbers: 15 = f, 20 = 14, 30 = 1e.

Here's the cool thing about hexadecimal: it works as shorthand for binary. One digit in hexadecimal holds as much information as four binary bits—so instead of 1101, programmers can simply write d.

ATTRACTING SEARCH ENGINE ATTENTION

There it is: your new e-business site, complete with a killer shopping cart, secure online payment, your earth-shattering catalog of ten thousand widgets, professional graphics, database compatibility, interactive Flash animations, and all sorts of other coolness. The problem is that only you and your dog know it exists. Follow the steps below to get the word out.

1. Write a twenty-five-word, search-term-rich description of your site and submit it to free and/or pay search engines and directories (Google, Yahoo, Live Search, Ask.com, etc.—instructions found by searching "submit to X").

2. Make your site dynamic. If you update or at least change content frequently, search engines recognize your site as active. Consider adding a newsletter or blog to your site and submitting content via RSS feed to relevant news sites.

3. Links: trade links with relevant (high quality) sites, and make sure

the anchor text of your links includes useful, relevant keywords. Consider getting an initial search-engine boost by buying links to pages with high page-ranks. Post to blogs and forums with links back to your content. Also, make sure all your links are current.

4. Consider pay-per-click marketing with Google or Yahoo (and be sure to track and calculate how much these clicks are worth to you in sales).

5. Gather customer e-mail addresses to which you can submit a newsletter. Offer a way on your site for visitors to submit their contact information and consider paying for advertising on existing, relevant e-zines or buying a customer list. Once you have a high-volume site with a vibrant and widely read newsletter, you can sell advertising space to tomorrow's little fish.

6. Beware any marketing service offering black-hat techniques such as link farms and keyword stuffing, which sound good and can boost your hits in the short term but will eventually result in search engines banning your site.

WHAT'S SO FRICKING COOL ABOUT THE HUMAN GENOME PROJECT?

In 2003, the Human Genome Project (HGP) succeeded in map-ping the more than three billion base pairs in the human genome (the sequence of human DNA). So far, researchers have sifted through this mass of data to define over twenty thousand genes with an estimated one hundred still lurking in the database. (In case you're getting a big head from the perceived complexity of our species, our number of genes is nearly two hundred times fewer than that of the single-celled *Amoeba dubia*). The HGP database has been dumped online and is now readily available to anyone interested in mining for information as part of a Ph.D. program or, say, in hopes of global domination through manipulating the very fabric of life itself.

But what has sequencing the genes of some dude from Buffalo, New York, done for us lately? (Besides providing the research funding necessary to transform major portions of the Garden State into an industrialized biotech belt.)

For starters, due to the HGP we are currently able to test much more accurately for genetic predisposition to diseases, including cystic fibrosis, liver disease, and breast cancer. The HGP database also provides a nexus for genetic researchers, organizing all known information about specific genes. This might not sound like much, but if you were a researcher who had tracked a cancer to a certain gene, by visiting the HGP database you could explore *all* other research done on this gene. Also, the techniques of genomics developed during the project allow more efficient research into the genomes of other living creatures—ones we can more ethically manipulate for the good of the world and/or domination thereof.

The future, though, is limitless (according to researchers in New Jersey who promise everything from everlasting life to the flying car, if only the money keeps flowing). Future applications are likely to include gene therapy (treating the underlying causes of disease rather than their symptoms), genomic manipulation of microbes for use in biofuels and carbon sequestration, precision exploration of evolution, the end of question marks in forensics, and supercows, which may or may not provide a viable transportation alternative to the flying car.

THE BENDS:*
RULES FOR
DECOMPRESSION

Believe it or not, the equation $PV = nRT$ is included nowhere else in this book. In short, this equation relates pressure and volume to amount of stuff and temperature: If you pack more stuff into a box, the pressure inside the box increases; if you heat up the same box, the pressure increases, too; but if you move the stuff from this box to a bigger one, the stuff spreads out and pressure de-

*Not to be confused with the second studio album of the English band Radiohead.

creases. Interestingly, $PV = nRT$ also means that when you quickly and dramatically decrease pressure, stuff can go from a liquid to a gas (because a gas has more volume and when pressure goes down, stuff spreads out to take up the extra space). Unfortunately for divers and those experiencing a loss of cabin pressure at thirty thousand feet, when the pressure drops, the liquid nitrogen in their blood changes quickly to gas, causing massive badness, including but not limited to death.

To prevent the bends, don't ascend too quickly while diving and avoid flights likely to catastrophically lose pressure. If you come up slowly, the microbubbles that form in your blood will be naturally expelled through your lungs. If you ascend too quickly, larger bubbles can form, blocking blood flow to your brain (contraindicated by the surgeon general). How slowly you must ascend from a dive depends on your maximum depth and the time you spend there. According to the U.S. Navy, you can spend up to 200 minutes at a depth of 40 feet with the recommended ascent speed of 1 ft/sec making 40 seconds of total ascent time. If you had spent this same, 200-minute dive at 60 feet, on your ascent you would need to spend a 69-minute decompression stop floating at 10 feet. If you spent just 80 minutes at 140 feet, you would need to spend just over 155 total minutes ascending, with stops at 40, 30, 20, and 10 feet.

A SAM LOYD MATHEMATICS PUZZLE

A trained cat and dog run a race, 100 feet straightaway and return. The dog leaps three feet at each bound and the cat but two, but then she makes three leaps to his two. Now, under those circumstances, what are the probabilities or possibilities in favor of the one that gets back first?

POWERFUL THINK TANKS AND THEIR IDEOLOGIES

It is every geek's dream to join a think tank and thereby rule the world with nifty numbers and influential ideas—for no think tank is completely without agenda. John Goodman of the National Center for Policy Analysis (not to be confused with the Emmy-winning actor of the same name, best known for his role as the beer-swilling husband on the TV series *Roseanne*) evenhandedly describes the difference in approach of first-rate liberal versus conservative think tanks, saying, for example, "The Brookings Institution is more likely to investigate unmet needs and ask what governmental programs could solve this problem. The NCPA [National Center for Policy Analysis] is more likely to investigate how government policies are causing the problem in the first place and ask how the private sector can be utilized to solve it." More partisan think tanks, such as Seattle's Discovery Institute write, for example, about their "belief in God-given reason and the permanency of human nature" in their mission statements.

On the other end of the political spectrum, the Tellus Institute hopes to "advance the transition to a sustainable, equitable, and humane global civilization."

But just how left and how right are these shadowy think tanks that control law, public policy, and thus the world as we know it? The best—but certainly not flawless—answer comes from a 2005 study by Tim Groseclose (UCLA/Stanford) and Jeff Milyo (Harris School Public Policy, University of Chicago), who used newspapers' citation rates of various think tanks to judge media bias (positing that if a newspaper cites a conservative think tank more than they cite a liberal one, the paper itself is more conservative). Of course, to explore media bias via their citation rates of think tanks, Groseclose and Milyo had to first define the relative conservatism/liberalism of the think tanks themselves. Generally their methodology states that because we can fairly accurately describe the political leanings of members of Congress (by Americans for Democratic Action scores), we should be able to describe the leanings of a think tank by how often these politicians cite it (if politician X is always blathering on about the findings of think tank Z, it's likely they share ideologies). Here are the Groseclose/Milyo rankings of the twenty think tanks most cited by Congress, from most liberal to most conservative (Groseclose, T., and J. Milyo 2005, "A Measure of Media Bias," *Quarterly Journal of Economics,* 120 (4):1191–1237):

1. Council on Hemispheric Affairs

2. Center on Budget and Policy Priorities

3. Children's Defense Fund

4. Economic Policy Institute

5. AARP

6. Amnesty International

7. Common Cause

8. The RAND Corporation

9. The Brookings Institution

10. The ACLU★

11. The Cato Institute

12. American Enterprise Institute

13. National Taxpayers Union

(Continued)

★The Web lights up with criticism of the ACLU's placement as slightly right of center. Groseclose/Milyo explain this placement as the result of the ACLU's opposition of the McCain-Feingold Campaign Finance bill, which congressional conservatives cited very often, skewing the results. Are other results skewed as well? Decide for yourself. (Groseclose and Milyo, both former fellows at conservative think tanks, calculated an overall liberal bias in the media, with print leaning substantially left of TV and radio.)

14. Citizens Against Government Waste

15. Alexis de Tocqueville Institute

16. National Federation of Independent Businesses

17. Center for Security Policy

18. National Right to Life Committee

19. Heritage Foundation

20. Family Research Council

EVERYDAY APPLICATIONS OF QUANTUM MECHANICS

Quantum mechanics has allowed us to more accurately describe the world—especially the very, very tiny bits of it. The field also helps us describe and predict interactions between elements, forming the theoretical basis of quantum chemistry. And quantum mechanics influences study in other fields as well, ranging from string theory to cryptography to computer science. But what does this mean to you and me? What current gadgets depend on quantum mechanics? Perhaps most important, could quantum mechanics one day lead to a viable flying car?

In fact, a good percentage of the things you plug into the wall depend on quantum mechanics.

Specifically, lasers and microprocessors would be impossible without our understanding of atomic function, first put forward by Niels Bohr in 1913. Basically, they depend on light emitted as a byproduct of excitable electrons jumping in and out of various orbits around their more steadfast protons. For the laser, this light is the goal, and for microprocessors, it is a conduit for information. Fiber optics, solar cells, even the little LED lights on your reading lamp depend on quantum mechanics (really, all of electricity itself depends on quantum mechanics, though in Edison's case invention came from tinkering rather than from quantum understanding). In a more high-tech example, to display images at the atomic level, the scanning tunneling microscope (STM) uses quantum tunneling, in which electrons' ability to act as waves as well as particles allows them to pass through (as well as reflect from) seemingly impenetrable substances. The STM translates this quantum bounce-back and tunneling into pictures.

Note: if there is any hope for a viable flying car, it will likely include quantum-influenced gadgets. However, cynics expect teleportation first, and possibly flying pigs.

AT-HOME EYE EXAM

Have years of monitor viewing blended your optical rod cells into slurried mush? Or perhaps your myopic vision is due to late nights spent reading manga by the light of a single LED held tented under your covers? Still, there remains hope that you, dear geek, have bucked the odds of your caste and retain ocular function. Wanna find out? Due to Hermann Snellen, you can.

Snellen's chart, which he developed in 1862, is rather deceptively low-tech; what looks at first to be a receding series of random letters is actually quite specific, including the set height and width of letters at exactly five times the width of the line used to draw them (and the width of this line equaling the gap in the letter C). Snellen's goal was to measure a person's sight relative to what a normal cross section of the population can see; thus, 20/20 vision means you see stuff at 20 feet that most people see at 20 feet and 20/40 vision means that what you see at 20 feet, others see at 40 feet (and means you should consider increasing the font size with which you usually interact).

To get a very rough estimate of your visual acuity, hold this book at arm's length (or otherwise place it about 2.5 feet from the tip of your nose), cover one eye, and start reading letters from the top. The smallest row you can accurately read determines your acuity. While each state is different, if you have less than 20/40 vision in both eyes, you may have to jump through hoops to receive a driver's license; if neither eye is better than 20/100, you may not be able to get one. If your maximum acuity is no better than 20/200, you are legally blind.

E	1	20/200
F P	2	20/100
T O Z	3	20/70
L P E D	4	20/50
P E C F D	5	20/40
E D F C Z P	6	20/30
F E L O P Z D	7	20/25
D E F P O T E C	8	20/20
L E F O D P C T	9	
F D P L T C E O	10	
P E Z O L C F T D	11	

FROM THE OFFICIAL RULES OF ROCK, PAPER, SCISSORS*

3.1.1. The player who has initiated the prime is under the strict obligation to maintain a constant priming speed so as to give his opponent every opportunity to "catch the prime."

3.2.0. The fist must remain in the closed position until the delivery of the final prime. The fist is the only acceptable hand position during the prime.

3.2.1. The fist must remain in full view of the opposing player and may not come in contact with any outside influences that inhibit the opponent's view.

3.3.0. Prior to the delivery of the final prime, the game may be called off for the following reasons only: rule clarification, decision clarification, or injury.

*Courtesy of the World RPS Society.

SIX SOMEWHAT FIENDISH CHESS PROBLEMS

As long as chess has existed, serious players have found themselves without partners to play with, late at night. Desperate times call for desperate measures, which result in the problems below.

WHITE TO PLAY AND MATE IN ONE MOVE

WHITE TO PLAY AND MATE IN TWO MOVES

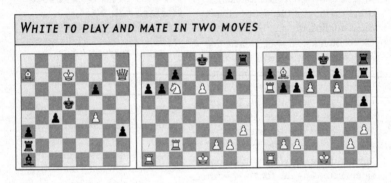

THE CLASSIC PONZI SCHEME

Before spam, phishing, packet interception, and other technology-assisted mugging, before the credit protection feature on your new card and before the sub-prime, variable-rate mortgage, before the Internet was even a twinkle in Al Gore's eye, there was the Ponzi scheme: investment in something without worth, with too-good-to-be-true dividends paid by using capital from later investors. Charles Ponzi's original scheme (Ponzi wasn't actually the inventor, just a very brash downstream user) was buying postal coupons—basically, the promise of a stamp—in a country where postage was cheap and then redeeming these coupons in the United States, where postage was expensive. It sounded great—the only problem was, it didn't work: too much red tape and too many logistics. But this didn't stop Ponzi from publicizing his Great Idea, and it certainly didn't stop people from investing in it. Ponzi waved his magic wand, promising that investors would double their money in ninety days. And he paid his first few investors, creating a massive buzz in a 1920s Boston that was newly gaga over investments of all sorts. About forty thousand investors contributed today's equivalent of $150 million. In fact, Ponzi had only invested about $30 in postal coupons. Unfortunately, after the *Boston Post* questioned the validity of Ponzi's scheme, enough people demanded their money back to sink the ship. Ponzi went to jail.

Maybe you've seen this incarnation of the Ponzi scheme:

> *Send five dollars to the first name on this list. Then cross out this name and add your name to the bottom of the list. Mail this letter to six friends. In a matter of months, you will receive thousands of dollars!*

This pyramid scheme doesn't even pretend there is a tangible product behind the "investment." Simply, the more people who pay into the system, the more the people higher up the food chain benefit. Of course, the people at the bottom of the chain mail don't get paid. Oh, and it's considered gambling, and by sending money through the USPS you are in violation of Title 18, United States Code, Section 1302, the Postal Lottery Statute (nothing but the facts, ma'am).

Modern Ponzi schemes abound: In 2007, the Second Life bank, Ginko Financial, promised 40–60 percent returns, prompting immediate, massive investment of Linden Dollars. Investors were Ponzied out of about $750,000, prompting calls for a Linden SEC.

POKERBOTS

The premise behind the pokerbot is simple: There are many, many bad players in online, low-limit poker games, and thus by playing a tight, mistake-free strategy, you will win over time. Unfortunately, because the worst players are in low-limit games and because Joe from Topeka takes his allotted thirty seconds every time he's confronted with a nickel raise, you might make a better hourly wage mowing lawns, flipping burgers, or participating in medical trials, even if you play multiple tables at once (see "Internet Poker: By the Numbers," page 44).

Enter the pokerbot: instead of doing the drudgery of playing mechanical, low-limit poker yourself, why not use a program to do it for you. Better yet, use many programs, each taking in a little money at a time.

There are many popular pokerbots available for immediate download. Simply search, click, pay, install, and go. Or, if you like, input your own formula set, teaching the bot how to play your way before setting it loose on the competition. Or better yet, get down with C/C++ and either write your own bot or tweak an existing one. Some bots allow you to automatically collude with other players at the table running the same software, further increasing your chances of winning.

Now, the question is, how long you can run your bot without your poker site of choice detecting it? (Even in the impersonal world of online gaming, there are ways to break your kneecaps, including freezing and/or appropriating your account.) There's an arms race between security and bots: Poker sites keep tabs on length of play, so pokerbots have evolved to frequently switch tables. Poker sites scan hard drives for common pokerbot software, so people now operate pokerbots from remote computers. Still, the most effective method of discovering a bot stems from the fact that bots can't chat. If you fear you may be playing against a Terminator, try striking up a friendly conversation.

NINE KNOCK-KNOCK JOKES LIKELY ORIGINATING IN WISCONSIN

WHO'S THERE?	PUNCH LINE
Hypothesis	Hypothesis your son, please let me in!
Little old lady	I didn't know you could yodel!
Toby	Toby or not Toby, that is the question.
Acid	Acid sit down and shut up!
Madame	Madame foot's stuck in the door!
Highway cop	Highway cop every morning with a Second Life hangover.
Chow Yun-Fat	Chow Yun-Fat who!? (joker proceeds to open a can of wushu whoopass on jokee)
Quaker	Quaker 'nother bad joke and I'll go Chow Yun-Fat on you!
Awkward silence	(. . .)

THE FIVE CANONS OF RHETORIC

Generally speaking, you want people to do what you tell them to do. In practice, this can be as simple as the Jedi mind trick ("These are not the droids you're looking for") or can be as difficult as arguing before the Supreme Court ("These are not the Floridian votes you're looking for"). No matter the situation, the ancient Greeks have got your back. Follow the five rules below to reduce the target of your persuasion to a malleable puddle of slobbering agreeability:

1. Invention: discover or invent creative arguments.

2. Arrangement: present these arguments in an organized manner.

3. Style: the rhetoric itself— make your argument *sound* good.

4. Memory: get your nose out of your notes.

5. Delivery: what would "*friends, Romans, countrymen!*" be without a sweep of the arm?

RICHARD

Wiseman of the University of Hertfordshire may or may not be funny. However, he is the world's foremost authority on what is universally funny. His 2001 study, called LaughLab, encouraged people from around the world to submit jokes and rate others, gathering more than 1.5 million opinions of what is and what is not funny. According to LaughLab, the universally funniest joke is as follows:

Two hunters are out in the woods when one of them collapses. He doesn't seem to be breathing and his eyes are glazed. The other guy whips out his phone and calls the emergency services. He gasps, "My friend is dead! What can I do?" The operator says, "Calm down. I can help. First, let's make sure he's dead." There is a silence, then a shot is heard. Back on the phone, the guy says, "OK, now what?"

CATCHPHRASES FOR THE MANAGEMENT OF EMERGENCY SITUATIONS

Warning: improperly performing the actions below can lead to discomfort and/or death. Fortunately, Good Samaritan laws make it extremely difficult to prosecute any well-meaning lifesaving attempts, so feel free to experiment! Also note the CDC's recommendation to wash your hands after any major disaster (printable "Clean Hands Save Lives" flyers, stickers, slide sets, and handout cards are available online).

EVENT	CATCHPHRASE
You are on fire.	*Stop, drop, and roll.*
You come upon an unresponsive or unconscious person.	*ABC: airway, breathing, circulation.*
The unconscious person is not breathing.	*CPR: 2 breaths, 30 pumps.*
Someone is choking.	*Heimlich maneuver: fist above belly button, shove up hard.*
Earthquake, tornado	*Duck, cover, hold.*
Flood	*FHG: Find Higher Ground.*
Defibrillation is necessary	*ABC: Attach, push button, char to a crisp.*

HOW TO CREATE A DUNGEONS & DRAGONS CHARACTER

Long before you go waving Yarkuch's Greatsword through the tangled passages of Torremor, the lair of the Obyrith Lord Pazuzu, you need to create a level I character. First, you will need a character sheet—either search the Web for a printable version (recommended) or make your own (but why?).

Now it's time to roll the dice. Despite your eagerness to untie your jingling pouch of multifaced dice, all it takes to determine your character's basic abilities for strength, dexterity, constitution, intelligence, charisma, and wisdom is a set of four good old d6 (six-sided dice). Roll 4d6 and drop the lowest score. Add the remaining three to get a score from 3 to 18. Do this six times and then choose to which attributes you will allocate these six scores. Don't cheat. Perhaps this is best done in the presence of your Dungeon Master, who will keep you honest.

Now choose a race. Depending on your attribute scores, certain races may or may not be available. For example you may only be an elf if your dexterity is more than 6, your constitution more than 7, and your intelligence and charisma more than 8 (find the full chart online or in the Player's Handbook). The race you choose will also modify your attributes.

Choose a character class: rogue, druid, cleric, paladin, ranger, wizard, sorcerer, bard, barbarian, or fighter. Again, your attributes may limit your choices, and your choice will modify your attributes.

Choose your alignment: How do you look at the world? Are you good or evil? This is a two-part descriptor using lawful/neutral/chaotic and good/neutral/evil (for example, you could be "chaotic evil" or "lawful good").

Determine your hit points. Consult the Player's Handbook to find your character class's hit die.

Name your character. If you're stuck, search "character name generator" and let the online tool spit out a name for you. Fill in your character's remaining background, including gold pieces, skills, feats, spells, equipment, height, weight, and appearance. The more detailed your character and the more you understand him or her, the more realistic your adventures will be.

A SAM LOYD MATHEMATICS PUZZLE

When the hour and minute hands are at equal distance from the six hour, what time will it be *exactly*?

SOMEWHAT ESOTERIC MACINTOSH KEYSTROKES

KEY COMBINATION	EFFECT
cmd-fn-ctrl-power	Reset Power Manager
cmd-opt-ctrl-power	Fast shutdown
cmd-opt-w	Close all open finder windows
cmd-delete	Move selected item to trash
cmd-shift-delete	Empty trash
Opt-"Empty Trash"	Empty even locked items
cmd-opt while booting	Rebuild the desktop file
cmd-opt-p-r	Zap the PRAM
cmd-opt-esc	Force quit
C during startup	Boot from CD
cmd-opt-shift-q	Logout immediately
cmd-shift-3	Take a picture of the screen
cmd-opt-shift-delete while booting	Bypass startup volume; seek alternate

FIVE NOT-TO-BE-MISSED TECH CONVENTIONS

A strong colony of *Coptotermes formosanus,* the Formosan subterranean termite, will produce over seventy thousand alates—winged females—which, for one brief night every year, swarm the skies together in search of mates. The diamondback rattlesnake, while primarily a rather antisocial species, spends winters in massive snake balls of a hundred or more individuals.

Similarly, geeks gather at the following yearly conventions:

CES: The VCR, Commodore 64, DVD player, and Atari's Pong console were all released in Vegas at the Consumer Electronics Show. Really, every geek needs to make a pilgrimage to the CES at least once in his or her lifetime.

O'Reilly Emerging Technology Conference: The Web materials state that, "O'Reilly conferences bring alpha geeks and forward-thinking business leaders together to shape the revolutionary ideas that spark new industry." Yum.

ICSE: You might have to travel for the International Conference on Software Engineering, but oh baby, is it worth it.

NextFest: Organized by *Wired* magazine, NextFest is the Disneyland of emerging technology. At this annual conference, playing with cool stuff takes the front seat.

Interop: What happens in Vegas affects the way the world experiences information. There are a handful of worldwide Interop IT conferences, but anybody who's anybody shows up at Interop's Vegas conference, usually near the end of April or the beginning of May.

MAP: RECORDED FINDINGS OF GIANT SQUID

Believe it or not, there are both giant squid (eight species) and colossal squid (*Mesonychoteuthis hamiltoni*), which reach lengths of up to forty-six feet, the giant squid being only fractionally shorter. Giant squid are found in all the world's oceans and the majority of its seas, and are known to eat fish and other squid

as well as fictional ships and submarines (the latter of which offer only fictional nutrition, and little if any of that to the leviathans, as literacy rates among giant squid are very, very low).

THE BASICS OF NUCLEAR ENERGY

The equation $E = mc^2$, with c equaling the speed of light, means that contained within a little bit of mass (m) is lots of energy (E). During nuclear fission, one unstable nucleus splits into two lighter ones, with any difference in total starting and finishing mass being expressed as energy. For example, an isotope of uranium, U-235, commonly absorbs one freewheeling neutron, making the very unstable isotope U-236, which then immediately decays into Kr-92 and Ba-141, releasing much energy and all sorts of other cool by-products. One of these by-products is more neutrons, which are absorbed by more U-235, which continues to go boom. In nuclear power plants, this chain reaction is controlled; in nuclear weapons, it is not. Nuclear power plants use the energy from this controlled chain reaction to heat water into steam, driving turbines and thus creating electrical power; nuclear weapons allow this heat (and radioactive by-products) to be released into the surroundings with massively destructive consequences. (A similar reaction can be engineered using plutonium-239.)

The crux (or, at least, *one* crux) is in obtaining U-235, as most naturally occurring uranium is the more stable U-238. Boosting the percentage of U-235 is known as *enriching*. Also crucial for those hoping to seriously blow stuff up is keeping the initial reaction contained until it has had the opportunity to chain-react into something big enough to do major damage. Even more difficulty is presented by slowing down the "freewheeling" neutrons to a speed at which they can be absorbed by the U-235 (this is often done by using heavy water, which despite its name is actually D_2O).

THE DEWEY DECIMAL SYSTEM

Most geeks are content to let Google do it for them. However, at very high levels of specialization, geeks may still be forced to sift through the stacks, in which case it's good to know a thing or two about Melville Dewey's famous system. Basically, the Dewey decimal system is a massive subject index, organized in ever-increasing levels of specificity. All of human knowledge is divided into the ten categories of General (000), Philos-ophy or Psychology (100), Religion (200), Social Sciences (300), Language (400), Science (500), Technology (600), Arts and Recreation (700), Literature (800), and History and Geography (900). Within each of these categories are ten more subdivisions and within these subdivisions are ten more. Because decimals could string on forever, you could theoretically move to ever more specific levels of subject categorization until every book had its own unique number. This isn't done—instead librarians know when to say when, and use the author's last name to distinguish within microcategories. After the first three digits, there is a decimal point, after which comes the real nitty-gritty of subject identification. For example, the book *Surely You're Joking, Mr. Feynman* is classified within Science (500) and Physics (530) and continuing until 530.0924 (which also includes the thrillers *Michael Faraday and the Dynamo* and *The Ultimate Einstein* and *The Mysterious Rays: Marie Curie's World*).

THE FINE ART OF THUMB TWIDDLING

While many pursue thumb twiddling only in hopes of increasing their text message WPM, it is in itself a surprisingly complex discipline, requiring technique, complex muscle memory, and patience. The best twiddlers count it a step toward Zen-like enlightenment (though the husbands/

wives/partners of many top twiddlers report concerns about OCD). Consider: will your thumbs touch or not? If they touch, will you keep them in constant contact or will they merely bump during each rotation? How deep will you twiddle? Thumbnail? First knuckle? The full length of the thumb? Do you allow a dominant rotational direction or strive for equality between front- and back-twiddling? Could you twiddle one thumb toward your fingers (front-twiddle) and the other away (back-twiddle)? What about your practice regimen? Are you open to partner twiddling? If so, will you contribute the right or the left hand? Are you a speed twiddler, attempting to increase your RPM, an endurance twiddler, looking to boost your hours, or a technique twiddler, hoping to develop the perfect twiddle rotation? How and at what depth will you interlock your fingers, forming the twiddle cradle?

While it didn't make Beijing and (as of writing) is unlikely to be considered as a winter sport for Vancouver (last-minute negotiations to include the twiddle as a perfunctory skating figure broke down), many enthusiasts hold out hope for London 2012.

THUMBS II: WRESTLING CHEATS AND THE TWF

If you haven't seen Thumb Wrestling Federation shorts on the Nicktoons Network, you haven't really lived. (For those without access to Nicktoons—shame on you. But luckily you can find the TWF online, too.) While most TWF takedowns follow the standard format of one thumb pinned under another, for better or for worse the association has also helped popularize alternate forms of pinning. Specifically, Senator Skull and his evil Sinistras are known for "buddy" play using the first finger (or less commonly the wraparound pinky) to snare unsuspecting opponents. Beware the quick count, both at the match's outset and while counting the pin; also beware arm twisting and distraction tactics. Proponents of thumb wrestling fair play include the English footballer Frank Lampard, a stalwart of the Chelsea Blue and frequent player on England's national squad—search "Frank Lampard thumb wrestling" for video evidence.

HOW TO MAKE CHAIN-MAIL ARMOR

Making chain mail is industrial knitting at its most tedious. But, a finished hauberk, pair of chaussures, or hooded coif will guard you against attack by bladed weapons as well as rudimentary projectiles—useful in home, office, and recreation. Consider watching period battle movies as you knit, both for technical inspiration and to stem the tide of boredom.

As you can see in this photograph (and as you probably already knew), chain-mail armor is made from many interlocking metal rings. Thus the first step in making chain mail is supplying yourself with these rings. You can buy precut rings online, or you can make your own. To make your own, buy a coil of steel wire—16 gauge is the strongest commonly used, but is hard to bend; for easier and quicker work, consider 18 or 20 gauge steel wire. Roll this wire around a mandrel, pipe, or other rod of desired circumference, creating a long, springlike coil. Pull the ends of your coil to slightly spread the links and then cut the length of your coil using tin snips or a hacksaw.

Now you will need to knit your mail. Use two pairs of pliers—one to hold your developing mail and the other to twist on new rings (curved needle-nose pliers work well; be sure to pad your hands or the handle, as you will be spending many hours crimping). Like historical European mail, consider using a four-to-one pattern, in which each link is clipped to four others (but unlike historical mail, you needn't rivet your rings together). Start by feeding four closed links onto an open one and then crimping the central ring shut. Be careful to fully close links, otherwise not only will they twist free, but they will also catch in your clothing and hair. From here, attach another open ring to two of the "free-floating" closed ones, also adding two more closed rings to

this new open ring to continue the pattern of four to one.

You will need to experiment to find your ideal knitting system. One successful strategy is to create long, three-wide "ropes" of mail with a center row of links closed around upper and lower rows. Then, once you have created many "ropes," use additional links to stitch them together. Look online for mail garment patterns.

MORSE CODE

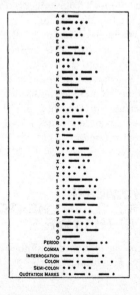

MECHANICS OF THE THEATRICAL FLY SYSTEM

In the theater, you cannot splice tape. You also can't depend on your audience to wait half an hour for a scene change (with the exception of intermission, which depends on Chardonnay to pacify the impatient proletariat). Thus the stage needs to function as a quick-change artist, with scenery, drops, scrims, and sometimes actors flying on and off stage. This requires very, very cool pulleys, which sometimes extend upward of seventy feet in a narrow, vertical fly space behind the stage.

The theater standard is the counterweight fly system, which functions similarly to most cable-and-pulley exercise machines: a stack of weights balances force on the other side of the wire—if the weight is heavier than the force pulling on it, it stays put; if the force is heavier, the weight is raised. The goal is to balance the weight of the desired curtains or scenery with counterweights such that one person's strength is enough to raise or lower it.

This picture shows the components of a common counterweight fly system. A are the hoisting cables, which lead up to pulleys at the top of the fly tower. B are the turnbuckles, which attach to D, the arbor, which holds the weight stack (E) and the counterweights themselves (F). At the base of the system is an anchored pulley (I) under which the purchase line (C) runs. Controlling the movement of the purchase line is a lever brake (H) attached securely with a locking safety ring (G). Thus the system is one giant loop—if the control lever is released, the weights can move up or down, allowing the purchase line to move up or down.

Generally, a number of these systems will be attached to a horizontal beam, called a batten, to which the actual scenery is attached. Along the theater's back wall is a locking rail that provides the base for a long rack of anchored pulley blocks and control levers.

A simpler system uses tied-off ropes with sandbags as counterweights.

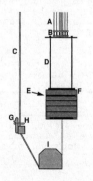

THE LONGEST AT-LEAST HALFWAY BELIEVABLE DESCRIPTOR FOR DESIGNER COFFEE

Half-caf double-tall triple-shot nonfat three-pump three-Splenda whole-milk-foam caramel macchiato in a double cup, no lid, with wings.

THE NINE MEMBERS OF THE FELLOWSHIP OF THE RING

GIMLI THE DWARF

His friendship with Legolas helped reestablish the bond between the Dwarves and Elves of Middle-earth. In addition to his inclusion in the Fellowship, Gimli traveled with Bilbo Baggins in *The Hobbit*.

PEREGRIN TOOK

Pippin, an exceptionally hairy but quite young Hobbit, drank Ent-draught with Treebeard and became one of the tallest hobbits at 4.5 feet tall (passing Bullroarer Took).

BOROMIR

The eldest son of Denethor II, Boromir was the Steward-Prince of Gondor and High Warden of the White Tower. Tempted by the power of the One Ring, he tried to steal it from Frodo, but later redeemed himself, giving his life while defending the Hobbit.

LEGOLAS THE ELF

Legolas was sent by his father, Thranduil, King of the Woodland Realm of Northern Murkwood, as a messenger to the council of Elrond at Rivendell, where he was to discuss the escape of Gollum from the elves' care, and where he was drafted into the Fellowship.

SAMWISE GAMGEE

Sam Gamgee was Frodo's stalwart companion, refusing to let Frodo travel to Mordor without him, along the way briefly becoming a Ring-bearer.

GANDALF

Somewhere between mortal and immortal, Gandalf was killed after an eight-day battle with a Balrog in and under the Mines of Moria. Upon his resurrection by Eru, the creator, Gandalf was known as The White.

MERIADOC BRANDYBUCK

At the Battle of the Pelennor Fields, Merry stabbed the Nazgul king in the back of the knee with his Dúnedain dagger, helping the shieldmaiden Éowyn kill the Nazgul and thus fulfilling the prophesy that the Nazgul could not be killed by man (but by Hobbit and woman).

ARAGORN

Heir of Isildur and the True King, Aragorn married the Elven princess Arwen, who renounced her immortality to marry him. He ruled the Reunited Kingdom for 122 years of peace and prosperity.

FRODO BAGGINS

Small in stature but big in heart, Frodo was the last Ring-bearer, who delivered the Ring to its destruction in the fires of Mount Doom. Frodo was Bilbo's adoptive heir and 78 years Bilbo's junior, both born on September 22.

A SAM LOYD MATHEMATICS PUZZLE

PROPOSITION—How much does the baby weigh if the mother weighs 100 pounds more than the combined weight of the baby and dog and the dog weighs 60 percent less than the baby?

A STRANGE THING SOMEWHAT NEAR REDMOND, WASHINGTON

On December 19, 1920, the Holstein heifer Segis Pietertje Prospect broke the world's record for the most milk produced in a year (37,361 pounds, as opposed to the 4,000-pound average at the time). In her day, the cow, nicknamed Possum Sweetheart, was visited by Jack Dempsey and the French commander in chief, Marshal Joseph Joffre. Today, you can visit her statue in Carnation, Washington, about twelve miles from Microsoft headquarters.

THE PETERS PROJECTION VERSUS MERCATOR MAP

Thank you, Aaron Sorkin, for using your political drama to point out the fact that we have been lied to: The world is not shaped the way we thought it was. The map we all grew up using, known as the Mercator projection, is reasonably accurate within fifteen degrees of the equator, but as you move toward the poles, distance is stretched, making, for example, Greenland look much bigger than it actually is. In fact, Africa has almost fourteen times Green-

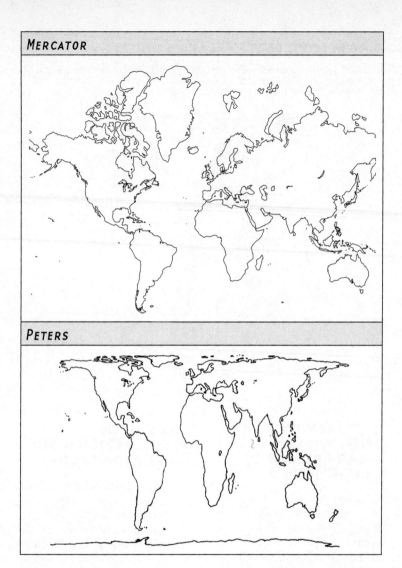

MERCATOR

PETERS

land's surface area, but they look almost equal on the Mercator. Here's why: imagine ripping open the globe and flattening it into the shape of an oval; now draw eleven dots along the equator and these same eleven dots along horizontals as you move toward the poles so that your map looks like this:

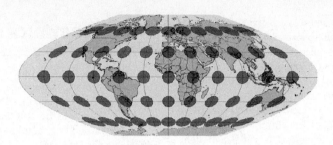

Now, you want your map to be a rectangle and not an oval, but when you stretch the top and bottom to make this possible you also expand Greenland. Despite its misleading shape, the Mercator map offers the advantage of representing navigational bearings as straight lines, and has thus been the standard since the time of exploration.

The Peters projection map represents land according to surface area and thus removes the potential for West-centric capitalist pigs using the world map as justification for NATO world domination.

Some Australians think the world looks like the map shown below, but they are wrong.

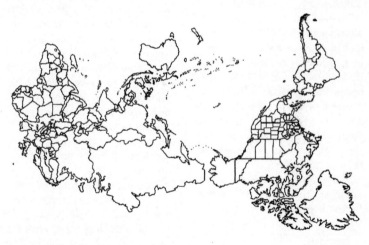

REFRACTION: HOW TO POP A CAP IN A CARP

If you haven't the infinite ammo of the late Hunter S. Thompson

or the lightning-fast trigger finger (and impressive spray radius) of a recent vice president, it actually takes considerable skill to shoot a fish in a barrel (exact difficulty proportional to size of barrel and fish depth and inversely proportional to size of fish). Some of this trickiness is due to refraction, or the change in speed and thus direction of light waves as they move from air to water.

Wait a minute?! Isn't the speed of light constant? Yes. But only in a vacuum. If you shoot light through glass, it travels only 0.67 times its original speed and if you shoot light through water it travels only 0.75 times its speed in a vacuum (in beer, 0.74). And the more you slam on the brakes, the more light changes direction. You can see this when you stick a straw in a glass. Refraction is also responsible for rainbows: As white sunlight refracts through atmospheric water, each frequency contained within this white light adopts a slightly different speed and thus refracts slightly more or less, spreading out into the immediately recognizable ROY-G-BIV spectrum. Thus, as seen in this diagram, if you are trying to shoot a fish at position R, it in fact appears at position L, and you will need to aim lower than it appears in order to hit it.

Note: shooting fish drastically decreases the chance of successful catch and release.

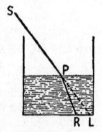

AHAB : *MOBY-DICK* :: SHIMOMURA : _____

If you answer this question correctly on an electronic version of the ACT or SAT II, your social security number will be automatically forwarded to admissions officers at CalTech, MIT, and the Indian Institute of Technology (not really). The answer, of course, is Mitnick—Kevin Mitnick, who, if he hadn't been reformed and reintegrated into American society, might joyfully have hacked the College Board Corporation to pirate said SSNs.

Mitnick's high-tech forays onto the murky side of the law started early. By age seventeen he was phreaking Bay Area phones, stealing free long distance, listening in on conversations, and making technology-assisted prank calls, including changing the class of service to make targets' home phones request 20¢ in order to make calls and rerouting directory assistance to lines of his choice, where Mitnick and his friends offered any number of fake phone numbers. ("Yes ma'am, that's seven, three, nine, four and a half. You *do* know how to dial a half, don't you?"). Unfortunately for Mitnick, his early hacks were brazen enough to be solvable by even standard FBI apes, and before he was twenty-eight, he had been arrested and convicted of computer-related crimes five times (though let it be said, his arrests were usually due to errors in human judgment, not in computer skill—once he was turned in by a friend and another time by a friend's girlfriend).

After being caught violating parole in 1992, Mitnick went underground, entering his most productive hacking period. It was during this time that he accessed Nokia, Sun Microsystems, Fujitsu Siemens, NEC, and Motorola systems (among many other alleged offenses), all while staying one cyber-step ahead of the law.

Then Kevin Mitnick picked on somebody his own size. In 1992 Tsutomu Shimomura was a senior fellow at the San Diego Supercomputer Center. Mitnick hacked Shimomura's home computer, stealing thousands of files. Shimomura made it his personal mission to nail Mitnick, setting up electronic listening posts and finally tracking down Mitnick's online cache of stolen information. Shimomura staked out the data and, though the dial-up calls used to access the info were painstakingly rerouted, Shimomura finally tracked the source to a cell phone in Raleigh, North Carolina. Armed with a cellular frequency finding antenna, he cruised Raleigh with a Sprint technician and pinpointed Mitnick's signal originating from a specific apartment complex. The next evening, FBI agents knocked on Mitnick's door.

Kevin Mitnick served forty months. He now runs his own computer security firm.

THREE BASIC TAP-DANCE STEPS

Step-Ball-Change: Start by marching in place, in time to music. Now, step backward onto the ball of one foot, then step with your flat forward foot, and finally bring the trailing foot back to its starting position. If possible, the step-ball-change should be a syncopated hiccup in time, with the backward step onto the ball of a foot coming between beats.

Cramproll: This is a modified jump in which you land first with the ball of one foot, then on the ball of your other, then on the heel of your first foot and finally on the heel of your second foot.

Flap-Heel: From a basic standing position, scuff the ball of one foot forward and then bring it down (this is the flap—think two syllables: fl-ap). Then bring down the heel of this forward foot. By alternating feet you can walk with the flap-heel. For optimal effect, practice this at the office while on the way to and from the watercooler.

TRAGICOMIC EVENTS IN THE LIFE OF FABIO

- On March 30, 1999, the hunky Italian supermodel was hit in the face by a goose while riding the

Apollo's Chariot roller coaster in Busch Gardens, Williamsburg, Virginia. Fabio was rushed to the emergency room at Williamsburg Community Hospital and later claimed his survival was "a miracle." It took one stitch to close the cut on his nose. The goose was killed. You can still find the video online.

• On November 7, 2007, Fabio was dining at a Los Angeles eatery with five female guests who had donated to the California Highway Patrol Foundation to earn the pleasure of his company. One of his guests snapped a picture of George Clooney, who was sitting nearby. Clooney was irritated and when Fabio approached Clooney's table to explain, the two sex symbols came almost to blows and had to be physically separated. Fabio said of the incident, "I just feel badly that it ruined the night of these women who paid to support charity. I am thinking of something to make it up to them."

• In addition to penning the modern classics *Champion, Rogue, Pirate,* and more, Fabio recorded an album titled *Fabio After Dark,* on which he waxes poetic about life and love over a background of what can only be described as porn music (offering evidence that Edison as surely as Einstein has doomed the human species). If you further investigate only one thing in this book, please, please make it this—you can find a copy of the album online. You will be a better person for it.

• After learning that object-of-competition Larissa had dated Fabio, Gil Hyatt of *Average Joe 2: Hawaii* left the show, claiming that "every guy would understand."

• Fabio is a spokesman for I Can't Believe It's Not Butter!

BE AFRAID. BE VERY AFRAID: THE CPSC'S TOP FIVE HOME HAZARDS

According to a 2007 press release by the Consumer Product Safety Commission, every year 33.1 million people are injured by consumer products in the home. No one is safe, and constant vigilance is required to avoid maiming and/or death (paraphrased). Here are the prime offenders:

1. Magnets: If a child eats your wedding ring, it will pass. If the same child eats both your wedding ring and a magnet, the two might attract through intestinal walls, creating a massive kink and making it very difficult to retrieve your ring.

2. Recalled Products: At cspc.gov, you can sign up for e-mail notification of recalled goods. With about four hundred recalls a year, you can rest assured that your inbox will be a constant source of terror.

3. Tip-Overs: You likely already know that vending machines are deadlier than sharks. But did you know that tipping TVs, ranges, and other furniture account for more than *ten times* the annual deaths of even killer soft-drink machines?

4. Windows & Coverings: The CPSC's press release states that "Kids love to play around windows," where they are at risk of strangulation and falling. While they suggest cutting looped cords, they fail to take into account children saved from falling out open windows by tenaciously gripping looped cords while awaiting the arrival of the fire department.

5. Pool & Spa Drains: Beware the frumious suction—a pool drain can hold you as surely as can a giant clam (featured horribly and unforgettably in the Chuck Palahniuk story "Guts").

TONGUE TWISTERS IN LANGUAGES OF FEWER THAN A MILLION SPEAKERS*

Welsh: *Oer yw eira ar Eryri.* (Cold is the snow on Snowdon.)

Maltese: *Toni taghna tani tina talli tajtu tuta tajba.* (Our Tony

*Courtesy of Simon Ager at Omniglot. com. Omniglot also includes recordings of many of these tongue twisters, though suspiciously, none of them is repeated ten times fast.

gave a fig because I gave him a good berry.)

Icelandic: *Ái á Á, á á í á.* (Grandfather from "Á" farm has a sheep in a river. Note: as you may remember, Iceland also produced Björk.)

Gaelic (Scottish): *Cha robh laogh ruadh luath a-riamh, is cha robh laogh luath a-riamh reamhar.* (A brown calf was never swift, and a swift calf was never fat.)

Gaelic (Irish): *Ná bac le mac an bhacaigh is ní bhacfaidh mac an bhacaigh leat!* (Don't bother with the son of the beggarman and the son of the beggarman won't bother you!)

Esperanto: *Serpo servu cin por cerpo el cerbo de serba cervo.* (May a billhook serve thee to scoop out a Serbian deer's brain.)

Manx: *Ta'n bear gaih gee burgeyr.* (The teddy bear is eating a burger.)

CONSENSUS

holds that the most difficult tongue twister in the English language is "The sixth sick sheik's sixth sheep's sick."

HOW TO WRITE YOUR NAME IN ELVISH

The Eldar of Middle-earth used Quenya, or High Elvish, for formal speech and writing, much the same way Europe of yesteryear used Latin. High Elvish also makes for a killer tattoo. The only necessary rule is to raise vowels above or below the letter they follow.

Letter	Symbol(s)	Note
A		
B		
C		
D		
E		when silent
F		
G		
H		
I		
J		
K		
L		
M		
N		
O		
P		
Qu		
R		as in "red" / as in "car"
S		alternate forms
T		
U		
V		
W		
X		
Y		consonant / vowel
Z		alternate forms

Elvish images courtesy of Ned Gulley at starchamber.com

CAFFEINE TOXICITY: HOW MUCH IS TOO MUCH?

There are four caffeine-induced psychiatric disorders recognized in the DSM-IV, the diagnosis manual of the American Psychiatric Association: caffeine intoxication, caffeine-induced anxiety disorder, caffeine-induced sleep disorder, and caffeine-related disorder not otherwise specified. And, as you know if you have ever had to walk low-Starbucks-density waste-lands, withdrawal can result in nausea, lethargy, and depression. But what of the classic, washed-up-child-star-style overdose?

The Mallinckrodt Baker Material Safety Data Sheet describes the lethal dose of caffeine as 192mg/kg in rats (note: does this imply study of multiple-kilogram rats? Potentially capybaras? Maybe Norwegian browns from the Bronx?). In humans, lethal toxicity is estimated at between 150 and 200 mg/kg, meaning that an average adult would have to consume between eighty and one hundred cups of coffee in a very short period of time. *Forensic Science International* reports a couple deaths from caffeine toxicity, all resulting from overdose of caffeine pills.

The moral seems clear: once you reach your seventieth cup of the afternoon, consider switching to Benzedrine, methamphetamine, or another similar stimulant.

LEGO ART

Sure, we're all familiar with large-scale LEGO construction. And we're aware that designers have made rather incredible things with the Technic series, including a sewing machine, bubblegum sorter, and about ten varieties of fully automatic LEGO machine guns (demonstrations of which are viewable on YouTube). But when do these ambitious LEGO projects take the small step from craft to art? Certainly

Nathan Sawaya, the full-time, freelance LEGO artist who has by now been featured in almost every major news source, including *The Late Show with David Letterman*, *Extreme Makeover: Home Edition*, and *The Colbert Report* (on which Sawaya revealed a life-size LEGO recreation of the host) has taken this step. To Sawaya, LEGO is only another medium, like oil, marble, or clay. Certainly it inherently generates more press attention than, say, papier-mâché.

Note: for knit algorithms, check out the work of Eleanor Kent.

THE SCIENTIFIC METHOD THE NASA WAY

The image on the following page is from the materials of the NASA SciFiles website. Notice that the icons imply that if your observations do not support your hypothesis, you should feel massively dejected for an unspecified period of time. Then you should blame your experimental design and devise further tests to get the data you wanted in the first place.

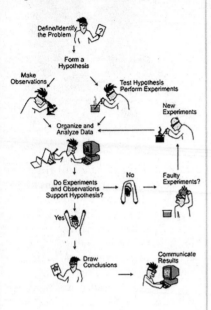

Define/Identify the Problem

↓

Form a Hypothesis

Make Observations

Test Hypothesis Perform Experiments

New Experiments

Organize and Analyze Data

Do Experiments and Observations Support Hypothesis?

No

Faulty Experiments?

Yes

↓

Draw Conclusions → Communicate Results

FOUR VERY DIFFERENT "BEST" AMERICAN BOWLING ALLEYS

RED ROCK LANES, LAS VEGAS, NV

With seventy-two lanes, over one hundred high-def flat-screen monitors used for scoring displays, and the ability to lower disco balls, hit the strobe, and flow the fog at the flick of a switch, the new $31 million Red Rock Lanes will bowl your mind. (We would expect no less from Vegas.)

SUNSET BOWL, SEATTLE, WA

The venerable Sunset Bowl is retro-kitsch and proud, with Sunday nights offering National Bowling Karaoke Idol contests. According to the editor's review at citysearch.com, Sunset Bowl is pushing toward a bowler-to-tattoo

A SAM LOYD MATHEMATICS PUZZLE

In pairs, the girls pictured here weigh 129 pounds, 125 pounds, 124 pounds, 123 pounds, 122 pounds, 121 pounds, 120 pounds, 118 pounds, 116 pounds, and 114 pounds. What is the weight of each one of the five little girls?

OUTWITTING THE WEIGHING MACHINE

ratio of one to one. It's open twenty-four hours.

SEIDEL'S BOWLING CENTER, BALTIMORE, MD

If Sunset Bowl is one end of a spectrum, Seidel's is the other. The most notable difference is the bowling itself—Seidel's is duckpin bowling, meaning smaller pins, smaller balls, and three shots per frame. Though there is some debate, Baltimore claims to have invented duckpin bowling around 1900. With the exception of live music Saturdays, it looks as if some of the sport's original inventors still bowl at Seidel's.

MINNEHAHA LANES, ST. PAUL, MN

The huge, somewhat dilapidated pink neon sign on top reads *Food. Bowling. Cocktails.* Inside is what you would expect—*exactly* what you would expect, and thus Minnehaha Lanes makes this list due to its representation of the Platonic ideal of bowling alley.

CORNELL UNIVERSITY'S "I TOUCHED CARL SAGAN" CONTEST

Carl Sagan, the great astronomer and popularizer of science, started teaching at Cornell University in 1968, quickly becoming the school's most famous lecturer. Despite (or more likely because of)

his pop image, Sagan lived apart from the Cornell community. A 1999 review of Sagan biographies in the *New York Times* described Sagan's Ithaca home as "a pseudo-Egyptian temple perched on the edge of a 200-foot gorge and protected by surveillance cameras and an iron gate." By the 1990s, Sagan was rarely seen and almost never by undergraduates. When the gents of Alpha Sigma Phi invited Sagan and his wife to dinner, the scientist referred them to his lecture agent. In 1994, the conservative newspaper *Cornell Review* announced the "I Touched Carl Sagan" Contest, promising a six-pack to any undergraduate who could provide photo evidence of "actually making physical contact with Dr. Sagan." Before the bet could be won, the university forced editors at the paper to close the competition, citing the eminent astronomer's privacy.

FOUR RECIPES USING ONLY FLOUR, BUTTER, EGGS, MILK, AND WATER

Look in your pantry (*pantry,* n.: a small, closed space connected to a kitchen, often with a door, in which food and utensils for food preparation can be stored). Perhaps a previous tenant left flour. Check for weevils. Open your refrigerator. Any chance it contains eggs, milk, and butter? If so, read on, dear geek. The goodness of cooked food is only minutes away.

DUTCH BABY

INGREDIENTS	DIRECTIONS	COMMENTS
5 eggs, 1½ cups milk, 1½ cups flour, half stick butter	Set oven to 425° and melt butter in deep (4-quart is best) baking pan. While butter is melting, mix remaining ingredients. Pour batter into melted butter and bake for 25 minutes, until very puffy. Serve hot, before implosion occurs.	Consider cheating the restrictive ingredients list by topping with something sweet (powdered sugar and lemon juice recommended).

DUMPLINGS

INGREDIENTS	DIRECTIONS	COMMENTS
½ cup milk, 3 eggs, enough flour to make stiff dough	Bring pot of water to boil. Mix all ingredients, adding enough flour to make the dough stiff and dry. Plop bits of dough into boiling water. When they float, they are done.	Comments: Serve with butter. Strong projectile for use with plastic spoon.

CRÊPES

INGREDIENTS	DIRECTIONS	COMMENTS
1 cup flour, 2 eggs, ½ cup milk, ½ cup water, 2 tbsp melted butter	Mix all ingredients. Batter should be runny. Pour into hot frying pan. Cook like a pancake.	Almost a pancake, but without the baking powder. Consider topping with something sweet.

PASTA

INGREDIENTS	DIRECTIONS	COMMENTS
2½ cups flour, 2 eggs, ⅓ cup cold water	Mix all ingredients. Knead with hands until small bubbles start to form. Sprinkle a little flour on rolling surface and roll out dough to desired thickness. Let dough sit for 20 minutes or until dry. Cut dough into strips and cook in boiling water as you would store-bought pasta.	If you are confused as to how one should cook pasta, give up and order Chinese food.

MOVIES FOR THE MATHEMATICALLY MINDED*

If you're reading this book, there's a better-than-not chance you've seen the movie (or read the book) *A Beautiful Mind*. Maybe you also remember *Good Will Hunting* and have perhaps heard of the movie *Proof*. But where, outside these big-name films, can you go for your fix of big-screen math scenes? Don't despair—simply watch one of the following movies today:

PI (1998)

A man goes bonkers while contemplating the mathematic, scientific, and theological implications of the number pi. Oh, and he's pursued by people who want to kill him.

STAND AND DELIVER (1987)

A high-school math teacher teaches inner-city kids calculus.

DIE HARD WITH A VENGEANCE (1995)

Bruce Willis and Samuel L. Jackson are given a five- and a three-gallon jug and must put exactly four gallons of water on a scale to keep a bomb from exploding.

*Courtesy of Arnold Reinhold at mathinthemovies.com.

I.Q. (1994)

Meg Ryan, playing Albert Einstein's niece, writes the Schrödinger equation describing the space- and time-dependence of quantum mechanical systems on a chalkboard (reason #1 why we love Meg).

INFINITY (1996)

This Richard Feynman biopic includes a calculating race between the scientist and a dude with an abacus. Feynman, using pencil and paper, adds slower, but multiplies faster and kills in the cube root competition (reason #1,243,891 why we love Feynman).

THINGS YOU WILL FIND WHEN YOU MISTYPE "MIT" INTO A SEARCH ENGINE

- MTI Whirlpools: "Design Your Experience." Offering surround-sound bathing.

- Motorsport Technologies, Inc: The ultimate source for performance parts, products, and high-performance engines.

- Three Mile Island Alert: Outcome and analysis of the accident and a current problems discussion.

- Too Much Information Comics: A Web comic starring "Ace, a young geek that's [sic] been kicked out of the house by his mom."

- Indiana Transportation Museum: Home of the nickel-plate steam locomotive No. 587.

- Integrative Manual Therapy: Using the interconnectedness of multiple body systems, therapists assist the body's own innate intelligence to take corrective action.

- Morgan Stanley Insured Municipal Trust: the stock quote.

BEACHES AT WHICH YOU ARE MOST LIKELY TO BE EATEN (BY SHARKS)

According to the International Shark Attack File at the Florida Museum of Natural History, Americans do not need a passport in order to experience a shark attack firsthand—the United States leads the world in number of confirmed unprovoked shark attacks with 837. Compare this to Australia's 329 and South America's scant 100 to fully appreciate the USA's global dominance in being gnawed upon by toothy fish.

NEW SMYRNA BEACH, FLORIDA

New Smyrna Beach's official city motto is "Catch the charm," but most people know it as the shark attack capital of the world. Luckily the sharks in question are only spinners and blacktips, which, while they may take frequent bites, tend to take small ones (though the New Smyrna Beach tourist board is unlikely to adopt the motto, "Oh, it's only a *little* shark bite" anytime soon).

BRISBANE, AUSTRALIA

The highest number of attacks is on the east coast, but the most fatalities are in the south where seal concentration and thus great-white numbers are higher. Take your pick. Attacks in Brisbane include the 2006 fatality of Sarah Kate Wiley, who was attacked by three bull sharks in chest-deep water.

GANSBAAI, CAPE TOWN, SOUTH AFRICA

Tourists flock to the area known as Shark Alley to cage-dive with great white sharks. Without the cage, you are simply lunch. YouTube is rife with footage of Gansbaai sharks.

KOSI BAY, SOUTH AFRICA

The Zambezi sharks of Kosi Bay are known for their forays into fresh water inlets in search of fish. They are also known for eating people.

THE RED TRIANGLE, CALIFORNIA

Bolinas, Stinson, and Point Reyes beaches just north of San Francisco are the chomping grounds of a massive concentration of great white sharks (the Red Triangle extends as far south as Big Sur). In fact, more than half the documented great-white attacks on humans have occurred within the Red Triangle.

NORTH SHORE, OAHU, HAWAII

The Banzai Pipeline is also Buffet Human. Fatal attacks include Courtney Marcher, who was never found, though her surfboard leash showed bite marks.

PRAIA DE BOA VIAGEM, RECIFE, BRAZIL

South America's hottest spot to see and be seen being eaten (forty-seven attacks since 1992, sixteen of which were fatal). South of Recife, two bull-shark birthing estuaries were sealed off to construct a shipping port, forcing the sharks into tourist waters.

THE DIGITAL PINHOLE CAMERA AND THE END OF ART

What do you do after art has broken all the rules—when the time-tested systems no longer apply? In music, after Stravinsky's *The Rite of Spring,* tonality was dead—just listen to the rhythmic closing minute, which is better understood using the vocabulary of techno or Hendrix-esque distorted noise than the rules of Western tonal music. No longer bound by the traditional rules, composers were forced to create their own. Schoenberg, Webern, and Berg explored serialism, Cage threw out the bathwater (and some would say the baby), continuing with the chaos of his own imagination, while Stravinsky went retro in search of rules, imposing upon himself the constraints of J. S. Bach (though Stravinsky's neoclassicism retained just enough cool modern twists to define it as a distinct product of the mid-twentieth century.)

So too with photography: through the discipline's history, artistic photographers have been limited by images in the physical world—even with burgeoning manipulations, they have depended on existing images as starting points. No longer. Today, photographers are almost completely free of the rules imposed by the real world (for an early example, image search "shark attacks helicopter"). What do we do without rules?

Like Stravinsky, some modern art photographers are mining the art form's history, imposing upon themselves the constraints of yesterday's technology (and as with Stravinsky, the combination of old techniques with modern twists results in something distinctly new and distinctly today).

Enter the pinhole camera, which was conceived as early as the fourth century B.C. as Aristotle and Euclid watched light patterns filter through a wicker basket. To impose the constraints of the pinhole on your multi-megapixel world is actually quite simple—just drill a hole in your lens cap and leave it on (best with an SLR, as some point-and-shoots won't allow you to power on with the lens cap in place). The cleanliness of your pinhole makes a major difference, so either use a very sharp drill bit or cut your hole carefully with an X-Acto knife. For even better results, drill a rather large hole in your lens cap and then cover it with self-adhesive aluminum foil wrap (or glue it on). Use a pin to punch a hole in the aluminum wrap.

Images from pinhole digitals offer a large depth of field. They can also be artfully fuzzy—recalling *Time* magazine shots from the 1950s or modern images from a scanning electron microscope.

EIGHT U.S. TOWNS WITH SEXUALLY EXPLICIT NAMES

- Beaver Lick, Kentucky

- Hooker, Arkansas

- Cumming, Georgia

- Tingle, New Mexico

- Horneytown, North Carolina

- Short Pump, Virginia

- Threeway, Virginia

- HooHoo, West Virginia

International Honorable Mentions:
- Dildo, Newfoundland, Canada

- Fucking, Austria

TWO IMPORTANT SUGGESTIONS FROM THE WORLD ROCK, PAPER, SCISSORS SOCIETY'S RESPONSIBILITY CODE

- Safety First! Always ensure that all players have removed sharp jewelry and watches.

- Think twice before using RPS for life-threatening decisions.

CLONE YOUR PET IN FIVE (NOT SO) EASY STEPS

In 2004, the *San Francisco Chronicle* reported that a Texas woman had paid $50,000 to become the first bereaved pet owner to have her recently deceased pet cloned. "I see no difference between Nicky and Little Nicky," said Julie (last name withheld for reasons that should be obvious). Of course, counting this the *first* case of pet cloning belittles the historical significance of Louis Creed's cat, Winston Churchill, or simply Church to his young daughter, Ellie. After Louis buried the recently flattened Church in the back of the sematary, Church returned to the Creed family, but something was amiss. The kitty was evil.

The question is: Is Little Nicky evil too?

There is suspiciously little mention of the continuing life of the mysterious Texan "Julie" and her little fur-ball of undead joy. Is the pair living happily, below the radar of the press, or was Julie quietly killed and eaten by the zombie cat? We may never know.

While the ethical and moral questions of cheating death itself are up for debate, cloning is undeniably a neat trick. You, too, can clone higher mammals by following these steps:

1. Capture nuclei from donor cells: Mechanically extract nuclei from the cells of your recently deceased pet by poking through cell walls with a very, very small syringe. Any nonreproductive cells will work.

2. Gather unfertilized eggs of same species. The technology for harvesting donor eggs has been around for years.

3. Switch nuclei: Use another tiny syringe to extract the nucleus from a harvested egg and replace it with a nucleus from your deceased pet. Currently, it may take many hundreds of attempts to do this without destroying the egg's viability.

4. Implant eggs into surrogate womb: Again, many of these eggs will not survive. If one does survive, it will mature in the womb.

5. Voilà! You now have a pet that is genetically identical to its donor.

PING-PONG DIPLOMACY

Before Nixon's historic 1972 visit to China, widely seen as the beginning of China's reintroduction into global politics and economics and thus the beginning of the end of Western civilization's world domination, there was Ping-Pong.

The year was 1971, and the U.S. table tennis team was in Japan for the Thirty-first World Table Tennis Championships, getting roundly thumped by almost anything with two arms and a paddle. (To be fair, Leah "Miss Ping" Neuberger had achieved much international success, winning the 1956 World Mixed Doubles Championship.)

PENNSYL-VANIA is the king of sexually explicit town names with Balltown, Big Beaver, Blue Ball, Climax, Desire, Intercourse, and Virginville. Who says the Amish are humorless?

One evening, the young player Glenn Cowan, described by a fellow teammate as a "hippie opportunist," missed the team bus. Instead, he hopped a ride with the Chinese team and struck up a friendship with the three-time world champion, Zhuang Zedong. When they stepped off the bus, waiting paparazzi ensured that the story became instant world headlines.

Soon after, Mao Zedong (no relation) invited the nine American team members to visit mainland China to play the role of Washington Generals to the Chinese team's Harlem Globetrotters. *Time* magazine called it "the *ping* heard round the world." Between severe Ping-Pong beatings, the U.S. team toured the Great Wall, chatted with factory workers, and attended the Canton Ballet. On the day of the team's gala banquet held in the Great Hall of the People, the United States lifted its twenty-year trade embargo with China.

SIXTEEN CLASSIC BUSINESS AND ECONOMICS BOOKS

Looking for riveting summer reading? If you are a true business geek, these books will fit the bill; if not, don't even consider opening these without stocking up on Super Glue and preplacing those eyelid toothpicks.

- *How to Win Friends and Influence People,* by Dale Carnegie (1936)

- *The Affluent Society,* by John Kenneth Galbraith (1958)

- *Capitalism and Freedom,* by Milton Friedman (1962)

- *Foundations of Economic Analysis,* by Paul Anthony Samuelson (1983)

- *The Functions of the Executive,* by Chester I. Barnard (1938)

- *Innovation and Entrepreneurship,* by Peter Drucker (1985)

- *The Seven Habits of Highly Effective People,* by Stephen Covey (1989)

- *The General Theory of Employment, Interest and Money,* by John Maynard Keynes (1936)

- *History of Economic Analysis,* by Joseph Alois Schumpeter (1954)

- *The Human Side of Enterprise,* by Douglas McGregor (1960)

- *Security Analysis,* by Benjamin Graham and David Dodd (1940)

- *Out of the Crisis,* by W. Edwards Deming (1982)

- *In Search of Excellence,* by Tom Peters and Robert H. Waterman Jr. (1982)

- *Good to Great,* by James C. Collins (2001)

- *My Years at General Motors,*
Alfred P. Sloan Jr. (1963)

- *An Inquiry Into the Nature and
Causes of the Wealth of Nations,*
by Adam Smith (1776)

THE SEVEN BEST COLLEGE PRANKS OF ALL TIME, IN NO PARTICULAR ORDER

THREE BILLION-DOLLAR BUSINESSES THAT STARTED IN GARAGES

One of the great mysteries in the evolution of human technology is the origin of the first garage, for the garage itself is a necessary component of innovation. Sure, in a pinch, a basement or a laboratory will work, but only due to

THE GREAT ROSE BOWL HOAX
At the halftime show of the 1961 Rose Bowl, fans held aloft secretly doctored flip-cards that spelled CALTECH—live on national television.
VETERANS OF FUTURE WARS
Princeton students demanded immediate compensation for probable service in future wars, igniting spin-off groups around the country.
THE MCDONALD'S CONTEST
Caltech students created a computer program that allowed them to generate a million entries to a McDonald's sweepstakes, thereby cleaning up on prizes.
PUMPKIN ON THE CLOCK TOWER
Cornell University students awoke one October morning to find a pumpkin speared on the lightning rod atop the precipitous clock tower. To this day, only the anonymous pranksters know how it got there.
THE SACRED COD
The staff of the *Harvard Lampoon* stole the five-foot-long Sacred Cod of Massachusetts, which hangs above the entrance to the chamber of the state House of Representatives.
GREAT DOME POLICE CAR HACK
A campus police car numbered π mysteriously appeared, intact, on the roof of MIT's Green Dome. Inside sat a dummy dressed as a patrolman, eating doughnuts.
WE SUCK
Following the formula of the Great Rose Bowl Hoax, students at the annual Yale-Harvard football game rigged the halftime cards, tricking Harvard fans into holding up cards that read WE SUCK.

their approximation of garage-ness. So how then was the *first* garage invented without there already being a garage in which to invent it? Many point to this paradox as evidence of a supreme power. No matter the origin, the businesses below have taken full advantage of the creative powers of the garage.

GOOGLE

In 1996, search engines scoured Web pages looking for users' search terms. A page in which the terms appeared five times would rank higher than a page in which the terms appeared four times. So, if you were selling inflatable chairs, you could guarantee strong search listings by including the words "inflatable chair" as many times as possible in your site's text, which to most visitors creates a rather uninspiring site. Larry Page and Sergey Brin hypothesized that a better way to rank search results was to explore the backlinks from other relevant sites, thus returning search results ordered by what the Internet already "knew." If they had been able to spell, the company they started in their friend's Menlo Park garage would have been called Googol (a 1 followed by 100 zeros). Their company's name is now a verb.

APPLE

In 1976, Steve Jobs sold his VW bus to buy circuitry. Steve Wozniak and Ronald Wayne assembled these Frankensteinian electronics into Apple I's on a workbench in Jobs's parents' garage. The two hundred computers of this first generation required users to connect transformers to supply two different AC voltages, purchase separately and then attach a keyboard, rig some type of (unincluded) monitor, and perhaps nail together a box to house the monstrosity. The more user-friendly Apple II stored information on cassette tapes. Now we have the iPhone.

HEWLETT-PACKARD

Silicon Valley itself was born in a 12 × 18 garage, leased for $45 a month by Dave Packard and William Hewlett in 1938. Their start-up cash: $538 (just over $7,000 in today's dollars). They flipped a coin to decide whose name would come first. In the true spirit of alchemist tinkerers, Hewlett and Packard jumped from invention to invention until finally deciding to focus on electronic test and measurement equipment. Disney bought eight of HP's 200A audio oscillators to test audio equipment for the movie *Fantasia*. The oscillator's inexpensive price of $54.40 was a reference to the 1844 slogan "Fifty-four forty or fight!" which was used to bully Canadians into a border treaty.

SEVEN MUST-SEE SIGHTS ON THE GEEK WORLD PILGRIMAGE

Microsoft Museum	4420 148th Ave NE, Building 127, Redmond, WA	You are not allowed in the factory. Only in the museum. Where there are no Oompa-Loompas.
Legoland	Jutland, Denmark	The genesis of every civil or mechanical engineer's career. Don't miss the LEGO re-creation of the Kennedy Space Center.
Studio Ghibli	Mitaka Inokashira Park, Tokyo	Creator of *My Neighbor Totoro, Spirited Away, Princess Mononoke, Howl's Moving Castle*, and more! Purchase tickets well in advance.
Palm Islands	Dubai, United Arab Emirates	A series of artificial, dredged-sand islands in the shape of palm trees. Palm Islands adds 520 K of beaches to the Dubai coastline.
Large Hadron Collider	CERN, Geneva, Switzerland (46°14' N, 6°03' E)	Hopefully the LHC will help physicists find their God Particle, the theorized Higgs boson.
The Lubyanka	Lubyanka Square, Moscow	You, too, can take a tour of this former KGB headquarters, whose reputation for high-tech spy gadgetry is as emphasized as its history of torture is deemphasized. Deviating from the tour is not recommended.
Bollywoodrome	Mumbai, India	A specially designed set on the Filmistan lot that offers a behind-the-scenes look at the Bollywood of yesteryear and the exciting directions of Bollywood today.

HOW TO LOAD A PAIR OF DICE

Warning: being caught with loaded dice can be highly dangerous both to you and to your role-playing characters.

Professionally loaded dice can be very, very slick. A popular model uses tunnels inside the dice, partially filled with soft wax; when a player breathes on, or tightly holds these wax-loaded dice, the wax melts, trickling downward and weighting the low side. This tunnel-based method of variable weighting can be accomplished with mercury or with a small magnet that is pulled through the dice tunnels by metal hidden in the table surface. In another, historically popular, method, dice were carved from a piece of wood that included a natural malformation, such as a pebble or spot of internal rot, thus showing no outward signs of tampering but being unequally weighted nonetheless. Yet another method includes slightly rounding or sharpening dice edges, though this can be easier to spot. The lowbrow, high-risk approach uses dice with only certain numbers, for example one die with only 5's and another with 2's and 6's for use with craps (requiring bluster, quick pickup, and/or sleight of hand).

However, the easiest and most surprisingly successful method of loading plastic dice is to cook them, either in an oven or in a microwave, with the number you want facing up. The heat gently softens the plastic, which almost imperceptibly pools lower, leaving the downward side slightly heavier than its opposite.

IF IT FEELS GOOD, DO IT: JEREMY BENTHAM'S HEDONISTIC CALCULUS

As an ethical hedonist, the English utilitarian philosopher and proto-bleeding-heart-liberal Jeremy Bentham (1748–1832) believed that right and wrong could be determined by weighing the "pleasures" and "pains" of any given action, with an action that produced more pleasure than pain being morally right. While this would be great by itself (in a geeky kind of way), what makes it truly spectacular is the fact that Bentham actually created an algorithm to define exactly how *much* pleasure and pain an action would cause. (His application of algebra to life decisions is echoed by at least one complete whackjob modern author. . . .)

To determine an individual's pleasure or pain from an action, Bentham suggested weighing *intensity* (pleasure's strength), *duration* (how long pleasure would last), *certainty* (the probability that the action will result in pleasure), *propinquity* (how soon the pleasure might occur), *fecundity* (the chance that the pleasure would result in further actions), and *purity* (the probability these further actions would be pleasures and not pains). He also added *extent*, taking into account the effects of said decision on other people.

We can only guess at the specific algebra Bentham used to compare these variables, and he left no note of how to quantify, for example, intensity of pleasure, but he envisioned his hedonistic calculus used for many decisions, including calculating jail sentences: Given a certain crime, Bentham thought it possible to determine the punishment that would outweigh the crime's pleasure and thus prevent future crimes.

PENCIL-AND-PAPER ROLE-PLAYING GAMES: GENRES AND MAJOR EXAMPLES

Genre	Major Examples	Comments
Fantasy	Dungeons & Dragons, Ars Magica, Warhammer, Call of Cthulhu, RuneQuest	The first and still the favorite RPG environment.
Science Fiction	BattleTech, RoboTech, CyberPunk, Blue Planet, Deadlands, Star Wars	We are the Transformer generation. . . .
Horror	World of Darkness, Vampire: The Masquerade, Werewolf: The Forsaken (both within WOD)	The game designers White Wolf have cornered the market in the horror RPG genre.
Superhero	Teenage Mutant Ninja Turtles, DC Heroes, Marvel Heroes, Champions	Crossover with the simpatico world of comic books was only a matter of time.
Universal Systems	GURPS, d20 System, FUDGE	Flexible playing mechanics applicable to any environment.
Espionage	Top Secret, Recon, d20 Modern, Merc 2000	Not a top genre, mostly due to success of video game versions.
History	Boot Hill, d20 Past, En Garde	A gateway drug to reenactment.
Manga	Big Eyes/Small Mouth, Mekton Zeta	Japanamania.

NOTHING BUT A GIGOLO

When a male anglerfish of the superfamily *Ceratiidae* is born, the clock starts ticking. The little dude must find a female before his infant energy reserves expire, or he will die. When he finds a female anglerfish, he bites her. Then he releases an enzyme that dissolves her skin and his mouth, fusing himself to the female anglerfish at the vascular level (they share blood—she is his only source of nutrition). Forevermore, the male anglerfish is little more than a sperm packet and a slight bump on the otherwise streamlined and independent modern female anglerfish. Whenever she's in the mood, the female anglerfish releases a hormone into her (and thus the male's) bloodstream, inciting the male to release sperm, thereby downloading DNA whenever needed.

SLINKY TRICKS

There comes a point in every geek's life when basic slinkying just isn't enough. You've *done* the stair trick, you've *done* the retractable cubicle-to-cubicle throw, and now you're ready for the next step in slinky tricks.

As your first next step, try the thumb-to-fingers rock. Hold your hand palm-up and place the inert slinky over your thumb. Hold up your first finger and rock your hand to transfer the slinky to this finger. Rock back and repeat. The cachet of this trick is similar to that of thumb twiddling.

If, whenever you take the moving walkway through the United Airlines tunnel in Chicago O'Hare Airport, you find yourself transfixed by the *Tron*-like sounds, you'll love this one: Bite a couple coils in the middle of a metal slinky, plug your ears, and drop the two ends so they bounce freely. What do you hear? Consider playing Floyd in the background and/or synching the experience with *Fantasia* or the movie *Baraka*.

Next, two variations of the stair trick: try it hand-to-hand, using a motion that mimics cupping, raising, and releasing rolls of belly flab. How many hand-to-hand steps can you get? Also try stacking books to create slinky obstacle courses. One advanced skill is the slinky spiral staircase, which involves banked turns.

Finally, if you are stuck in the jungles of Southeast Asia with no exit strategy, consider using the following trick pioneered by the U.S. Marines—throw a slinky into a tree for use as a makeshift shortwave radio antenna.

THE famous slinky jingle (*It's Slinky, it's Slinky, for fun it's a wonderful toy. It's Slinky, it's Slinky, it's fun for a girl and a boy*) was co-opted by the cartoon *Ren & Stimpy*, which substituted the words *It's Log, it's Log, it's big, it's heavy, it's wood! It's Log, it's Log, it's better than bad, it's good!*

A SAM LOYD MATHEMATICS PROBLEM

Here is a famous prize problem that Sam Loyd issued in 1882, offering $1,000 as a prize for the best answer showing how to arrange these seven figures and the eight dots so they would add up to 82: . 4 . 5 . 6 . 7 . 8 . 9 . 0 .

Out of several million answers, only two were found to be correct.

OUR COLUMBUS PROBLEM

FIND HOW TO ARRANGE THE FIGURES 4 . 5 . 6 . 7 . 8 . 9 . 0 . IN AN ARITHMETICAL SUM WHICH ADDS UP THE NEAREST TO 82 SEE OUR GREAT PRIZE OFFER Send your answers on the following blank

NAME — DATE

ADDRESS

ANSWER

LOYD

GREAT FEATS OF RUBIK'S CUBISM

In 1982, Knoxville, Tennessee, hosted the World's Fair. Over six months, more than 11 million people visited the city, mostly to see the large display of a Rubik's Cube, which ennobled the entrance to the fair's Hungary Pavilion. (Note 1: not the food court; note 2: it must have been the Rubik's Cube that drew crowds, because it certainly wasn't Cherry Coke, which debuted at the fair.) In the two years preceding the fair, the cube had sold 100 million units.

Fast forward to the present day. Granted, a 2 × 2 × 2 puzzle is fairly basic, but that doesn't negate the wonder of Lukasz Cialon's 1.01-second solving record. (Cryptically, his quote accompanying the record at www.speedcubing. com is "not LC. pzdr." Is this cubist code?) Holding the record for the more standard 3 × 3 × 3 puzzle is Andrew Kang (7.12 seconds), who cut his speed-cubing teeth while working at a football concession stand. ("Out of nowhere a 7.12 pops up. I was spazzing like no other.") To date, the king of the Professor's cube (5 × 5 × 5) is Takayuki Ookusa, who rocked a 1:25.78 during the 2007 World Championship. (In fourth place in this category is Michael Gottlieb, who may or may not be the same as the well-known New York City lighting designer.)

The debate rocking the speed-cubing world is the relative meaning, for example, of a 7.12-second solve by someone whose average is otherwise well into the double digits. Certainly a lucky cube can be serendipitously set for success and self-submitted results are notoriously difficult to verify. For heroes, purists instead tend to look to the likes of Harris Chan, with his 10.64 average for 3 × 3 × 3 or Marc van Beest with his 50.65 average for 4 × 4 × 4. As of this writing, the world's top player in the traditional Rubik's Cube category is Ron van Bruchem of the cube-fertile Netherlands, who has also been one of the sport's great ambassadors.

As you could probably have guessed, speedcubers are prone to bouts of oversubmission to online video sharing sites, and thus many examples of freakishly quick Rubik's work can be seen on YouTube.com.

CHEMICAL EQUATION PUZZLES: IF THESE ARE FUN, YOU ARE A GEEK

Newton posited that matter is neither created nor destroyed. While any role-playing gamer with a mage capable of casting Meteor Swarm or Magic Missile knows this to be untrue, still, teachers of Chemistry 101 hold to Newton's idea when forcing on high-school and undergraduate students their narrow-minded approach to balancing chemical equations. How-

ever, we geeks don't much mind. Chemical equations are neat little math puzzles, and thus we will allow the world at large to retain its mistaken idea that chemical two-plus-two always equals four.

The first step in balancing a chemical equation is learning to read the equation itself. Elements are abbreviated as in the periodic table, and any subscript describes how many atoms of the preceding element are in a given molecule. (For example, H_2O contains two hydrogen atoms and one oxygen atom—duh.) Reactants are listed before the arrow and chemical products are listed after the arrow. Take a look at the equation below in which natural gas (methane) reacts with oxygen to create carbon dioxide and water, as would happen on a common gas burner or if you hold a match near the back end of a cow:

$$CH_4 + O_2 \rightarrow CO_2 + H_2O$$

On the surface, this all looks well and good, but on closer inspection, where the hell did the extra hydrogen go (there are four on the left and only two on the right) and where did we get that extra oxygen atom (there are two on the left and three on the right)? Were atoms created and destroyed by the level III mage in the sky? No, in fact, the imbalance of elements in this reaction means we need unequal numbers of each of these molecules to create a complete reaction. Here is the same equation, giving Newton the benefit of the doubt:

$$CH_4 + 2O_2 \rightarrow CO_2 + 2H_2O$$

The coefficients of two in front of O_2 and H_2O mean there are two of each of these molecules (the coefficient applies to the entire molecule, not just the first element). Now we have the same amount of each element on the left as we do on the right. And thus is the balance of the universe restored.

Now, an example that looks tricky (but is not) in which calcium chloride reacts with silver nitrate solution to yield a white precipitate of silver chloride. (Notice the subscript 2 outside the parentheses—this means there are two complete NO_3 "chunks" in this molecule, but it doesn't double the Ca as it would have if the two had been used as a coefficient.)

$$CaCl_2 + AgNO_3 \rightarrow AgCl + Ca(NO_3)_2$$

We can balance this equation using the following coefficients:

$$CaCl_2 + 2AgNO_3 \rightarrow 2AgCl + Ca(NO_3)_2$$

Now that you are an expert, try balancing the equations below (no fractions allowed in your coefficients, you slacker!):

BEWARE YOUR FOOD

The summer months are risky— in addition to shark attacks and boredom-related deaths due to midseason baseball, they're the time of food poisoning. If you live in Florida or California, you should be especially vigilant, as you are susceptible to all three (the most baseball teams, the most shark-infested beaches, and—according to the CDC—the most restaurant outbreaks of food poisoning, with a combined 143 in 2007). In all, the CDC estimates that food-borne diseases every year cause approximately 76 million illnesses, 325,000 hospitalizations, and 5,000 deaths (salmonella alone costs the United States upwards of $5 billion annually in medical care and lost productivity). One can only imagine the sheer volume of liquid effluvium generated by these 76 million people. (Actually we can do better than only imagining: A large tank truck of the kind commonly used to transport gasoline has a capacity of around 6,000 gallons; taking a conservative estimate of 0.5 gallons of effluvium per sickened person results in over 6,000 gasoline tankers per year filled with human waste materials due to food poisoning. No, no—no need to thank me.)

Especially virulent are the

$H_2 + N_2 \rightarrow NH_3$	$NH_3 + O_2 \rightarrow NO + H_2O$
$NaCl + BeF_2 \rightarrow NaF + BeCl_2$	$FeCl_3 + Be_3(PO_4)_2 \rightarrow BeCl_2 + FePO_4$
$Ca(OH)_2 + H_3PO_4 \rightarrow Ca_3(PO_4)_2 + H_2O$	$C_2H_6 + O_2 \rightarrow CO_2 + H_2O$

days surrounding the Fourth of July—heat-speeded bacteria-blooms, the ubiquity of meat products, and the overall unsanitary conditions of Uncle Sam's barbecue argue for renaming the event Uncle Salmonella's.

PHOENIX CHAMBER OF COMMERCE: "YES, BUT IT'S A DRY HEAT"

It is 50°F. If you live in Seattle, you're wearing a thick cable-knit under your hooded R.E.I. poncho and shivering uncontrollably despite your death grip on a Vente mochaccino. If you're in Boulder, Colorado, you're wearing shorts while adjusting the sun umbrella at an outdoor café on Pearl Street, waiting for your microbrew to arrive. (This, in a nutshell, is why Microsoft employees are so productive and why UC Boulder is a party school.) This difference in experience bespeaks the relative uselessness of mercury in determining temperature as experienced by human skin.

Being geeks, atmospheric scientists are aware of this problem and have developed various indices for use in transforming atmospheric data to better describe the temperatures we feel. Traditionally these indices add variables for wind chill (used to make cold temperatures colder) and humidity (used to make hot temperatures hotter). For example, the National Weather Service uses the following formula to compute degrees of wind chill

(where T is the air temperature and V is wind speed):

$$\text{WindChill}(°F) = 35.74 + 0.62T$$
$$- 35.75(V^{0.16}) + 0.43T(V^{0.16})$$

And Heat Index is approximated with the following formula (R is relative humidity):

$$HI = -42.38 + 2.05T + 10.14R$$
$$- 0.22TR - 6.83 \times 10^{-3}T^2$$
$$- 5.48 \times 10^{-2}R^2 + 1.29 \times 10^{-3}T^2R$$
$$+ 8.53 \times 10^{-4}TR^2 - 1.99 \times 10^{-6}T^2R^2$$

Fortunately, online calculators are available for both. In the year 2000, the private company Accu-Weather introduced the copyrighted equation RealFeel, which takes into account not only wind chill and humidity, but also solar intensity, precipitation intensity and type, elevation, and atmospheric pressure. Bravo, private-sector geeks, bravo!

WHATEVER HAPPENED TO HARRY ANDERSON FROM *NIGHT COURT?*

Harry Anderson's magician schtick from the bench of *Night Court* was much more than mere schtick. In fact, before becoming an actor, Anderson worked as a street magician (thus making the list of comedians who have paid their dues, alongside the likes of Steve Martin). After *Night Court,* touring for post-*Court* spin-off stand-up gigs, and a couple successful TV character-acting jobs, Anderson in the summer of 2005—with near-presciently terrible timing—opened Oswald's Speakeasy, a nightclub in New Orleans's French Quarter, throwing open the doors just in time to welcome Hurricane Katrina. Though initially Anderson was a stalwart of the New Orleans reconstruction scene, in 2006 he and wife Elizabeth sold the speakeasy and moved to Asheville, North Carolina, citing as a reason, the reelection of mayor Ray Nagin.

According to the IMDb, Harry Anderson's first wife, Leslie, is a certified witch.

ULTIMATE FREEDOM: GOING COMMANDO

King Tutankhamun was buried with 145 loincloths. William Wallace wore no underwear at all. Is this reflective of their establishment versus antiestablishment views? Perhaps. Consider John Coltrane, who stopped wearing underwear at age eighteen, feeling that it restricted his artistic freedom. Or the bra burners of the 1970s, who eschewed undergarments to symbolize political and social freedom. The recommendation that U.S. military personnel do without in order to reduce the occurrence of (pardon the French) crotch rot, is widely reported—thus the origin of the term "going commando."

Underwear propagandists claim the garments provide enhanced comfort, warmth, and hygiene, but who are they kidding? With today's increased standards of personal hygiene and comfortable, rip-stop fabrics, underwear serves as only a mild aphrodisiac and as a first line of defense for the mildly incontinent. (Note: though American pop singers, and anyone else for that matter, should be aware of the line between discreetly going commando and outright exhibitionism; this line, of course, is based on skirt length and the likelihood of being photographed while stepping out of a chauffeured car.)

For those interested in taking the first step toward a less inhibited lifestyle, check out the Aussie jeans aptly known as *freeballers*. They include built-in boxers and a button fly.

THE U.S. military's recommendation for the strategic removal of undergarments was taken a step further by the Liberian warlord Joshua Blahyi, known to friend and foe as General Butt Naked for his habit of leading naked troops into battle while wearing nothing but boots.

HOT WHEELS CARS RELEASED IN 1968 AND 1969

Look through your childhood closet. Does your old, hot-pink Hot Wheels Beach Bomb have surfboards strapped to the sides, or do they stick out the back window? If they stick out the back window, you will not be able to launch it down your Super-charger Sprint Track, but your disappointment might be slightly tempered by the $70,000 you may be able to get for the defective car at auction (as paid by Bruce Pascal in 2000). In general, scan your closet for any early Hot Wheels in pink, which was considered a girly color and used sparingly—making it the rarest and thus the most valuable color.

Still, just because it's old doesn't

1968	1969
• Beatnik Bandit	• Brabham Repco F1
• Custom Barracuda	• Chaparral 2G
• Custom Camaro	• Classic '31 Ford Woody
• Custom Corvette	• Classic '32 Ford Vicky
• Custom Cougar	• Classic '36 Ford Coupe
• Custom Eldorado	• Classic '57 T-Bird
• Custom Firebird	• Custom Charger
• Custom Fleetside	• Custom AMX
• Custom Mustang	• Custom Continental
• Custom T-Bird	• Custom Police Cruiser
• Custom Volkswagen	• Ford MK IV
• Deora	• Indy Eagle
• Ford J-Car	• Lola GT70
• Hot Heap Python	• Lotus Turbine
• Silhouette	• Maserati Mistral
	• McLaren M6A
	• Mercedes-Benz 280SL
	• Rolls-Royce Silver Shadow
	• Shelby Turbine
	• Splittin' Image
	• Torero
	• Turbofire
	• Twin Mill
	• Volkswagen Beach Bomb

necessarily mean it's priceless. Most of the cars on the list are worth between $100 and $500.

VALUE-BASED FANTASY FOOTBALL: DEFT, NOT DAFT, IN THE DRAFT

Fantasy football is a rare nexus of geek and meathead cultures. Enticingly, it is a nexus we geeks should rightly dominate, providing at least cursory psychological payback for games of flag football played in middle-school PE class. If only there were a way to snap a towel through fiber-optic lines (see quotes widely misattributed to Bill Gates, pages 172–173.

As any fantasy football website makes immediately clear, the most important time in your fantasy season is draft day. And, as you can easily find at these same sites, there are myriad strategies for drafting a winning team (most notably, build your team around a stud running back, though some debate this theory). However, below these rather obvious surface suggestions lurk the strategies we geeks can and should use to dominate the virtual sports world:

1. Before draft day, rank players by desirability, and then box your list into tiers. It may not be worth taking the first running back of the second tier if others who are generally comparable may remain in later rounds; instead, look to pick the last remaining player in a higher tier (maybe a QB or WR). Another way to say this is to pick the player who offers the largest projected point differential over remaining players. This is value-based drafting in a nutshell.

2. If you think a star player's stats are due to overall team quality, consider drafting a backup player on that team in later rounds. For example, any WR catching Brady in 2007 would have put up numbers, especially without Randy Moss pocketing anything airborne.

3. Look for indicators of breakout or breakdown years. For example, a contract year can provide just the motivation a player needs to put up some stats. For whatever reason the third season seems to offer breakout potential for wide receivers. And beware the curse of the thirty-year-old running back, which can immediately doom your fantasy season (see the Shaun Alexander debacle of 2007; ah, the heartbreak of the Seattle sports fan!—always a bridesmaid, never a bride!).

4. Fantasy owners will generally fill their starting rosters before drafting backups. Use this to your advantage: If everyone else has already drafted a QB, you may be able to safely wait for another couple rounds before doing so yourself. Keep a position checklist of the opposing owners' picks.

OH SHIT! IT'S THE SCIENCE FAIR!

It's Tuesday night. Who knew the science fair was on Wednesday? Actually, your child has known for months but neglected to mention it or, in fact, do any-thing whatsoever about it until tonight. You know that if he or she is laughed at, it will destroy any semblance of burgeoning academic confidence, leading to delinquency and eventually to work in the sex industry and/or as a freelance writer. Never fear. Choose from the projects below:

SIMPLE HOVERCRAFT	
MATERIALS	*INSTRUCTIONS*
• Plywood: one sheet • Plastic sheet • Duct tape • Leaf blower or shop vac • Small plastic disk (coffee lid or other) • Short wood screws • Saw, drill, staple gun, scissors, screwdriver	**1.** Cut a plywood disk big enough to sit on. **2.** Cut a hole in the disk (off-center) just big enough to fit leaf blower nozzle. **3.** Cover one side of disk with plastic sheet (fold edges over and staple them in place on top). **4.** Place small plastic disk over plastic sheeting in exact center of wood disk. Use wood screws to fasten in place. **5.** Cut about six egg-sized holes in plastic sheet, ringing your plastic disk and about three inches from it. **6.** Attach leaf blower and blast off!

METAL CHALLENGE: THE ORANGE LIGHT	
MATERIALS	*INSTRUCTIONS*
• Oranges • Brads, nails, wires, or other "spikes" of various metals, including copper, iron, aluminum, lead, zinc, tin, silver, etc. • Copper wire • 4–10 small flashlight bulbs • Optional: voltmeter instead of lightbulbs	**1.** Your goal is to compare the electro-chemical potential of your metals. To do this, you will make batteries from different metals and connect these batteries to lightbulbs—the brighter the bulb the higher the difference between the two metals. (Some metals want to give up electrons and some want to gain them; if you have a metal from each side of the spectrum, you have a powerful battery.) **2.** Here's how: Plug two brads (of different metals) into an orange—one on either side. Attach a wire to each brad and touch the two wire ends to a flashlight bulb. Bingo! The bulb should light! Repeat this with different combinations of metals, creating a display of your orange-powered flashlights of varying intensities.

ANTACID CHALLENGE	
MATERIALS	*INSTRUCTIONS*
• Various commercial antacids (Maalox, Mylanta, Tums, Rolaids, Pepto-Bismol, etc.) • Bromothymol blue (a weak acid/base indicator available at pool/spa stores) • 2-to-1 water to vinegar mixture	**1.** You will be testing the effectiveness of various commercial antacids. To do so, you will attempt to neutralize a standardized acidic solution (the 2-to-1 water/vinegar mixture of defined volume). Into the acid solution, drop a standardized quantity of antacid. Then, once the antacid has had time to work, test the solution's resultant pH using bromothymol blue, which goes from yellow to green to blue as it gets more alkaline (more yellow is more acid). Be sure to standardize your quantities throughout.

SOLAR COOKER	
MATERIALS	*INSTRUCTIONS*
• Two cardboard boxes of different size (the larger with a removable lid) • Tinfoil • Heavy plastic wrap • Knife or other cutter • Tape	**1.** Line small box with aluminum foil. **2.** Nest small box inside the larger so the open side of the smaller box is flush with the top of the larger. (You can support the underside with crumpled newspaper.) Tape in place. **3.** Cut a three-sided flap in the lid of the larger box that matches the size of the smaller box. Line the underside of this flap with aluminum foil. Cover the flap opening with clear plastic. **4.** Place food in small box, replace large box lid, and use reflective flap to direct sunlight. Consider not using turkey as a test food.

QUASIMODO: MASTER OF PERMUTATIVE GROUP THEORY

To ring traditional church bells, a team of human operators pulls ropes that spin the giant bells, some weighing several tons. The mechanics of the system impose strict rules on what can be played. Gone entirely is melody, replaced by the idiomatically frenetic and somewhat cacophonous sound of cascading tones played for maximum note density. Within the two seconds it takes a bell to rotate, the tones are slightly offset so that each bell rings before any one bell sounds twice.

So instead of playing melodies, church bells are rung in rows—patterns that describe the order of bells. The pattern of highest to lowest in a six-bell tower is described as 123456 and is known as *rounds.* Simply ringing rounds over and over would quickly get monotonous, but because the weight of human ringers can only slightly slow or accelerate the bells, it is possible to change a bell's ringing order by only one position from row to row. Following these rules, diagram 1 shows the row pattern known as *plain hunt* or *original,* in which the maximum of three bell "switches" is followed by two switches, taking twelve rows to return to rounds. There are many methods that allow starting and ending at rounds without repeating a pattern, including *plain bob minor,* shown in diagram 2. Since bell ringers are not permitted visual aides like this one, they instead memorize the path of the lines (as shown) that define the place of their bell in each pattern.

In a *full peal,* every permutation is rung without repeating a row (starting and ending at rounds). Thus, at two seconds per row, it takes about half an hour to play a full peal in a six-bell tower (720 permutations). To play this same full peal on eight bells would take just over 22 hours (40,320 permutations).

```
123456
214365
241635
426153
462513
645231
654321
563412
536142
351624
315264
132546
123456
```

Diagram 1

Plain Bob Minor

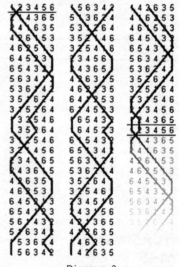

Diagram 2

IM AT YOUR OWN RISK

First there was BlackBerry thumb, and now iPod finger. This, according to the American Society of Hand Therapists, which coined both terms (in a major marketing coup for their member therapists). But before you dismiss these and other technogenic repetitive strain injuries as figments of future class-action hopefuls' imaginations, consider OSHA's estimate that RSIs affect hundreds of thousands of workers and cost the U.S. economy more than $20 billion a year in worker's compensation claims. Good old carpal tunnel syndrome affects almost eight million Americans. According to the ASHT, you can take the following steps to minimize your risk: Use a straight-wrist grip, take a break every hour (as if . . .), raise the device to eye level to avoid neck strain, get a good chair, and switch hands frequently.

If the aforementioned steps aren't realistic, avoid using any device that requires a power source.

GREAT MOMENTS IN CITIZEN JOURNALISM

The population density of Earth is 112 per square mile and rising. In 2007, nearly 3.3 billion people subscribed to cell phone service. This means that wherever and whenever news happens, someone is likely to see it and that someone within this viewing population will think, "Wow, instead of finding higher ground, I think I'll stand here and shoot pictures of this rapidly approaching giant wave." Until recently, these shots

of death and destruction would have made *America's Funniest Home Videos* (especially if said shots involved testicular damage); now, they're news. Below is a list of the top scoops made by everyday Joes and Janes:

• Rodney King beating: user-generated content before user-generated content was cool. George Holliday videotaped King's 1992 beating by four white police officers, resulting in massive backlash against the apparently racist LAPD.

• 2004 tsunami: the aforementioned "big wave"—230,000 people were killed, but some survived to post images.

• Sheffield dust-up: in 2005, Keith Whamond whipped out his digital camera to capture Yankee Garry Sheffield's scuffle with an intoxicated fan in Fenway Park's right-field bleachers.

• Execution of Saddam Hussein: proving that nothing is private, video footage of Hussein's final drop appeared online shortly after his 2006 execution.

• Lotticide: in 2002, speaking of the 1948 presidential candidacy of the segregationist Strom Thurmond, Trent Lott said, "When Strom Thurmond ran for president, we voted for him. We're proud of it. And if the rest of the country had followed our lead, we wouldn't have had all these problems over the years, either." Bloggers put this directly between the eyes of every American computer-user. Result: TKO—bloggers 1, Lott 0.

• Rathergate: two months prior to the 2004 presidential elections, Dan Rather of the CBS News program *60 Minutes* went public with documents that offered an excoriating picture of GW's service with the National Guard. Like gerbils on Agent Orange, bloggers took to the Web to question the documents' authenticity. Result: TKO—bloggers 1, Rather 0.

• London bombings: though every major news source covered the 2005 London bombings, the most immediate photos came from cell-camera-wielding citizens trapped on the subway.

• Hurricane Katrina: Amid governmental disorganization, citizens led the online charge to publicize routes to safety and the location of aid resources, and later to reunite family members via online message boards.

• Virginia Tech shootings: Jamal Albarghouti, a graduate student, captured the sounds of gunshots and screams in the background of his much-played cell-phone video.

• The Iraq War: soldiers' blogs provide the first inklings of trouble in "Mission Accomplished" paradise.

THE QUOTABLE BILL GATES

• There's nobody getting rich writing software that I know of.

• Success is a lousy teacher. It seduces smart people into thinking they can't lose.

• There are no significant bugs in our released software that any significant number of users want fixed.

• Just in terms of allocation of time resources, religion is not very efficient. There's a lot more I could be doing on a Sunday morning.

• It's possible, you can never know, that the universe exists only for me. If so, it's sure going well for me, I must admit.

• About three million computers get sold every year in China, but people don't pay for the software. . . . As long as they are going to steal it, we want them to steal ours.

• Microsoft has had clear competitors in the past. It's a good thing we have museums to document that.

Note 1. Quotes widely misattributed to Gates include the following:
• Tell you what—I'll buy your right arm for a million dollars. I give you a million bucks and I get to sever your arm right here.

- The day is coming when every knee will bow down to a silicon fist, and you will all beg your binary gods for mercy.

- Windows 2000 already contains features such as the human discipline component, where the PC can send an electric shock through the keyboard if the human does something that does not please Windows.

Note 2. The Gates Foundation gives around $1.5 billion every year to education and global health.

Note 3. Microsoft company checks in the name of this author can be sent via Three Rivers Press.

TELEPORTATION USING EINSTEIN-PODOLSKY-ROSEN (EPR) ENTANGLEMENT

Traditionally, the crux of teleportation has been its seeming contradiction of the Heisenberg uncertainty principle, which states that you can never measure and thus know all the information contained within an atom (the more you measure, the more you disturb, until the thing no longer looks like what you started with). Without knowing the makeup of the original object, how could you replicate it across space?

The answer is spooky, or to be precise, *spooky action at a distance.* In a (vastly oversimplified)

nutshell, this spooky action describes the ability of a particle to influence the state of another particle without these particles ever having any measurable interaction. In other words, particles separated by space know things about each other they should not. This has allowed the following procedure:

Particle A is scanned and thus changed, but the information gleaned is transferred spookily to a new particle B, which has had no contact with A. Based on the information it picks up, particle B becomes an exact replica of particle A (but since particle A was completely farked—not to be confused with FARC, the Revolutionary Armed Forces of Colombia—the procedure is technically teleportation and not replication). If you want to severely damage your frontal lobe, consider that this procedure actually requires the intercession of a third particle, C, which acts as an information carrier, but must visit particle B (the result) *before* visiting particle A (the model), and thus transmits its information backward in time.

Yes, this is very, very spooky. But, according to IBM researchers, the technique has been used in the lab to teleport photons, coherent light fields, nuclear spins, and trapped ions. The application of EPR entanglement is also seen as a promising step toward a quantum computer or Internet.

ROCK, PAPER, SCISSORS: ALTERNATE SYMBOLS

Believe it or not, it is possible to eventually become bored with standard RPS. Should you find the spark gone even when throwing the notoriously feisty scissors, consider spicing up your life with one of the following variations:

- Bear, Salmon, Mosquito

- Bear, Ninja, Cowboy

- Nuclear Bomb, Boot, Cockroach

- Microwave, Kitten, Tinfoil

- Village Chief, Tiger, Mother-In-Law

- Elephant, Person, Ant

A SAM LOYD PICTURE PUZZLE

As you can see, the chain in this box is broken into thirteen unjoined pieces. The task of this French blacksmith (and thus yours) is to mend this chain, linking it together in one unbroken loop, and then to replace the links into a box of the same dimensions shown.

Sam Loyd's Endless Chain Puzzle.

FOR mind-numbing funness, visit Dave Lovelace at www.umop. com, where you can learn to play multiple-weapon RPS, like the RPS-25 shown on page 174.

CARTOON WOMEN WHO HAPPEN TO BE VERY HOT

This list intentionally omits Disney characters (Ariel, Esmerelda, Belle, Mulan, Pocahontas, Cinderella, Jasmine, Jane, Jessica Rabbit, etc.), as well as anime characters, the latter of which are nearly impossible to search online without also finding porn. The list (whose members are callously referred to by some as CILFs) includes only characters whose hotness is ancillary to their function within their cartoons.

• Veronica: ah, the question that has plagued male geeks since Pep Comics #22—Betty or Veronica? As Betty is a bit brain dead (and panders to the meathead demographic with her stuffed bears and auto repairs), this list instead chooses Veronica—whose vindictive evil is somehow magnetic.

• Jem: yes, the show was initially a Hasbro marketing ploy, and yes, you could only watch it if you claimed to have lost Rock, Paper, Scissors to your little sister, but seriously—*Showtime, Synergy!*

• The Baroness: if you think this G.I. Joe dominatrix is hot, check out the lead in the 70s-era pulp spy novels of the same name.

• Britney and Quinn: these two tarts from the show *Daria* represent everything geeks despise—and secretly yearn for.

• The White Queen: aka Emma Frost, this villain-turned-heroine is pure sex in white lingerie and a shoo-in for this list.

• Smurfette: admittedly the inclusion of Smurfette in this list sullies otherwise pure childhood memories. Oh well.

• She-Ra: an easy inclusion (as would be Wonder Woman).

• Daphne: Internet wisdom claims that while Velma cannot compete with Daphne's obvious pulchritude, the bespectacled, mousy crime-solver is the series's true hottie. Jinkies! It's a tough call.

• Rogue: while Rogue merits only #4 on IGN Entertainment's list of top ten X-babes (behind Emma Frost, Jean Grey, and Psylocke and just ahead of Storm), her utter unattainability—skin-to-skin contact can result in death—allows comic readers to amplify their longing by sharing in comic characters' unrequited lust.

• Cheetara: This fleet-footed Thundercat makes our collective battlestaff grow.

HIGHLIGHTS FROM THE NATIONAL ASSOCIATION OF ROCKETRY'S SAFETY CODE

While many promote model rocketry to pyromaniac geek middle-schoolers as a positive alternative to setting structure fires, the National Association of Rocketry offers the following guidelines (and more!) that seem designed to restrict said pubescent geeks to the toy side of the toy/antiaircraft-missile spectrum.

2. I will use only certified, commercially made model rocket motors, and will not tamper with these motors or use them for any purpose except those recommended by the manufacturer.

7. If my model rocket weighs more than one pound at liftoff or has more than four ounces of propellant, I will check and comply with FAA regulations before flying.

8. I will not launch my rocket at targets, into clouds, or near airplanes, and will not put flammable or explosive payload in my rocket.

To learn more about model rocketry, consider subscribing to *Sport Rocketry* magazine or, if you are a middle- or high-school student, participating in the Team America Rocketry Challenge. (Yes, it is actually called Team America.)

THE HIDDEN HISTORY OF ICONIC SPORTS TEAM NAMES

• The Brooklyn (now L.A.) Dodgers are so named after a pejorative applied by Manhattanites to Brooklyn residents. In the late nineteenth century, they implied their superiority by teasing their eastern cousins about the necessity to always be on the lookout for trolleys—thus "trolley dodgers," later shortened to "dodgers."

NONE of the team names in United States mainstream sports can hold a candle to the following names drawn from the annals (as it were) of world soccer:

• FART: a Norwegian women's soccer team
• Deportiva Wanka: a Peruvian soccer team
• Fukien AA: a Hong Kong soccer club
• Orange Crushers: a Guam soccer club
• Cockburn City: an Australian soccer club
• Admira Wacker: an Austrian soccer club

- The Calgary Flames originated in Atlanta in 1972. Actually, the flames themselves originated with General William Sherman during the Civil War when he torched the aforementioned Athens of the South.

- New York Knicks: Generations of New Yorkers claim to be direct descendants of Father Knickerbacker, despite the original Diedrich Knickerboker being a fictional character used by Washington Irving to narrate his political satire *A History of New-York from the Beginning of the World to the End of the Dutch Dynasty* (the so-named style of pants/shorts came later).

- While there are precious few lakes in Los Angeles County, there are quite a few in the Lakers' original home of Minneapolis. (And the Utah Jazz originated in New Orleans.)

- Phillies: In 1883, the team was known as the Philadelphia Quakers, then briefly as the Blue Jays (1943–44), before settling into the cheese-steak-eating, Big Head–worshipping Phillies briefly popularized by John Kruk.

Note: The completion of the $270 million, 32,000-person Wankdorf stadium, new home of the Swiss football team Young Boys, spawned the Reuters headline "Young Boys Wankdorf Erection Relief."

HYPNOSIS 101: HOW TO MAKE YOUR FRIENDS ACT LIKE CHICKENS

Like hacking, it is much easier to hypnotize someone once his or her firewall is down. Thus, you will need to find a way to gain your victim's confidence before you can exert your evil will, perhaps couching your hypnosis in terms of relaxation or memory techniques.

The first step is to make your victim comfortable. Ask him to sit or lie down. Then, in a soothing voice, ask your victim to close his eyes and focus on his breathing. Have him drift his consciousness into various body parts, relaxing each part in turn. Offer encouragement. Repeat for ten to fifteen minutes. Beware of any interruptions.

Voilà—your victim is now susceptible to your will, and will be for about the next ten minutes. Use your time wisely.

When bringing someone out of hypnosis, use one of the clichéd endings, such as, "I will count down from five, and when I reach zero, you will open your eyes, feeling alert and rested, and will forget that I have made you scratch around the watercooler while clucking, flapping your arms, and pecking at imaginary grubs while the rest of the office dissolved into hilarity."

Note: The previous description of hypnosis is massively unethical. If you make your friends and/or family act like chickens, you are going to hell.

'80S DANCE MOVES THAT DESERVE RESURGENCE

Some argue—and they may have a point—that every time someone commits the following dance moves to print, they doom future generations to repeat the mistakes of the 1980s. These doomsayers posit that even after 80s dance moves recede from our cultural memory, books such as this will lie dormant, like pods from the movie *Aliens,* waiting for discovery by some future teen, at which time they will burst forth to infect another generation.

The Running Man. Hop as you bring one knee up, then slide your grounded foot back as you bring down your raised foot, landing on this foot directly underneath you (as if running in place). Repeat. Consider combining with churning butter or other seriously funky hand movements. The Running Man and its variation, the Roger Rabbit, are basic repertoire for any aspiring 80s dancer.

The Typewriter. Hop sideways, alternating your toes in and out.

Funky Alien. Push a fist out from underneath your shirt to imitate alien birth from your abdominal cavity. For added effect, draw alien face on your fist and periodically let it peek from your neck hole.

TOUCH-TONE TUNES: THE KEYS TO SUCCESS

If you have perfect pitch, go no further. However, if your mind is open to the microtonal tuning systems of the Orient, you can employ rhythm to make up for what these songs lack in completely accurate pitch. To play these songs, it is imperative that you know them well before taking to your phone's keypad.

"Lean on Me"	"Working on the Railroad"	Olympic Fanfare
4, 4569, 9654, 45665 4, 4569, 9654, 45614 654, 99996, 69654, 456655 4, 4569, 99654, 9666154	42454864, 66426 42454864, 6662265 55556541, 6644556 44455446, 61621	3, 9, 91231, 2222, 32112312 3,9,91231,2222,32112321
Horn of the *General Lee*	"99 Bottles of Beer"	*Monkees* Theme Song
321112369993	6661116666, 9992229 333,3333, 1112236666	665466, 444445556 445564, 4444551
"You Are My Sunshine"	"California, Here I Come"	"Happy Birthday"
15333,35311 1536#, #963 1536#, #9631 153,35531	8888981 333 3634	112163, 112196 11085563, 008121

Hangin' Tough. Pioneered by NKOTB. Left arm high in the air. Wave it back and forth (like you just don't care).

Popcorn. Hop side-to-side in time with the music while shaking your head in the opposite direction and smiling as if Molly Ringwald had just agreed to be your prom date. This should be as cheesy as possible and is thus best performed ironically (as, in all honesty, are most of these steps).

Popping. Like the robot in its percussive tensioning of isolated muscles. Best accomplished to electro-funk.

Waving. An outgrowth of popping—stretch out your arms and start a wave at your fingertips that travels the length of your arms, ending at your far fingertips. Consider multi-person waves.

The Smurf. One heel up, the other down. Switch to the beat.

The Sprockets Dance. C'mon—don't pretend you don't know it.

Dance Imitates Life. The shopping cart, the fishing pole, the sprinkler, milking the cow, churning butter, mugging the goat, etc.

Dance Imitates 80s Personalities. The Hammer Dance, She Bop, Axel Rose, Risky Business, the Ed Lover, the Icky Shuffle, etc.

THE EVOLUTION OF LINK, THE GAMING CHARACTER

In 1986, when Link first appeared in Nintendo's Legend of Zelda, he looked to be in his midteens, implying a birth year of around 1971. However, despite many physically, intellectually, and emotionally demanding trials while traveling through Hyrule in search of the Master Sword and Light Arrows needed to defeat Gannon, Link appears to have aged little since this time, implying that the aging rate for the Hylian species is different from that of humans. While bending the rules of aging, Link also disobeys the rules posited by the linear, one-way progression of time. For example, in The Legend of Zelda, Link is a young boy, and Gannon has stolen the Triforce of Power; in Ocarina of Time, Link is *still* a young boy and still hot on the trail of Gannon and the Triforce, but this time he is a tree-person; in The Wind Waker, Link—again a young boy—travels a flooded planet Hyrule to rescue his sister from the Helmaroc king, who is controlled by a surprisingly undead Gannon. (This multiplicity seems to prove physicists' many-worlds theory.)

Throughout, the brave but reticent Link's only spoken line in addition to grunts and cries is "Come on!" which he yells in The Wind Waker. It is worth noting that Link has never been seen in the same room as Orlando Bloom, who played Legolas in Peter Jackson's film version of Lord of the Rings.

MacGYVER WINE MAKING

Almost anything that contains sugars can be made to produce alcohol as it decomposes—fruit of any type makes especially good wine (or, as it is commonly referred to in the business, "hooch"). In the following recipes, extract juice from your fruit (if not inherently juicy, this may require pouring boiling water over it and letting it sit for forty-eight hours) and mix together all ingredients *minus the sugar and yeast*. Add a crushed Campden tablet to stop any wild yeasts from influencing the batch. Then, use a hydrometer to measure the wine's specific gravity, and add sugar to adjust the specific gravity to the desired level. Add the yeast of your choice and let ferment for five to seven days (until reaching a specific gravity of 1.010–1.025). Then, transfer to a carboy and ferment for another thirty days, until it dips below a specific gravity of 1.000. At that point, add ascorbic acid to avoid making vinegar and nuke it with potassium sorbate to avoid any further fermentation. Sweeten to taste and bottle. Consume while listening to bluegrass and/or petting hound dog and/or shooting at squirrels from your porch.

Raspberry Wine	Dandelion Wine	Huckleberry Wine	Plum Wine
3–4 lbs raspberries 2¼ lbs sugar ½ tsp acid blend ½ tsp pectic enzyme ⅛ tsp grape tannin 7 pints water yeast/nutrient	3 qts dandelion flowers 1 lb golden raisins 1 gallon water 3 lbs sugar 2 lemons 1 orange yeast/nutrient	4 lbs huckleberries 2½ lbs sugar 1½ tsp acid blend 7¼ pts water yeast/nutrient	6 lbs plums 3 lbs sugar ½ lb barley 1 orange ½ tsp pectic enzyme 1 gallon water yeast/nutrient
Prickly Pear Wine	**Persimmon Wine**	**Chokecherry Wine**	**Elderberry Wine**
5–6 lbs prickly pears 2½ lbs sugar 1 tsp acid blend 1 gallon water yeast/nutrient	3 lbs persimmons 2½ lbs sugar 1 tbsp acid blend ½ tsp pectic enzyme 7 pts water yeast/nutrient	2½ lbs chokecherries 2½ lbs sugar 1 tsp acid blend ½ tsp pectic enzyme ¼ tsp grape tannin 7 pts water yeast/nutrient	3 lbs elderberries 2 lbs sugar 3½ qts water 2 tsp acid blend ½ tsp pectic enzyme yeast/nutrient

THE MATHEMATICS OF SPAM FILTERS

The English mathematician and Presbyterian minister Thomas Bayes was born in 1702 and died well before the incorporation of Microsoft in 1975 or CERN's 1991 publication of the World Wide Web project. Before Bayes, statisticians had been able, given the number of black and white balls in a barrel, to predict the likelihood of drawing a ball of a certain color. Bayes's theorem provided tools to describe—having drawn a certain number of balls—what the ratio of black to white balls remaining in the barrel was likely to be.

Fast forward to the Bayesian spam filter, which says, If you tell me whether a specific e-mail is white or black, I will be able to tell you about the composition of your inbox. To do this, a modern filter compares words in new mail to words in messages marked spam, using the following formula, in which Pr(spam/words) is the percentage that an e-mail is spam, Pr(words/spam) is the probability of finding given words in a spam e-mail, Pr(Spam) is the probability that any e-mail is spam, and Pr(words) is the probability of finding the given words in any e-mail:

$$\text{Pr(spam|words)} = \frac{\text{Pr(words|spam)} \times \text{Pr(spam)}}{\text{Pr(words)}}$$

This formula needs to be trained—it doesn't work very well until you teach it which words are high indicators of spam. Therefore, a Bayesian spam filter uses artificial intelligence to learn your needs. If you work in a lending office, you may want to read e-mails that contain the word *refinance;* by keeping these in your inbox, your spam filter learns this is a desirable word. If you repeatedly mark e-mails containing the word *Pen1s* as spam, your filter will eventually be able to reach a threshold of spam certainty (say, 95 percent) and automatically throw these messages away.

E-mails that contain only images mixed with random words are trickier for spam filters.

PETER PIPER PICKED A KEPPLER-POINSOT POLYHEDRON PATTERN

Copy and cut five of this shape. Cut anywhere a triangle's short side touches a long side. Fold the long lines backward and the short lines forward (taping or gluing the tabs to hold it in place). The tab marked N is where the next of the five pieces will attach; the side marked P is where this piece attaches to the previous one. When joined, you will end with the shape immediately recognizable as a great stellated dodecahedron (or "spiky-ass ball" if for some reason you happen to be unfamiliar with complex polyhedra).

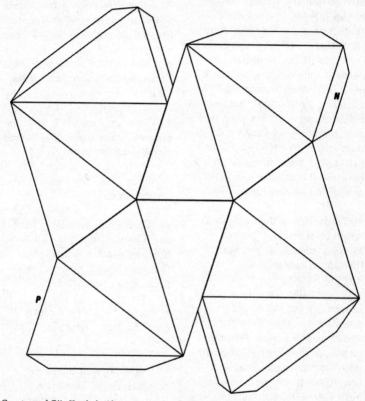

Courtesy of Gijs Korthals Altes at www.korthalsaltes.com.

AUDIENCE PARTICIPATION GAGS REQUIRING PROPS IN *THE ROCKY HORROR PICTURE SHOW*

There are more than three hundred customary verbal responses to the film, almost all of which contribute to a viewing experience that's NC-17 at best. For example, in the first, rather innocuous paragraph spoken by the film's disembodied lips, the audience responses reference edible underwear, sex play with fruit topping, and aimed ejaculation. It gets worse (or deliciously better . . .) from there. Included here are the instances of participation that involve props.

• Throw rice as the newlyweds Ralph Hapshatt and Betty Munroe exit the church near the film's beginning.

• When Brad and Janet are caught in a rainstorm, Janet holds a newspaper, the *Plain Dealer,* over her head. If in the back row, simulate the rainstorm with a water pistol; if sitting toward the front, cover your head with a newspaper, à la Janet (if at all squeamish, consider leaving head and eyes covered throughout film).

• When flame shows on the screen during the song "Over at the Frankenstein Place," hold up a lighter or the legal equivalent— a flashlight.

• When the movie's lead, the transvestite, bisexual scientist Dr. Frank-N-Furter, thrice snaps his rubber gloves, snap along.

• Noisemakers greet the end of Frank's creation speech.

• When Brad cries "Great Scott!" throw rolls of Scott's brand toilet paper in the air.

• Offer confetti along with the Transylvanians at the end of the Charles Atlas song.

• When Dr. Frank-N-Furter proposes a toast, give it to him— throw toast in the air.

• When Frank dons a party hat, do the same.

• When Frank asks if we heard a bell (while singing the modern librettist's masterpiece "Planet Shmanet Janet"), provide the noise with your own bell.

• Frank: "Cards for sorrow, cards for pain." Response: throw cards.

• Optional props include a bouquet, rings, doughnuts, sponges, and a paper airplane.

Note: It defies logic that Susan Sarandon received an Oscar for her role in *Dead Man Walking* and not for her sensitive yet clear-eyed portrayal of Janet Weiss in RHPS.

THE LONGEST WORDS IN MANY LANGUAGES

There are many caveats accompanying languages' longest words. Do you allow hyphenation? Do you allow place names? Do you allow medical and chemical terms? Drawing on the rules of Scrabble, the longest word in the English language is *ethylenediaminetetraacetates,* at twenty-eight letters (which, of course, would not fit on a Scrabble board). The longest nonchemical word in English is *electroencephalographically,* at twenty-seven letters. The longest one-syllable English word is *scrootched,* at ten letters. In German, a suborganization of a prewar shipping company on the Danube was known as the *Donaudampfschiffahrtselektrizitatenhauptbetriebswerkbauunterbeamtengesellschaft.* In French, the longest word is *anticonstitutionnellement,* which means—as you might guess—"anticonstitutionally"; similarly the longest word in Spanish is *anticonstitucionalmente,* and the longest in Portuguese is almost identical. In Italian, *precipitevolissimevolmente* means "as fast as you can." While there is intense Internet debate over Norway's longest word, the word describing the chairman of the Norwegian Supreme Court (*høyesterettsjustitiarius*) is the consensus favorite. In Dutch, the word *hottentottensoldatententententoonstellingsterreinen* refers to the tents of the Hottentot soldiers. Certainly, the word *hääyöaieoionta* (having to do with the intentions of the wedding night) is not Finland's longest, but it is perhaps the world's most difficult to pronounce correctly.

CREVASSE RESCUE USING COOL PULLEYS

Enviros and the evil scientists paid by megacorporations to deny global warming both agree that Earth's climate warms and cools in cycles. Generally, like a playground swing, the higher the oscillation in one direction, the higher the corresponding swing in the other. This means that, while flip-flops made from recycled tires may currently be a hot

IF you are not among those who consider hyphenated chemical names to be cheating, then the world's longest word is the description of the Dahlemense strain of the tobacco mosaic virus, at 1,185 characters long, starting with *acetyl* and ending much later with *serine.*

investment, before long (geologically speaking) we will be roaming the permafrost with (cloned) mammoths. So buy a good coat.

Along with the upcoming, post-global-warming ice age will come the increased daily danger of crevasses—giant cracks in glacial ice, which may or may not be covered by a thin layer of snow and thus pose as solid ground. The first step in protecting yourself from crevasses (which can suck you in as surely as the burrow-bound Sarlaac in the Dune Sea) is, whenever you walk, do so as part of a rope team. A two-person rope team is adequate if you are both very skilled, but rope-pooling with three or more is safer and in the frozen future will allow you to use walking lanes denied to smaller teams. If a fellow member of your rope team falls into a crevasse and cannot ascend the rope, you will need to pull him or her out. With three or more team members remaining on the surface, you may be able to "haul tuna" simply walking backward to raise your team member.

However, with fewer than three, you will need to engineer a bit of mechanical advantage as shown in this picture provided by the Association of Canadian Mountain Guides (who have retained their expertise in roaming mammoth-infested glaciers). As you can see, padding the lip of the crevasse with a pack keeps the rope from cutting into the snow (jaunty chapeaus also appear necessary). In this picture, the rescuer has dropped a loop

of rope to the fallen climber, who has clipped the loop into a carabiner so that it runs through like a pulley. Above, one end of the loop is secured and the other end runs through another pulley (connected to the anchor). This free end then passes back through another pulley (clipped to the rope) and is yanked by the rescuer. Without friction, this system offers a three-to-one advantage (you have to pull three times the distance, but with only a third of the force). With the realities of system inefficiency (a rope running through a 'biner doesn't pull smoothly, and even a Teflon-coated pack would provide some unwanted friction), it will still be useful to have two people hauling on the loose end.

ORIGAMI FROG HIGH JUMP CHALLENGE

Many geeks adhere to stiff paper theory (SPT), holding that frogs made of expensive company letterhead will jump higher than those made of flimsy copy paper. However, while SPT adds giddyup to any origami amphibian, it also adds weight. The trick is to find a paper that offers the happy combination of high spring at low weight. In this regard, linen papers tend to underperform; so too do cardboard mailers, as they lead to bulky, bullfrogesque hoppers. Like the Mongols conquering much of the known world with their invention of the compound bow (horn and sinew grafted into the wooden grip), some forward-thinking geeks have developed a Frankensteinian technique whereby cardboard legs are grafted onto a lightweight paper body, but this technically falls outside the rules of traditional origami and thus in most arenas is considered cheating. And remember when choosing your frog's overall dimensions that success doesn't necessarily depend on the size of the origami frog in the fight but rather on the size of the fight in the origami frog.

In addition to choice of paper, pay special attention to precise construction and to the technique of your frog stroke. Push directly down on your frog's hopping mechanism and you will lose spring due to a slow release (you can't release your hand faster than your frog's recoil); stroke too far forward and you risk losing precious compression. Instead, geeks know that a confident but gentle stroke from the frog's nose, ending off its backside, produces maximal hopping power.

If comparing origami frog jumping heights in an online forum, be sure to account for altitude and humidity at your test site, both of which drastically affect performance (higher humidity leads to damp and thus somewhat flaccid frogs; higher altitude allows less air resistance, though it can provide cardiovascular challenges for the frog's operator).

Here are plans:

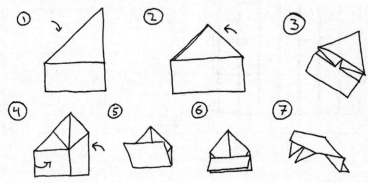

THREE MORE PENCIL AND PAPER GAMES

SPROUTS

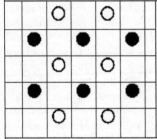

1. Start with two or three dots on a page.

2. A move consists of two steps— draw a line between two dots (or to itself); and mark a new dot anywhere on this line.

3. Your new line may not cross any existing line.

4. Once a dot has three lines coming out of it, it is closed.

5. Whoever makes the last possible move wins.

PIPELAYER

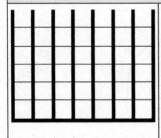

1. In a grid like the one shown, one player is trying to connect white dots to move from the top of the board to the bottom; the other player is trying to connect black dots to move from left to right.

2. Take turns drawing short horizontal or vertical lines.

3. You can't cross your opponent's lines. Don't get blocked!

FOUR IN A ROW

1. Imagine this grid is an open board of the kind used to play Connect Four.

2. One player is Xs and the other is Os. Take turns "dropping" your shape into the game board, where it falls down to rest on the lowest open spot.

3. The first person to make four in a row wins.

A SAM LOYD LOGIC PUZZLE

The goal of the game shown below is to knock over the last standing pin. With each throw, Van Winkle or his opponent can knock down any one or two (adjacent) pins. The little man of the mountains (who can be seen flipping Van Winkle the bird) has just knocked over pin number two, and now it is Van Winkle's turn to let it rip. Which play ensures that he will win the game?

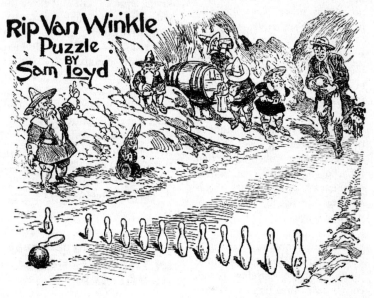

COFFEE ALTERNATIVES

At work in your cup of hot coffee is a complex pharmacopeia of chemicals, the combination of which has the potential to see you safely through the morning. While the effects are caffeine-dominated, the components of this cocktail gently raise and lower various body functions resulting in everything from boosted cognitive performance to higher blood pressure to a reduced risk of gout. But what if your early morning lover has lost its luster? (And the ever expanding array of choices at your local chain coffee shop has started to look like the desperate pandering of new-is-better marketing.) Maybe it's time to try one of the following:

• Yerba maté. From deep in the heart of South America comes this flavorful drink borne of a species of holly plant. Maté contains caffeine but also related compounds of the same type (xanthines), which offer a similar but slightly different psychoactive pick-me-up. No, maté is not cocaine, and no, it has never been clinically proven to be addictive.

• Black tea. Use only if you like the taste. It has half the caffeine of coffee. Drink with extended pinky finger.

• Chai. If you are neither a turtleneck-wearing poet nor a complete wuss, your only option for chai is masala chai, which contains a bracing mixture of cardamom, cinnamon, ginger, pepper, and cloves.

• Anything containing guarana. The guarana bean contains three times as much caffeine as the coffee bean. Brazilians, who consume mass quantities of guarana soft drinks, claim the drug offers caffeine's energy boost without the accompanying jitters.

• Hippie witch brew. The magazine *Mother Earth News* recommends a blend of crushed acorns, burdock root, California coffeeberry, carob, chicory, dandelion, and sow thistle. Try asking for this at Starbucks. See what happens.

THE COOL THING ABOUT DIVIDING BY SEVEN

One divided by seven equals 0.14285714; two divided by seven equals 0.285714; three divided by seven equals 0.4285714; four divided by seven equals 0.5714285714; five divided by seven equals 0.714285714; six divided by seven equals 0.8571485714. How frickin' cool is that? While certainly described elsewhere, this pattern was independently discovered by a friend of this author's "when doing some math one day in college, which is what sociology majors do between happy hours."

PERSON NEVER SEEN IN THE SAME ROOM AS BATMAN

Linus Torvalds.

SELECTIONS FROM THE SOCIETY FOR CREATIVE ANACHRONISM'S RULES FOR ARMED COMBAT

III-B1: Striking the opponent with excessive force is prohibited.

III-B7: A fighter shall not deliberately strike a helpless opponent.

IV-B1: If a combatant intentionally places an illegal target area in the path of a blow, the combatant forfeits that attached limb as if it had been struck in a legal target area.

V-B1b: The minimum effective thrusting blow to the face shall be a direct touch and the maximum shall be substantially lighter than to other parts of the body.

V-C1: An effective blow to the head, neck, or torso shall be judged fatal or completely disabling, rendering the fighter incapable of further combat.

VII-A3: Flails are expressly prohibited.

VIII-A: Siege engines or structures may be used in combat during melees and wars in accordance with the rules set forth in the *Siege Engines Handbook*.

VIII-C1: A blow from a siege-class ammunition to any legal target area shall be judged fatal or completely disabling.

XI-D: If an injured person is conscious, they may be asked if they would like assistance. No conscious person will be forced to accept treatment without his or her consent. No non-combatant shall enter the combat area until summoned by a marshal.

Courtesy of Society for Creative Anachronism's *Marshal's Handbook*, 2007, www.sca.org.

THE WORLD'S WORST SOMEWHAT-MODERN NATURAL DISASTERS

If you're a tourist hoping to experience disaster of biblical proportions, you won't do better than a trip to mainland China, which boasts seven of the modern world's top ten natural disasters. While you missed out on the fertile years of the 1920s and 1970s, there is no telling when disaster may strike again! Note: In 2002, twenty-five people in China's Henan Province were killed by hail.

1. In the summer of 1931, China's Yellow River flooded, and up to eight million people drowned or died of ensuing disease and famine.

2. The same river flooded in 1887, killing upward of a million people.

3. On November 13, 1970, the Bhola cyclone struck Bangladesh, killing between 500,000 and one million people.

4. In 1839, a cyclone in India killed upward of 300,000 people.

5. In 2004, the Indian Ocean tsunami officially killed 283,100 people.

6. In 1976, China's Tangshan earthquake killed a government-reported 242,000 people, but estimates of the death toll range as high as 655,000 people.

7. When China's Banqiao Dam failed in 1975, approximately 231,000 people were killed.

8. In 1920, an earthquake in China's Gansu province claimed at least 200,000 lives.

9. Another Chinese earthquake, this one in Xining, killed 200,000 people in 1927.

10. In 1935, the Yangtze River flooded, but human deaths were limited to a mere 145,000.

THE WORLD'S WORST SOMEWHAT-MODERN NATURAL DISASTER MOVIES

If you're a moviegoer hoping to experience horrendous acting and/or cinematography of biblical proportions, what better than a trip down memory lane with the following ill-received and wonderfully cultish disaster classics? The conventions of the genre ensure that you can pick the disaster that most deeply resonates with your unconscious directly from the title.

1. *Earthquake:* The people of Los Angeles are assaulted by an earthquake of unimaginable magnitude. The audience feels their pain.

2. *Night of the Comet:* A comet wipes out all but two L.A. valley girls, who are forced to fight zombies to survive. Seriously.

3. *Avalanche:* Rock Hudson and Mia Farrow, trapped at a ski resort. Stops short of *The Shining* and *The Donner Party*.

4. Though *Volcano* (1997) stars the venerable Tommy Lee Jones and the unattainable Anne Heche, its tagline says it all: "The coast is toast."

5. *The Day After Tomorrow:* A disaster grab bag, featuring hurricanes, tornados, tidal waves, floods, and an ice age that threatens to overtake vehicles traveling in the right lane.

6. *Meteor:* An eight-kilometer-wide chunk of the asteroid Orpheus is heading toward Earth. The only hope is to nuke it. Acting in this clinker are the redoubtable Sean Connery and Henry Fonda. We can only imagine that both stars' reaction to the premiere must have included firing their agents.

7. *Armageddon:* According to IMDb, "When an asteroid the size of Texas is headed for Earth, the world's best deep core drilling team is sent to nuke the rock from the

inside." Big oil, eat your heart out.

8. *Deep Impact:* According to IMDb, "Unless a comet can be destroyed before colliding with Earth, only those allowed into shelters will survive." Too bad Robert Duvall and Téa Leoni couldn't track down Bruce Willis and his deep core drilling team.

9. *The Core:* According to IMDb, "The only way to save Earth from catastrophe is to drill down to the core and set it spinning again." Too bad Aaron Eckhart and Hilary Swank couldn't track down Bruce Willis and his deep core drilling team.

A BRIEF HISTORY OF LASER WEAPONS

With only a quick stop at your local box store, you can be ready to pop a conventional cap in someone's ass; however, charring said ass to a crisp using a laser or other ray weapon is not so easy. This is because—despite many decades of government promises—laser weapons do not currently exist (despite the ubiquity of industrial cutting lasers and promises by high-school tech-ed teachers that one false move with a pointer will render your lab partner a cyclops).

One of the earliest claims of ray-gun success was by Nicola Tesla (who else?), who in 1937 pub-lished a treatise titled "The New Art of Projecting Concentrated Non-Dispersive Energy Through the Natural Media." The schematics of his "teleforce weapon" are suspiciously missing (having perhaps suffered a fate similar to that of the Ark of the Covenant, which is stored in a vast government warehouse to the benefit of unwitting humankind).

Later, Ronald Reagan spent many billions of dollars trying to scare Soviet scientists into believing the United States was, in fact, technologically able to create laser weapons capable of zapping ICBMs out of the sky. This sparked projects with badass-sounding acronyms like MARAUDER and MEDUSA and MIRACL, but almost no measurable results (other than a precedent for massive defense spending on pipe dreams).

The crux, in the cases of almost all types of ray weapons, is in generating the needed energy using a method that is more portable than the standard nuclear power plant. Also difficult is the plasma breakdown of air when hit with massive energy, known as "blooming"—as the air breaks down, so too does the laser it conducts. Any particulate matter in the air greatly enhances blooming—bullets push dust and smoke aside; laser weapons have to burn through them.

What this means is that you should content yourself for now with your trusty Star Trek phaser, which, while the nadions it fires can be seen to travel much slower than the speed of light, can be set for *stun* in addition to *kill*.

RARE NORTH AMERICAN BIRDS AND WHERE THEY CAN BEST BE SEEN

Common Name	Scientific Name	Conservation Status	Best Seen In	Notes
Xantu's murrelet	Synthliboramphus hypoleucus	Vulnerable	Channel Islands, CA	After breeding, disperses to sea
Snail kite	Rostrhamus sociabilis	Least concern	Everglades, FL	Ground-nesting bird of prey
Kirtland's warbler	Dendroica kirtlandii	Near threatened	Lower peninsula, MI	Depends on jack pine seed
Garganey	Anas querquedula	Least concern	Rare in U.S.	Attempts to turn Smurfs into gold
Lucifer hummingbird	Calothoras lucifer	Least concern	TX, AZ, NM	Male in white underpants; female is buff below
Gyrfalcon	Falco rusticolus	Least concern	Northern MT	Largest of all falcon species
Fork-tailed flycatcher	Tyrannus savanna	Least concern	Rare in TX	Mostly Central and S. America
Blue-footed booby	Soula nebouxii	Least concern	Channel Islands, CA	From the Spanish *bobo* ("stupid fellow")
Murphy's petrel	Pterodroma ultima	Near threatened	Off Pacific Coast	Member of the gadfly petrels
Pink-breasted titnipple	Mammarius aureolis	Somewhat threatening	Grand Teton N.P., WY	The male of the species is much smaller

MARITIME SIGNAL LANGUAGE

Like Egyptian hieroglyphics, signal language can be phonetic or representational: Flags stand for letters but also have their own meanings. For example, the three bars of J mean "on fire, keep clear" (as if the flames weren't clue enough), and the four squares of U signal "You are standing into danger." In actual usage, these flags are also color coded, so as to avoid implying, for example, that all Dutch ships are on fire and all Jamaican ships are in need of help and/or are stopped.

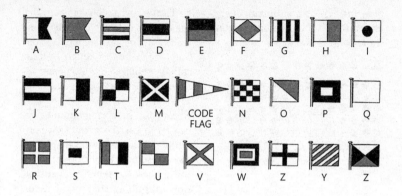

THE QUOTABLE XENA: WARRIOR PRINCESS

XENA TO GABRIELLE ABOUT JOXER: He would crawl fifty miles on broken glass just to sweat in your shadow.

LEAH: Life as a priestess to the virgin goddess Hestia isn't all that hard. The most important rule is to know who you are.
GABRIELLE: Believe me, if I have to go the rest of my life without companionship, knowing myself won't be a problem.

XENA: Oh, we don't have to run for it. I'm going to slap these bitches silly.

XENA: I will crush his head like a peanut between the thighs of doom!
GABRIELLE: For once, Xena, I'd like to be the Roman noble and you be the slave.

GABRIELLE: You did it! When your village was destroyed, you were infected with bloodlust. But you overcame it!

A RECORDER FINGERING CHART

By the Middle Ages, the recorder had reached its modern form (proved by the discovery of a fourteenth-century, eight-hole recorder in a latrine in the German city of Göttingen). Now, due to its inexpensive construction, ease of playing, and the difficulty of making truly horrendous accidental noises while playing (as opposed to the clarinet, trombone, or violin), the recorder is the go-to instrument of choice for elementary school music programs across the country. There remains nothing quite like the sound of twenty-nine fifth-graders simultaneously attempting "You Are My Sunshine" on the soprano recorder.

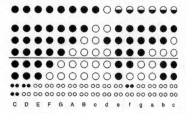

INTERESTING BITS OF EGGSHELL PHYSICS

While the facts below are best termed trivia, there is, in fact, a way to win money or beer using eggshells: Hold a sharp knife upright and set half an eggshell on its point. Bet that your dupe cannot pound the handle of the knife into a table with enough force to cause the tip of the knife to puncture the shell. He or she won't be able to, but if you hold the knife handle loosely, allowing it to rebound slightly as it hits the table, it will punch through the half shell.

• A hard-boiled egg will spin easily (and may author smoky 1950s detective novels).

• A fresh egg will sink in water and an older egg will float; this due to an ever increasing air space.

• The stringy coils inside the egg are not (as is commonly held) made of rooster semen; rather, they are bands of tough protein called chalazae, which act as shock absorbers to the yolk.

• During the spring equinox, an egg is no easier to stand on end; neither is it easier to balance an egg at the equator. (Proponents of these theories point to a direct, upward pull exerted by the moon in the first case and the sun in the second.) However, by shaking an egg to break its chalazae, you can release the yolk, lowering the egg's center of gravity, thus making it easier to balance.

• A fresh egg looks cloudy because carbon dioxide present at birth hasn't yet had time to escape.

• An eggshell may have as many as seventeen thousand tiny pores, through which it can absorb flavors.

• The eggshell is composed mainly of calcium carbonate and thus mixing crushed seashells with chicken feed improves shell strength.

• Like the Taj Mahal, the egg's domelike shape evenly distributes force applied to its top.

ALTERNATE PATHS TO SUCCESS

DEMOCRATIC PRESIDENT	REPUBLICAN PRESIDENT	TECH MOGUL
1. Debate club	1. Eagle Scout	1. Online gaming
2. Student body president	2. Football team	2. Band
3. Ivy League college	3. West Point	3. MIT/CalTech
4. Rhodes Scholarship	4. Military	4. Social deviance
5. Law school	5. Get stars/medals	5. Mad genius
6. Public defender	6. Optional stint in private sector	6. Accumulate wealth
7. State government	7. Senator/governor	7. Hostile takeover(s)
8. National spotlight	8. Success!	8. Success!
9. Success!		

BUSINESS MOGUL	ROCK STAR	NOBEL LAUREATE IN LITERATURE
1. Debate club	1. Play with fire	1. Suffer
2. Ivy League college	2. Inhale	2. Small liberal arts school
3. Powerful fraternity, and/or college secret society	3. Join band	3. Continue suffering
4. Intro investment banking job (Wall Street)	4. Eat ramen noodles	4. Publish short stories in literary mags
5. MBA: Harvard/ Wharton	5. Play gigs	5. Still suffering
6. Return to Wall Street	6. Get arrested	6. Write about suffering
7. Climb corporate ladder	7. Play more gigs	7. Teach at small liberal arts school
8. Success!	8. Sell out	8. Success! (Though still suffering)
	9. Success!	

SUPERHEROES, THEIR NEMESES, POWERS, SECRET BASES, AND WEAKNESSES

	POWERS	*NEMESIS*	*SECRET BASE*	*WEAKNESS*
Green Lantern	Power ring generates plasma bolts, force fields, etc.	Legion of Doom	Satellite Watchtower	Needs ring
Silver Surfer	Master of universe's cosmic energy	Fantastic Four, Galactus, Thanos	Nomadic	Own fractured soul and periodic allegiance to evil Galactus
Batman	Inventions, gadgets	Joker, Penguin, Riddler, etc.	Bat Cave	Own fractured soul
Superman	Almost limitless	Lex Luthor	Fortress of Solitude	Kryptonite
Captain Marvel	Wisdom, strength, stamina, power, courage, speed	Doctor Sivana	Rock of Eternity	None
Wonder Woman	Brain power concentrated in muscle energy (more in late versions)	Baroness Paula von Gunther	Themyscira	None
Hulk	Strength and invulnerability	The Thing, the Abomination	Avengers Mansion	Uncontrolled anger
Wolverine	Animal powers	Sabretooth	Xavier Institute for Higher Learning	Own fractured soul
Aquaman	Water powers, strength, speed	Ocean Master	Hall of Justice	Air
He-Man	Strength, pulchritude	Skeletor	Castle Greyskull	Sentimentality

THE MATHEMATICAL DEFINITION OF AN EULER BRICK

The famous brick borne of the mathematician Leonhard Euler is a cuboid with unequal integer edges and integer face diagonals (if the space diagonal was also an integer it would be called a perfect cuboid, though currently no perfect cuboids have been found). While this sounds simple, the smallest Euler brick has sides of 240, 117, and 44.

The edges of the Euler brick satisfy the following equations (where d, e, and f are the face diagonals created by a box with sides a, b, and c):

$$a^2 + b^2 = d^2$$

$$b^2 + c^2 = e^2$$

$$a^2 + c^2 = f^2$$

I CAN'T BELIEVE IT'S A LOOPHOLE!

Here it is—April 14—and time again to start worrying about taxes. Wouldn't it be easier for the IRS to simply offer a basic geek credit in recognition of the fact that you will almost certainly find $32,000 of sneaky, obscure write-offs? Lawmakers, take note: Perhaps geek certification should be recognized as another exemption on the standard W-4 form. Until then, don't forget the following tricks:

• If the primary reason for a visit to your vacation property can reasonably be considered work (e.g., you are doing a bit of maintenance on the lake cottage before renting it for the summer season), this time is not taxed as "personal use." (Likewise, if you rent out your vacation home for fewer than fourteen days in a calendar year, you can pocket the cash.)

• Use child labor to your advantage! If you put your son or daughter on your payroll, he or she can open an IRA, is subject to a lower tax rate than if you had kept the money, and is exempt from Social Security taxes. Likewise, paying a spouse from your sole proprietorship allows him or her to open a separate retirement account.

• If a doctor specifically recommends exercise, you can write off your gym membership and/or any other "weight loss expenses."

• While your dog doesn't quite count as a dependent, don't forget to write off pet moving expenses and expenses incurred for guard dogs (you can deduct the percentage of dog expenses that matches the percentage of time your Chihuahua spends guarding the house).

• To protect a one-year windfall, in addition to buying a (big) first home, consider blinding yourself, which will allow you to check the coveted box 39A.

- If you are planning to be busted in possession of a large quantity of illicit drugs or moonshine, be sure you visit your state's department of revenue beforehand to pay your illicit drug tax. Affix the needed stamps to your "product."

- Consider holding business meetings in Caribbean countries where you can write off expenses: Honduras, Trinidad and Tobago, the Dominican Republic, Barbados, Costa Rica, etc. It's much harder to write off meetings in Europe.

Note: Employing family members and/or deducting pet expenses is effectively volunteering for an audit.

OCARINA SONGS FROM *THE LEGEND OF ZELDA*

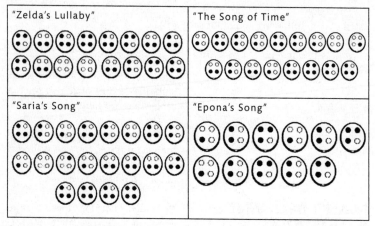

Courtesy of www.clayz.com, where you can also find audio examples.

TOILET TRAIN YOUR CAT

Woe be unto ye who messes with the world of the cat. In terms of specific woe, you can expect everything from shredded furniture to endless sulking to sneaky deposits of urine, discoverable only once they have thoroughly wrecked the carpet and/or floor-boards behind the couch, should ye artlessly attempt feline potty training. But oh, the rewards of training done right! No more stench of ammonia filtering from the litter box in the corner of the laundry room! No more scouring of late-night infomercials for the perfect hands-free disposal system! No more subtly plotting ways in which your wife's cat could "accidentally" encounter your neighbor's Rottweiler! Just follow the steps below and when in doubt, take it slow!

• First, explain to your cat that you are not trying to kill him/her. Nor are you in any way impinging upon his/her right to urinate and/or defecate wherever and whenever he/she sees fit. Nor are you implying that you would appreciate it if he/she urinated/defecated in the toilet. You are only implying that said cat might *prefer* urinating/defecating in the toilet, and as his/her servant, you are willing to offer help as wanted. Repeat the following mantra: "It is I who is being trained, not the cat. Ohmmmm."

• Slowly and in stages likely totaling the life expectancy of your cat, move the litter box toward the bathroom. If your cat pees on the rug, move the litter box back to the last successful spot and wait.

• Once the litter box is in the bathroom (oh joy!), slowly build a platform under said box, raising it glacially closer to the height of your toilet. If your cat is pliable (as if . . .), you might add a phone book per week; if your cat is a cat, consider the weekly addition of the Sunday sheet of newspaper containing the *Garfield* comic strip.

• Throughout and forevermore, be sure to leave the toilet seat down and the lid up.

• Now slowly scoot the litter box onto the toilet itself (at the pace of continental drift).

• Once the litter box is firmly atop the commode, start shearing away bits of the box. Start with a small hole in the box's center and cut away the box until nothing remains. The crux is leaving enough box to allow the system's continued stability—a mistake

ONCE you have mastered the Zelda basics you can, in fact, use your ocarina skills to play other songs, including the following:

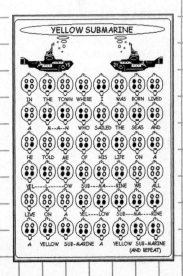

here can result in a wet, pissed-off cat, whose twin outlets for angst are your home and your person. During this stage, encourage cat to place feet on toilet seat, rather than in litter box. Herein lies the art.

• Eventually you will have cut away the litter box entirely and your cat will be hanging it over the rim. Congratulations: you have entered a very elite club. However, from this point forward you may have to forgo hosting dinner parties with non-cat-owning guests.

Note: An alternate strategy employs a metal bowl as a transition between litter box and toilet bowl—find a bowl that fits snugly in your commode. Start with it in the litter box and then transfer it to the pot.

TURTLE ART

FORWARD 25

RIGHT 90

FORWARD 25

RIGHT 90

FORWARD 25

RIGHT 90

FORWARD 25

Does this ring a bell? In the programming language Logo, these simple commands draw a square. The idea behind Logo is that of a trained turtle with a pen strapped to its tail walking on blank paper. In fact, this is exactly what "Irving" did—MIT's robot turtle, constructed in 1969 to test an early version of the language. If you are a geek of certain age, you spent many grade-school evenings writing lengthy Logo programs on graph paper, which, if you were lucky, your math teacher would let you test during recess. Today, you can write and test your Logo programs online at www.sonic.net/~nbs/webturtle/.

THE JOYS OF FANGRAPHS.COM

It's game five of the 2005 World Series. The Cardinals are down 4–2 in the top of the ninth, two outs, two men on. Albert Pujols steps to the plate. Unfortunately for Pujols, there's a 92.4 percent chance the Cardinals will lose the game (though the chances were 96.3 percent against before Jim Edmonds walked and 98.9 percent against before Eckstein's single). This, according to www.fangraphs.com, which (generally) measures game situations against past situations of the same type to determine probable outcomes. Unfortunately for the Astros, Pujols knocked it out of the park, making the score 5–4 and giving the Cardinals an 81.1 percent chance of winning, which they did after two Astros grounders and a fly ball.

Imagine this: In the top of the ninth, you bet $10 on the Cardinals with a bookie who was tracking the odds in real time and thus offered you 89.9-to-1 odds (.989/.011). When the Cardinals won, you pocketed $899. Nice.

SIX STEPS TO COLLEGE ACCEPTANCE

According to *U.S. News and World Report*, in 2008 the country's most selective university was the Julliard School of Music, with a scant 7 percent acceptance rate. Yale and Harvard both weighed in at 9 percent. This, of course, is measured against the pool of applicants who had the gall to apply to these schools in the first place (and back up this gall with an application fee). Follow the steps below to avoid being on the losing end of these massively discouraging statistics.

1. Apply early. Many colleges accept a much higher percentage of early-decision applicants than they do from their standard applicant pool. Pick your dream school and submit before November 1.

2. Volunteer. Every applicant to the country's top schools has a 4.0 GPA, racked up enormous SAT and ACT scores, was concertmaster in the state orchestra, ran cross-country, and won the science fair. Not all candidates volunteered at their local at-risk after-school program. It doesn't hurt to highlight this volunteer involvement in your essay, in a way that demonstrates how your interest in this specific cause evolved organically from your background.

3. Excel. Have a 4.0, enormous SAT and ACT scores, be concertmaster in the state orchestra, run cross-country, and win the science fair. Be sure your GPA includes your school's hardest classes. Don't trade GPA and test scores for increased extracurricular involvement.

4. Befriend and impress specific teachers. Starting early in your high-school career, groom the teachers whom you will eventually ask for references.

5. Top choice! If a school is your top choice, let them know. If the school knows you will attend if accepted, they may be slightly more likely to offer admission.

6. Contribute. Demonstrate specific skills that will contribute to the college environment. If possible, make professors at your school of choice aware of these skills, so that said professors can advocate for your acceptance. For example, get recruited by a school's engineering competition team.

FOLDING INSTRUCTIONS FOR A MASSIVELY COMPLEX PAPER AIRPLANE

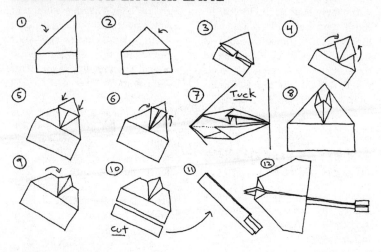

ARE YOU HOT? YOUR COMPUTER KNOWS

Interestingly, the method used by Australian scientists Massimo Piccardi and Hatice Gunes to calculate facial beauty is similar to the method used by fangraphs.com determine probable baseball outcomes: Their software compares features of a new situation (in this case, any given face) to features of a known situation (in this case, 215 faces of models and actresses), to make inferences about the present situation (if the ratios of the face being measured match those of actresses and models, the face is attractive). According to Australian news source the *Age*, the good doctors' software predicts facial beauty to within 1.5 points (on a scale of 1–10) of a human panel voting on the same face.

Lest ye think the good doctors have undertaken frivolous research, they point to their software's application in determining outcomes of plastic surgery, both in quantifying gains and in avoiding possibly unnecessary procedures.

Enterprising hackers are exploring the possibility of remotely accessing computers' built-in webcams to automatically determine users' attractiveness and then posting these ratings on social networking sites.

A SAM LOYD LOGIC PUZZLE

In this version of the game Dots and Boxes, the players take turns drawing a segment that connects two of the letters in the grid (as shown). The goal is to complete boxes. If a player completes a box, they may draw another segment. It is the sitting girl's turn. What is her best play?

THE BOXER'S PUZZLE

THE TURING MACHINE

The Turing machine is quite simple: It is a tape divided into cells, a head that reads and writes 1's or 0's in these cells, and a set of instructions telling the machine four things—based on the state of the machine (1), and the symbol it reads (2), it should assume another state (3) and either write or erase the cell or move left or right one cell. (This can be represented by a "program": $<State_0, Symbol, State_{next}, Action>$.) This is where it starts to get tricky: The tape is infinitely long, making the machine's "memory" infinitely large (and relegating the Turing machine to the realm of thought experiment). This seemingly simple machine can be programmed to compute almost any numerical function. Not only that—the construction known as a Universal Turing Machine can, like a DNA strand that incorporates new instructions added by a retrovirus, "eat" other machines. Simply put, you could lay the configuration and instructions for all Turing machines ever constructed onto the infinitely long tape of one machine (which would, at this point, certainly be capable of world domination). In fact, in 1950, Alan Turing argued that because the mind functions at the neural level as a series of operations, his simple machine could emulate the functions of the brain itself—thus Turing is considered one of the fathers of artificial intelligence.

A SAMPLING OF YIDDISH WORDS ADOPTED INTO THE COMMON LEXICON

YIDDISH	MEANING	SAMPLE
bubkes	nothing	Bubkes I got.
chutzpah	nerve	It took chutzpah to point out the toilet paper attached to the boss's shoe.
farklempt	choked up	Oy, I'm getting a little farklempt, talk amongst yourselves!
goyim	non-Jewish people	After the favorable review in the *Times*, the Brooklyn deli was packed with goyim.
kakameyme	crazy	He threw all his gelt into some kakameyme scheme.
kibitz	to gossip or meddle	She spent the whole party kibitzing in the corner with Hertzela Katz.
kvetch	to complain, a complainer	Quit your kvetching.
mazel tov*	cheers, congratulations	Mazel tov on the promotion!
mensch	a good guy	Sure, he's a mensch.
meshuggener	crazy person	Get a couple drinks in him and he acts like a meshuggener.
mishmash	conglomeration, hodgepodge	He threw a mishmash of vegetables into the pot.
nudnik	pest, bore	His little sister was such a nudnik.
shmendrik	fool, idiot	Don't be such a shmendrik!
shmutz	dirt, stuff	He spilled a bunch of shmutz on his suit jacket.
shtick	a routine	The singer couldn't carry a tune, but what shtick!
shvitz	sweat	Oy, am I schvitzing!
tuchis	butt	He slipped on the ice and fell right on his tuchis.

*Not to be confused with the famously flammable cocktail of similar name.

THE PROBLEM WITH SEMAPHORE

The primary problem with semaphore is that not only are you acting geeky, but by the activity's nature (waving flags to attract attention) you are doing so in a very visible way. Thus it is commonly understood that every semaphore communication starts with the unsignaled phrase *Look at me! I'm a geek!* which is then followed by the message itself (as in "Look at me! I'm a geek! It seems as if your scoutmaster is being eaten by a bear!"). Provided here is the semaphore alphabet as well as depiction of the proper semaphore-signaling outfit.

A-(1) B-(2) C-(3) D-(4) E-(5)
F-(6) G-(7) H-(8) I-(9) J-(10)
K L M N O
P Q R S T
U V W X Y
Z NUMERALS FOLLOW SIGNALS FOLLOW ATTENTION INTERVAL

BODY TRICKS WE LEARNED IN MIDDLE SCHOOL THAT INDUCE ZOMBIFIC POSSESSION AND/OR ALTERED STATES OF CONSCIOUSNESS AND PERCEPTION

1. The Completed Church Steeple. Clasp your hands, intertwining your fingers. Hold them clasped tightly together for at least thirty seconds—the longer the better. Then, raise your index fingers as if imitating a church steeple with an open top. Watch the tips of your fingers close inexorably together.

2. Harmonic Rotation. Stand or sit while rotating your right leg in a clockwise circle. Draw a six in the air with your right hand. What direction is your leg rotating now?

3. Women Are from Venus, Men from Mars. Stand with your derriere and heels touching a wall. Reach down to retrieve something small from between your toes. (Men will likely fall forward, while a naturally lower center of gravity may allow some women to touch the floor without toppling.) Similarly, stand three foot-lengths from a wall and use your hands to lower yourself until your forehead touches the wall. Stand up without help from your hands (or from momentum). Again, many women can, while almost all men can't.

4. The Doorway Trick. This is an old standby. Stand in a door frame and push outward/upward with your hands for at least thirty seconds. When you move out from the door frame, your arms will rise above your head as if possessed by zombific force.

5. Feet Through the Floor. Lie on your back and close your eyes. Have a friend hold your feet up at an angle. Relax. Go to your happy place. After a minute or two, have your friend slowly lower your feet. It will feel as if they are falling through the floor.

SLIGHTLY COMBATIVE AND/OR VIOLENT TWO-PERSON GAMES

The obvious evolution of these games is boxing, wrestling, or gladiatorial combat with accompanying mass spillage of blood (and can quickly revert to such, should participants fail to set ground rules for decency and good-natured combat). They are also best performed by the very stupid. As such, their inclusion in this book requires justification: While each is physical, winning requires skill and cunning—unlike dodgeball, if pitted against meathead competitors, geeks will win these games. If still in doubt as to these games' geek pedigree, a quick visit to www.fingerjoust. com will put your mind at ease. Beware: participation in any of the following can act as a gateway between violence experienced in video games and movies and the expression of violence in real-world settings.

• Finger Jousting. Clasp hands with your opponent as if arm wrestling in the air. Each person should raise his or her index finger to point at the other person. Now, try to poke your opponent in the chest.

• Hand Slap. The classic game in which one player hovers his or her hands face down over an opponent's hands (face up), who tries to slap the top of the first person's hands before he or she can remove them. Be quick, grasshopper.

• Flamingo Death Match. Players face each other in positions of maximal body twistage—one leg twisted around the other and arms twisted in front. The players then crash into each other with the intention of toppling the other. The loser is whoever first touches to the ground any body part other than the one foot used for hopping.

• Shin Kicking. Participation in this game without the acknowledged purpose being intentionally ironic stupidity requires an IQ of less than 80. Simply, combatants face each other with their arms on each other's shoulders and then try to kick each other in the shins.

• The Rope Game. Stand facing your opponent, about two paces apart. Hold between you a length of rope (some versions recommend passing this rope around your back and then holding it in the opposite hand). Now pull and loosen the rope with the intent of throwing your opponent off balance. The first to move a foot or drop the rope loses.

BECOME A BILLIONAIRE TODAY THROUGH THE POWER OF NO-LOSE BIDDING!

With a group of friends, classmates, or coworkers, offer to auction a $20 bill. One more rule: both of the top two bidders must pay their final bid. Imagine that person A and person B are foolish enough to join your auction, with person A bidding 25¢ and person B overbidding to the tune of 30¢. Obviously this should escalate—who wouldn't bid $7 to earn $20, especially if this could keep you from losing money you previously bid? As bidding passes $10, you—the auctioneer—earn money. However, the auction is far from over. As the two bidders reach $20, it becomes obvious they will not earn money on this transaction—but how much are they willing to lose? For example, if person A has bid $19 and person B bids $20, wouldn't person A be smart to bid $21 in order to win the auction and thus lose only $1 as opposed to paying $19 for a second-place bid? According to game theory (and with players of infinite resources), without collusion, there is no logical end to this bidding war, and you will soon be a billionaire, minus $20.

However, if your bidders recognize their peril at the auction's outset and are not prevented from colluding, they can quickly agree to let one or the other win the auction at a low price and split your $20.

THE QUOTABLE *KUNG FU*

It is the *Tao Te Ching*? Is it Buddha? Confucius? Mencius? The course materials from a Chinese anger management seminar? No! It's the 70s TV series *Kung Fu*!

• Avoid rather than check; check rather than hurt; hurt rather than maim; maim rather than kill. For all life is precious, nor can any be replaced.

• I seek not to know the answers, but to understand the questions.

• Do not see yourself as the center of the universe, wise and good and beautiful. Seek, rather, wisdom, goodness, and beauty, that you may honor them everywhere.

• If you plant rice, rice will grow. If you plant fear, fear will grow.

• When you cease to strive to understand, then you will know without understanding.

• Become the calm, restful breeze that tames the violent sea.

• To suppress a truth is to give it force beyond endurance.

• When you can take the pebble from my hand, it will be time for you to leave.

IT'S THE GREAT CIRCLE (CHARLIE BROWN)

You probably thought the shortest distance between two points was a straight line. This is true, unless you are literally trying to get from point A to point B and said points happen to be in the literal world, which is a sphere (nearly). In this case, the shortest distance between two points is an arc, specifically an arc of the great circle defined by these two points. (Let's take a step back—*great circle*, n: a circle on the surface of a sphere, whose center is the center of the sphere; alternately, a circle that has the same circumference as the sphere on which it is drawn. Alternately—the circle that divides a sphere into two equal hemispheres. Thus the equator is a great circle, but other parallels are not.) This leads to the following counterintuitive flight paths:

- The shortest route from Houston to Calcutta travels over the North Pole.

- To get from Seattle to London, you fly over Baffin Island and south-central Greenland.

- To get from Melbourne, Australia, to São Paulo, Brazil, you fly nearly over the South Pole.

- Flying from New York City to Tokyo takes you over the Bering Strait.

THE BASICS OF GOLDEN AGE GEEK BRITCOM

Ah, British humor! How we love to bask in your wry, absurdist glow! How we long to stumble across your late-night rebroadcast marathons, deep in the recesses of triple-digit cable television! How we yearn to endlessly rewatch your short-attention-span skits, most of which follow the general format *I am a toff but happen to not be wearing pants,* until we can quote them verbatim while standing around the sidelines after being theatrically killed at a Society for Creative Anachronism reenactment battle!

- *Blackadder.* Edmund Blackadder, played by Rowan Atkinson of *Mr. Bean* fame, is an English noble of declining fortunes who stumbles through some of the high- and low-lights of Brit history.

- *Fawlty Towers.* The title hotel is run by Basil Fawlty (played by John Cleese, who also cowrote the series), a social climbing, miserly paranoiac. Legend has it the character was inspired by the proprietor of a hotel where the Monty Python cast once stayed while filming.

- *Red Dwarf.* Dave Lister is the universe's last remaining human being and is aided in his quest to pilot the title ship back to Earth by a hologram, a cat-like creature evolved from a pet named Frankenstein, the ship's (male) computer (named Holly), and a Series 4000 mechanoid robotic servant named Kryten. For extra geek points, you can read the books.

- *Monty Python's Flying Circus.* If you are reading this book, you are already familiar with MPFC, which produced sketches including "The Dead Parrot," "The Lumberjack Song," "The Ministry of Silly Walks," "The Spanish Inquisition," and "Nudge, Nudge."

THE NECESSARY HOME SAFETY DEVICES

With global warming, the HIV/AIDS crisis, the threat of terrorism, potential nuclear proliferation in extremist states, ongoing and ever-shifting pockets of genocide, natural disasters seemingly on the increase, and second thoughts about your choice of preschools for your three-year-old, it is hard enough to sleep without having to also worry about being robbed. Installing the following safety devices will allow you to sit atop your hoard like the unholy lovechild of Ayn Rand and the dragon Smaug, without needing to sleep with one eye open in order to protect your loot from the destitute and desperate proletariat (let them eat cake!):

• Acoustic sensors: highly sensitive microphones mounted in your walls (inappropriate for occupied homes or those with naturally high ambient noise).

• Infrared sensors: in addition to detecting warm bodies, an infrared sensor can also detect heat change due to fire and/or malfunctioning home appliances.

• Microwave sensors: these use Doppler radar, measuring the waves that normally bounce back from a wall or other home object. If something is moving within the sensor's field, the waves will return compressed or expanded (à la Doppler).

• Photoelectric sensors: a light is pointed at a sensor, which is tripped if the light beam is broken. The sneaky part is the light, which is commonly infrared and thus invisible to would-be intruders.

• Magnetic detection: though this sounds relatively cool, it actually refers to a metal-to-metal circuit that, if broken, triggers an alarm. These can be as basic as a connection inside your window locks or as complex as mesh screens built into your walls that detect thieves equipped with reciprocating saws and/or directed explosive charges.

• If you like, connect all these goodies to your computer, allowing you to remotely access your streamed video security footage and get break-in messages sent directly to your mobile phone (as if you weren't already compulsive enough about your inbox).

UNDERSTANDING THE SUBPRIME MORTGAGE DEBACLE

To the lay consumer, the term *subprime* sounds like a good thing ("Wow, if prime rate is what banks charge their best borrowers, then *subprime* should be even better!"). It's not. In fact, it is worse and sometimes much worse. Subprime loans are those extended to iffy borrowers at rates high enough to justify the risk. "Sure," banks say, "some of these iffy borrowers will default, but the extra money we get from charging 14.99 percent interest on this home equity account will make up for these few defaulting cases." Unfortunately for banks, their haste to extend sketchy credit coincided with the bursting of the housing bubble, which meant that all of a sudden banks were left holding loans worth more than the collateral and also that many, many more borrowers than banks had predicted proved unable to meet their loan payments. Prices in the housing market, flooded with foreclosures, desperate sellers, and builders who failed to foresee the end of the boom years, further slumped.

If the crisis had been limited to banks and borrowers, this might not have been such a big deal. But many banks bundled these iffy loans and passed along the debt to third-party investors via Mortgage Backed Securities (MBSes, which are proving similar in risk and potential detrimental effects to the ROUSes of *The Princess Bride*). Basically, big financial companies bought the debt from banks and offered them as investment opportunities to people looking to ride the bubble ever upward. As borrowers defaulted, the monthly payments to these MBSes dried up, and the financial institutions were left "holding their asses," as the phrase goes.

Oops.

Also going down with the ship were the firewall companies designed to mitigate this risk (dealers in collateralized debt obligations and structured investment vehicles), which were simply overwhelmed by the ever growing snowball of badness that landed in the middle of their celebratory housing-bubble *cum* stock-market-bubble cake.

Of course, the response of the credit markets (after high-decibel profanity and/or jumping from Wall Street windows) was to stanch the bleeding. The availability of credit dried up. This is bad for everybody, because credit is how deals get done; without it, would-be homebuyers as well as businesses considering mergers, acquisitions, and expansion are hamstrung. Usually with housing prices down, homeowners would jump at the opportunity for a deal, but without available loans, there is no jumping (except from the aforementioned windows).

The morals of the story: greed trumps sense, and when a wolf (or predatory lending institution) offers you a cookie, beware.

FOUR PAIRS OF VELCRO SHOES AVAILABLE NEW FOR BELOW $34.99

• Izod Men's Bravura: a sporty leather slipper with stylish Velcro Z-closure. Perfect for the home office or trips to the mailbox in your boxers.

• Rockport Ellery Velcro Men's Walking Shoes: like the Izod but with traditional two-strap Velcro closure, with octopus tentacle sucker traction pattern.

• Dexter Men's Bowling Shoe: be the envy of your league.

• Propet Men's Walker: according to the manufacturer, these shoes offer "that 'broken-in' feeling as soon as you take them out of the box."

DEVELOPMENTAL MILESTONES

You know your child is a genius. Your child's grandparents know he/she is a genius. So why do the other parents in your playgroup shoot you sideways looks when little Ricky continues to eat rocks at twenty-four months? Provided below is a chart that will only make things worse. Read this at your own risk and then discount everything therein, continuing in the belief that your child is perfect.

AGE	MOTOR SKILLS	COGNITIVE STUFF	LANGUAGE AND SOCIALIZATION
6 MONTHS	• Bites rocks and anything else within reach of grubby little hands • Gleefully pummels long-suffering family Labrador with rattle • Wants to dance; can't quite pull it off	• Opens mouth for spoon as if readying for parental avian regurgitation • Mimics you (stage I)	• Highly narcissistic when presented with mirror • Laughs, screams, squeals, and babbles (similar to Sam Kinison)
12 MONTHS	• Pinches Cheerios, raisins, and dad's nipples if dad is foolish enough to leave them exposed when trying to initiate sleep • Can also poke dad in the eye, pour water on him, throw blocks at him, etc. • Crawls within range to do any of the preceding	• Has gained purposefulness ("I want to pinch dad's nipples; I will crawl close enough to do so") • Mimics you as if neurally linked	• Has gained empathy ("Dad is distressed because his nipples hurt; I will be distressed, too") • Terrified of anyone but mom and long-suffering Labrador
18 MONTHS	• Gets naked quickly and without warning • Walks; runs as if perpetually constipated • Scribbles on walls, appliances, and long-suffering family Labrador	• Identifies things in book *Where the Wild Things Are*; potentially mimics roaring, gnashing teeth, rolling eyes, and showing terrible claws. • Knows what is expected; refuses to comply	• Says 8–10 words (mom, dad, Labrador, poop, etc.) • Makes feelings known • Attempts to control surroundings
24 MONTHS	• Gets into every closet, drawer, box, cubby, and nook in the house • Drinks with a straw; feeds now-collaborating family Labrador with a spoon	• Takes apart anything within ability • If given the chance, goes up • Programs in Logo and BASIC	• Listens to *Where the Wild Things Are* over and over (and over) • Uses hundreds of words in rudimentary sentences

DAVID COPPERFIELD'S ATTEMPT TO DISCOURAGE THE HUDDLED MASSES

In 1983, who didn't enjoy a good form-fitting, robotic silver jacket, open to a dramatic V at the neck? As seen in his YouTube video showing the disappearance of the Statue of Liberty, certainly David Copperfield cannot be counted among the style dissenters. In this video, Copperfield raises a curtain between a live audience and the Statue of Liberty, and seconds later the curtain drops to reveal searchlights passing through the space where the statue recently sat. The trick, created by Jim Steinmeyer, has not been officially explained, but in his book *Bigger Secrets,* William Poundstone opines that Copperfield's illusion required a rotating seating area, which pointed the audience to a manufactured "empty zone" at sea, or that the audience was composed of paid actors looking at a much smaller model of the statue. The true secret may never be revealed (insert crooked eyebrow here).

ODE TO NPR

A snapshot of one Sunday's NPR programming: satellite images of nitrogen emissions that allow us to infer a region's dominant religion based on decreased emissions on the Friday, Saturday, or Sunday holy day (*Weekend Edition*); scientists in New Zealand working to remove the methane-causing bacteria in cows and sheep (*Climate Connections*); an appearance by the Ultimate Fighting champion Chuck "the Iceman" Lidell on *Wait, Wait, Don't Tell Me;* the background music of *All Things Considered* provided by Jaco Pastorius, Sonny Rollins, Taj Mahal, and Sex Mob.

Oh NPR! Anywhere, anytime if in need of geekery, we must only scan the clusters around 89.1, 102.1, or 106.9 for your endearing mixture of highbrow hilarity, quirky science, political insight, news, interviews, geek eye by the sports guy (Frank Deford), and social commentary (with traffic reports, weather, and the überalluring voice of Terry Gross, to boot!).

We don't even begrudge the fund drives, which allow geeks to alleviate our liberal elitist guilt with an act of giving that neatly mimics the cleansing of the soul offered by answering a Falwellian/Robertsonian/Grahamsian/Swaggartian call for cash. The extent of our addiction is revealed when, instead of switching the station, we choose to listen to the familiar voices of our NPR commentators desperately describing the waning minutes of a funds-match opportunity.

(Technically, *Car Talk, This American Life, Fair Game,* and other geek standbys of this author's Sunday programming on KCRW Santa Monica are provided by PRI, not NPR—but still, you say tomayto, I say tomahto.)

A TIMELINE IN PICTURES: BADLY BROKEN ARM

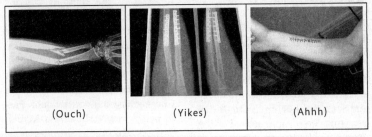

| (Ouch) | (Yikes) | (Ahhh) |

Courtesy of Charlie Bosmore.

ANOTHER LOOK AT PSEUDOSCIENCES

• A crystal filters and otherwise transforms light. Why not also the vibrations, chrakas, and electromagnetic fields of the human body? Crystal healing was common in the ancient civilizations of Egypt, India, and China, as well as among the Inuit.

• Trees need water to survive, and root systems will expand into water-rich areas to supply trees with this water. If you were holding a representative of this root system—say a Y-shaped branch—you would undoubtedly feel its natural pull toward water. If you honed your skills, you could follow this pull to underground water sources, using the procedure known as dowsing.

• Quantum physics tests the edge of our mind's grasp of reality. Scientists tout the possibility of teleportation, time travel, and existing in two states at once; so, too, does Vedantic Hinduism. Thus, quantum physics proves the validity of the Veda (Deepak Chopra: "Our bodies ultimately are fields of information, intelligence, and energy. Quantum healing involves a shift in the fields of energy information, so as to bring about a correction in an idea that has gone wrong").

• Newton tried it. So did Plato. Pope John XXII, too. Likewise Tycho Brahe, Ernest Rutherford, and Roger Bacon. In fiction, Dante and Gargamel were obsessed by it. Of these, only Rutherford succeeded—in 1919, he turned nitrogen into oxygen. Unfortunately, even Rutherford's results fell short of the transformation of lead to gold these alchemists desired.

THE QUOTABLE X-FILES

MULDER: Sometimes the only sane answer to an insane world is insanity.

MULDER: After three hours I asked him to summon up the soul of Jimi Hendrix and requested "All Along the Watchtower." You know, the guy's been dead twenty years, but he still hasn't lost his edge.

SCULLY: Your contact, while interesting in the context of science fiction, was, at least in my memory, recounting a poorly-veiled synopsis of an episode of *Rocky and Bullwinkle*.

MULDER: Sometimes the need to mess with their heads outweighs the millstone of humiliation.

SCULLY: Oh, brain sucking parasites.

MULDER: Do you realize how hard it is to fake your own death? Only one person has pulled it off—Elvis.

MULDER: It's a conspiracy wrapped in a plot inside a government agenda.

THE ANSWER TO THE ULTIMATE QUESTION OF LIFE, PART I

To the existentialists—Nietzsche, Kierkegaard, Sartre, Camus, et al.—there is no God and thus no absolute judge of morality or reality, and humans are free to make their own (i.e., while you look at a round, red fruit and say tomato, I might say focaccia; and while a God-influenced society might consider murder a crime or sin, existentialism-influenced figures like Dostoyevsky's fictional Raskolnikov do not . . . necessarily). This leads to the existential crisis of suddenly finding oneself alone and without purpose in a big, impersonal world.

The answer, say the existentialists, is to accept your isolation in this world and to revel in the fact of your own existence. This can be easier said than done. Especially when existentialists disallow the crutches of religion (remember, there is no God), science (just another way to put the world in artificially clean boxes), and even rationality (Sartre called rationality "bad faith" and emphasized the world's fundamental irrationality).

THE ANSWER TO THE ULTIMATE QUESTION OF LIFE, PART II

42.

THE 0.15 OF A TOPIC: THE ANSWER TO THE ULTIMATE QUESTION OF LIFE, PART III

6.3.

BRAINS, BRAINS!

You wouldn't be much without your brain; however, you would also be less likely to attract zombies. Admittedly, this is a difficult trade-off.

Presumably there is something special about the human brain, as zombies are rarely seen lusting after or consuming the brains of lesser species. While we can only guess what this special something might be, in the chart below you can see many differences between the human brain and those of said lesser species.*

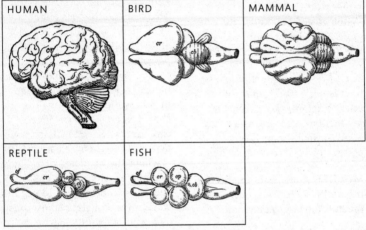

*of = olfactory, op = optic, cr = cerebral hemisphere, cb = cerebellum, m = medulla oblongata

HOW TO PROGRAM UNIVERSAL REMOTE CONTROLS

• RCA: Turn on the component you want to control. Press this component's button on your remote control (the ON-OFF button will turn on). Press and hold the component button with the ON-OFF button, which will turn off and then back on, at which point you can release both buttons. Press and release the PLAY button until the component turns off. Press and release the REVERSE button until the component turns on. Press the STOP button to save your code.

• GE: Search online for your component's three-digit code. Turn on the component you want to control. Press and hold the remote's CODE SEARCH button until the indicator light turns on, at which point you may release the button. Press and release the desired component's button. Enter the component's three-digit program code.

Jensen: Search online for your component's three-digit code. Turn on the component you want to control. Press and hold the remote's DEVICE key until the indicator light turns on. Release the device key and immediately enter the three-digit component code. Press the POWER key to check your work.

• Sony: Search online for your component's two-digit program code. Simultaneously press the remote's OFF and MUTE buttons. Press the indicator button for your desired component. Enter the two-digit program code and press the ENTER button.

• Zenith: Very similar to GE.

SINUS INFECTION, BEGONE!

When mired in a sinus infection, haven't you wondered about the possibility of attaching a small-craft bilge pump to your face and sucking everything free? It turns out your face comes pre-equipped with a natural bilge pump—the vomer bone—which acts as the keystone of your sinus system. Unfortunately, the vomer bone is buried under the cartilage of your septum, making it a bit difficult to operate the pump handle. Instead, alternately push your tongue to the top of your mouth and press with one finger between your eyebrows. Keep at it. After twenty seconds, your congestion will loosen and stream out your nose (keep a bowl or other receptacle handy).

YE OLDE WEB ACRONYMS

• CGI: The Common Gateway Interface processes data you submit, allowing you to interact with Web content. Commonly used in search boxes.

• FTP: File Transfer Protocol allows you to quickly transfer large files from one computer to another (commonly used to upload material to the Web).

• HTML: Hypertext Markup Language is the common programming language behind the Web pages you view (as interpreted by your browser).

• IP Address: Your Internet Protocol address is your computer's unique online ID number.

• ISP: Internet Service Providers sling connections via modem.

• RSS Feed: Embedding a site's Really Simple Syndication feed on your site allows you to access your target site's content from the comfort of your own page. It also alerts you immediately to new content and is thus commonly used to monitor news sites.

• TCP/IP: The software that spawned the Internet.

- URL: Every Web page has a unique Uniform Resource Locator, which includes its domain name.

- XML: Watered down HTML, useful for databases and other sites that require standardized pieces that reappear in many places.

THE WORLDS OF NORSE MYTHOLOGY

Much of what we know of Norse mythology comes from the works of Snorri Sturluson (1178–1241). And we thought Snorri was that uncle who tried to get kids to drink aquavit at holiday gatherings or the bass player on the Stan and Doug *Yust Go Nuts at Christmas* album. Tolkien, eat your heart out.

- Asgard: land of the Æsir or spirits/gods.

- Vanaheimr: land of the Vanir, or minor gods (also a Norwegian metal band).

- Midgard: land of the humans (literally "middle enclosure," or to Tolkien "Middle-earth").

- Muspelheim: realm of fire, the fire giants, and their master Sutr, whom you would not like to meet in a dark alley or, say, during Ragnarok, when Sutr will rush forth to burn almost everything, including the gods.

- Niflheim: land Later, Niflheim beca as Hel, the resting pla who had not died hero (also a Swedish speed-me band).

- Álfheimr: world of the elve Álfheimr is also the ancient name of the Swedish province now known as Bohuslän, where during the summer months elves can still be seen harvesting the region's official flower, the wild honeysuckle.

- Svartálfaheim: the underground home of the Norse dwarfs. In Svartálfaheim, dwarfs combine the sound of a cat's footfall, a woman's beard, the roots of a mountain, the sinews of a bear, the breath of a fish, and the spittle of a bird to craft the silken *gleipnir* that binds the mighty wolf Fenrisulfr (who, at Ragnarok, will burst free of the *gleipnir* to devour Odin).

- Jötunheimr: world of the giants. Pyrmr, king of the giants, stole Thor's hammer. This proved a mistake—in retribution, Thor killed not only Pyrmr, but also the entirety of his giant lineage.

- Johnjacobjingleheimr: world of the never-ending family road trip.

ARCH PHYSICS

Imagine a vertical tower of blocks placed on a table. The weight of

the blocks pushes straight down and is balanced by blocks below pushing straight up (and eventually by the table, floor, and Earth pushing up to balance the force of the blocks; if forces didn't balance, the blocks would either sink down or float up). The same is true of an arch: The forces balance, only it is as if you bent your block tower over like a slinky. This bending of your block tower into the shape of an arch leads to slightly more complex directional forces (vectors), with one force vector pointing directly down as each voussoir (aka "block") is pulled toward Earth, one pointing down and out as blocks are pushed from above, and the balancing vector of lower blocks pushing up and in. Everything is in balance, grasshopper. As you can see in this diagram, each voussoir is pushed from above and pushes on a voussoir below; in contrast, the keystone pushes outward in both directions to balance the forces of both voussoir half-arches. If you ever doubt the organic power of the arch (shame on you!), visit Utah.

HOW TO TAP A MAPLE TREE AND CONDENSE SYRUP

According to a bulletin produced by the University of Maine, you first need to find a maple tree at least ten inches in diameter, measured four and a half feet from the ground. After purchasing a commercial tap, use a sharp bit to drill the appropriate size hole (at a slight upward angle, allowing the sap to run downward). Do so when the temperature is above freezing to minimize the risk of splitting the tree. Hang your covered bucket to collect sap. When you have collected the desired amount of sap, boil it to condense—working outdoors is recommended. As sap boils down, add more, always keeping at least a couple inches in the pan. Use a hydrometer to measure the syrup density: Between 66 and 67 percent sugar is optimal. Filter the syrup through cheesecloth into sterilized canning jars.

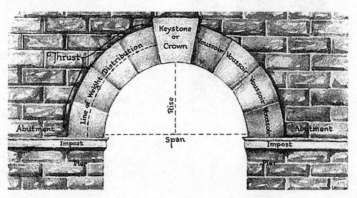

HOJUJITSU ROPE RESTRAINT

Once you have successfully opened a can of jujitsu whoopass on would-be assailant X, you will need to somehow restrain him/her until the cops arrive to cart him/her away. Enter the traditional Japanese martial art of hojujitsu, or tying into restraints (not to be confused with shibari, its erotic cousin). Traditionally, samurais applied this hojujitsu restraint in the field to accused but not convicted prisoners, and thus the technique allows a prisoner to be bound securely, but without the humiliating use of knots. (Note: it is not recommended that you search the Internet in the presence of minors for further information on this subject.)

WHISTLE PHYSICS AND AIRPLANE WINGS

Our ears pick up vibrations, and thus the crux of creating any musical sound is in inducing air to vibrate. In a saxophone, the vibration is produced by a buzzing reed; in a trumpet, your lips buzz; on a piano, strings vibrate. In a flute or whistle, the vibration is caused when the air you blow into the mouthpiece (1), is split by the sharp edge of the labium ("lip") (2), creating an oscillation in the voicing mouth (3), which sets the whole sucker a-vibrating (6). The longer the tube allowed by the plunger (4), the longer the resonant wavelength of the tube and thus the lower the tone produced. (The harder you blow, the higher the sound's amplitude, but the wavelength, and thus the pitch, doesn't change).

On an airplane, the leading edge of the wing acts like the labium, splitting the airstream into two paths—one that travels over the wing and one that travels under. Due to the curved shape of the wing's top, the air above must travel farther than does the air below to rejoin at the same point at the back of the wing. As this airstream has to rejoin simultaneously (to avoid leaving a vacuum), the air on top has to travel a bit faster than the air below. Faster air leaves low pressure (thank you, Daniel Bernoulli), and with lower pressure on top of the wing than below it, the wing lifts up. Interestingly, near the speed of sound, Bernoulli goes screwy and thus vibrations à la the tin whistle threaten to tear apart supersonic jets (if not designed by very experienced aeronautical geeks). Note: outside the wind tunnel, rarely do geeks perform firsthand tests of supersonic planes, for obvious reasons.

Perhaps, instead of the illogical and draconian practice of forcing airline passengers to turn off cell phones and laptops, the FAA should investigate the idea of dewhistling passengers prior to takeoff.

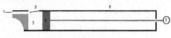

Courtesy of Berndt Meyer.

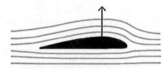

Courtesy of Dan Pope.

SPECIES IN D&D, MIDDLE-EARTH, *WINNIE-THE-POOH*, AND MAGIC: THE GATHERING

Can you sort these fantasy species by the world that spawned them?

- abishai
- Balrog
- Barrow-wight
- beholder
- blink dog
- bugbear
- chaos beast
- doppelgänger
- drow
- eladrin
- Ent
- fell beast
- frost worm
- great spiders
- heffalump
- hell hound
- Hobbit
- Myr
- Nazgûl
- phasm
- purple worm
- Saproling
- Skulk
- Thrull
- Uruk-hai
- Valar
- winter wolf
- yugoloth

PIMP YOUR CUBICLE: FIVE MUST-HAVE GADGETS*

- Sun jar: this nifty LED light recharges when placed in the sun, allowing you to bring (a replica) of actual sunlight into your cave-like geek domain, thus periodically reminding you of the existence of an outside world.

- Binary clock: rather than expending the time and effort needed to convert decimal-based digital clocks to information you can understand, go right to the source.

- Desktop personal air conditioner: your coworkers—sweaty and profane; you—cool and collected.

*All gadgets accessed on thinkgeek.com.

- USB webcam rocket launcher: not only can you fire rockets over cubicle walls deep into enemy territory, but if you are chatting with someone who also owns a launcher, you can remotely control said launcher, co-opting and firing your enemy's own rockets from close range.

- Shock ball: bringing hot potato to a new, more painful level.

THE RUBE GOLDBERG MACHINE

While this book intentionally skirts mention of fraternities (for reasons that should be obvious), the good gentlemen of Purdue's Phi Chapter of Theta Tau deserve an exemption. (Their motto is "the nation's oldest, and still foremost, Fraternity for Engineers.") Among their officers are the positions "Local Rube Goldberg" and "Nat'l Rube Goldberg." These two hardy and intrepid souls are in charge of organizing the annual machine competition, which has grown since its inception in 1983 to become Purdue's largest non-sports media event. The seemingly mundane tasks in this engineering contest have included squeezing orange juice, shredding paper, and making a cup of coffee. However, the machines that accomplish these tasks can be half-room behemoths of multitiered mechanical gadgetry, utilizing seemingly countless inane steps to accomplish the task. This, in accordance with the design ideals of Rube Goldberg, whose namesake machines were first defined in *Webster's Third New International Dictionary* as "accomplishing by extremely complex, roundabout means what actually or seemingly could be done simply." Included here is a modern-day example of a Goldberg-inspired machine.

Courtesy of Stephen VanDyke.

ELEVEN WAYS TO MAKE MONEY ONLINE

1. Online storefront. Sell anything, using a website as a catalog. If you would rather not deal with shipping, inventory, etc., consider using your storefront to point to another storefront that does the actual order fulfillment.

2. Market second-party products. Sites like Amazon will pay you to market for them (Amazon affiliates program). Build a book widget and stick it on your site. If your site visitors click the widget and buy from Amazon, you get a cut.

3. Charge to post, à la Monster .com, Craigslist, or the many other sites that charge users a small fee for the privilege of posting their information.

4. Sell ads. Once you have a massively successful site of any kind (judged by page-views per month), you can sell space to big-name advertisers. Until then, consider adding Adsense and tweaking your content until the automatic ads become relevant.

5. Freelance. Offer a service: Either use your own website to troll for clients, or search and complete listed online freelance jobs. Consider offering online support for semiobscure open-source software or opening an online brokerage.

6. Subscriptions. Create content or service that people will actually pay for. You wanna play World of Warcraft? Pay your monthly fee.

7. Sell photos. Stock photography sites are booming. Add your pix to the mix and earn cash automatically every time someone downloads them.

8. Flip Web addresses. Speculation in the domain-name game can cost less than $5 a pop. Know of an upcoming movie title? Buy it quick, then sell to a movie studio for profit.

9. Blog for pay. This is a paid job, like any other paid job, but you can do it in your boxers. Frequently, sites pay for reviews.

10. Virtual economy. Work in Lindenbucks, World of Warcraft gold, or another virtual commodity with real-world value.

11. Gamble. See the sections on pokerbots (page 125), the Iowa futures market (page 97), and the economics of Internet poker (page 44).

A MASSIVELY COOL DIAGRAM OF A SYNAPSE

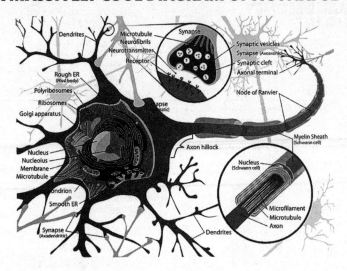

A SAM LOYD SLIDING-TILE PUZZLE

In how many moves can you transpose the whisky bottle and the scrubbing brush?

PANGRAMS IN MANY LANGUAGES

Language	Pangram	Translation
Catalan	Jove xef, porti whisky amb quinze glaçons d'hidrogen, coi!	Young chef, bring whisky with fifteen hydrogen ice cubes, damn!
Dutch	Sexy qua lijf, doch bang voor 't zwempak.	Sexy of body, though scared of the swimsuit.
French	Portez ce vieux whisky au juge blond qui fume.	Take this old whisky to the blond judge who smokes.
Icelandic	Kæmi ný öxi hér ykist þjófum nú bæði víl og ádrepa.	If a new axe were here, thieves would feel increasing deterrence and punishment.
Italian	Ma la volpe, col suo balzo, ha raggiunto il quieto Fido.	But the fox, with her leap, has reached the quiet Fido.
Serbian	Ljubazni fenjerdžija čađavog lica hoće da mi pokaže štos.	A kind lamplighter with grimy face wants to show me a stunt.
Spanish	Whisky bueno: ¡excitad mi frágil pequeña vejez!	Good whisky, excite my frail, little old age!
Portuguese	Um pequeno jabuti xereta viu dez cegonhas felizes.	A curious little red-footed tortoise saw ten happy storks.

A *pangram* is a sentence that uses every letter of the alphabet at least once. First, a couple in English: (1) Junk MTV quiz graced by fox whelps. (2) Waltz bad nymphs, for quick jigs vex. (3) How quickly daft jumping zebras vex!

DATING TELLS

It's true—to be successful in the free-market environment of the singles bar, male geeks may require the edge afforded by a little extra information of the sort herein provided.

If things are going well, she will:

• Increase her angle of incidence off vertical as her upper body leans in your direction.

• Mirror your movements—for example, responding in kind as you reach for a drink, cross your legs, or rest your head on your hand.

• Lower drink from initial defensive posture.

• Refrain from fidgeting.

• Point feet and body toward you like a solar array catching sunlight.

- Allow her pupils to widen, leading to increased blink rate.

- Engage actively in conversation, asking questions and paying compliments.

- Touch body parts—hers or yours.

THE QUOTABLE FUTURAMA

FRY: Full price for gum!? That dog won't hunt, Monsignor.

FRY: Ugh, it's like there's a party in my mouth and everyone is throwing up!

Rᴇмᴇмвᴇʀ that song? The one that goes da-da-Daa-da? Too bad you don't remember the title, artist, words, or, really, anything other than half a bar of catchy melody. Never fear! Technology will save you!—www.midomi.com will match your singing, whistling, or playing to a database of millions of songs.

BENDER: My life, and by extension everyone else's, is meaningless.

BENDER: Comedy's a dead art form. Now tragedy, that's funny.

LEELA: Look, Fry, you're a man and I'm a woman. We're just too different.

PROFESSOR: Everyone's always in favor of saving Hitler's brain. But when you put it in the body of a great white shark, ooohh! Suddenly you've gone too far!

ZOIDBERG: Stop! Stop! If you interrupt the mating dance, the male will become enraged and maul us with his fearsome gonad!

ZOIDBERG: . . . And that's how I got my new shell. It looks just like the shell I threw out yesterday, and I found it in the same Dumpster, but this one had a live raccoon inside.

HERMES: What's that you're hacking off? Is it my torso? It is! My precious torso!

ZAPP: The best way into a girl's bed is through her parents. Have sex with them, and you're in.

SPECIES COUNTERPOINT

The theory of Western tonal music offers rules for writing more than one note at once. Obey the rules and things sound good; disobey

(Continued)

FIRST SPECIES

- Note against note.
- No unisons except beginning and end.
- Use only consonant intervals (thirds, fifths, sixths, octaves, and tenths), but avoid parallel fourths, fifths, and octaves.

SECOND SPECIES

- Two notes against one.
- Only consonant intervals in first half of measure.

THIRD SPECIES

- Four notes against one.
- Consonant intervals on accented first and third beats.

FOURTH SPECIES

- Suspended notes, often creating dissonance on accented beats and resolving on unaccented beats.

them and your composition can sound like a middle-school band warming up. Like Einstein's theory of general relativity having its genesis hundreds of years earlier when humans noticed that things fall toward Earth, so too did the music of Wagner evolve in a direct line from the one-line chant music of composers such as Palestrina. In the samples on the previous page, an example of this one-line chant is included as the bottom line or cantus firmus (CF). To the CF are added successively complex accompaniments. The consensus Grand Pooh-Bah of counterpoint is Bach.

THERE IS NO EASTER BUNNY

• Eggs and rabbits were common fertility symbols of the ancient world. Today, come the spring equinox, we continue to worship the pagan, egg-laying bunny (with a massive display of consumerism).

• Saint Nicolas of Myra presented three impoverished girls with dowries so they would not have to become prostitutes. His modern incarnation was created and popularized by the nineteenth-century cartoonist Thomas Nast. Come winter solstice, it's time to worship the jolly old elf (with a massive display of consumerism).

THOUGH Uncle Sam doesn't quite make the cut as a Big Three mythical figure in American culture, his story remains cool: After his birth from the initials U.S. on meat rations during the War of 1812, Uncle Sam has appeared on recruiting posters, as a Grateful Dead mascot, and as the undead antagonist of the 1997 horror film that shares his name. Come the Fourth of July, it is time to worship the old coot (with a massive display of gluttony, inebriation, and firepower).

• In the eighteenth-century French fairy tale "La Bonne Petit Souris," the title mouse changes into a fairy before hiding under an evil king's pillow and knocking out all his teeth while he sleeps. In American culture, the fairy brings us money.

RACISM AND GENOCIDE IN THE MMORPG LINEAGE II

Lineage II is a massive multiplayer online role-playing game in which characters exist, act, and interact in an elves/orcs/swords/monsters fantasy world. The currency of this world is adena, with which avatars purchase equipment, skills, etc. Unfortunately, adena doesn't grow on trees. Your avatar must accumulate adena through combat, quests, and other tasks. Your character can and will accumulate adena in the normal progress of play, but most L2 players choose to "farm" adena, jumping through the rather mundane hoops needed to accumulate enough adena and thus quickly create a rather kick-ass character ('cause who wants to role-play a gimp?). The character class that can most quickly generate adena is the female dwarf.

There is, in fact, another way to accumulate adena without spending endless hours solo hunting green and blue con mobs: Pay someone to farm adena for you. Yes, using American dollars on sites like eBay, you can purchase adena for your character.

The supply that meets this demand is provided, in large part, by Chinese companies that pay employees around $3 a day to play Lineage II with the sole purpose of gathering adena (or by automated bots that do the same). Of course, commercial adena farmers play female dwarfs.

In her 2006 paper for *Games and Culture* magazine (vol. 1, no. 2, pp. 199–213), Constance Steinkuehler describes the result: "a whole new form of virtual racism has emerged, with an in-game character class substituted for real world differences between China and America." In Lineage II, non-adena-farming, largely American players initiate periodic pogroms, cleansing the game of perceived adena farmers—i.e., they commit genocide of girl dwarfs (of course, some innocent avatars are "cleansed" in this process). So deep is the association between Chinese players and avatars that farm adena for resale that American L2 players are likely to distrust—and at times go out of their way to kill—any avatar they suspect is being played by a Chinese operator.

The question, Steinkuehler asks, is whether labeling an avatar with the in-game insult "Chinese" will remain a comment about an avatar's gaming style, or whether this moniker, in fact, affects real-world racial perceptions.

FUTURE COOLNESS AS PROMISED BY NASA

Since the days of the first Mercury capsules, rockets have been propelled by combustible chemical fuels, using the rule of equal and opposite, similar to J. K. Rowling's blast-ended skrewt. Technological advancement has been limited to better fuels, offering more bang per kilogram (though decidedly not more bang per buck). Enter VASIMR, or variable specific impulse magnetoplasma rocket. First a word about plasma: it's a very cool type of gas that is highly electrically conductive (to massively oversimplify things). As you can see in the NASA diagram, VASIMR uses nuclear-generated electricity to ionize hydrogen, helium, or deuterium fuel into plasma, which is then heated by a laser death ray to add some zip and finally directed by electromagnetic fields out the back of the hypothetical rocket craft (shooting it forward like the aforementioned skrewt). There are a couple benefits of hydrogen: It is an effective radiation shield and is found almost everywhere in the known universe, allowing a ship to blast off with only enough hydrogen to power it to another hydrogen source (i.e., Mars).

INFORM AND INTERACTIVE FICTION

It is the calendar year 948 GUE, and you are standing near a white house. Inside the house are a brass lantern, an empty trophy case, and an engraved sword. Under the rug, a trapdoor leads into the Great Underground Empire (beware the grues, trolls, etc.). Playing perfectly, you can restore the twenty-one Treasures of Zork to the trophy case and finish the game in exactly 236 moves. Good luck.

As good as Zork was, it is but the progenitor of a massive and ever growing library of interactive fiction, with other standouts including Planetfall, Amnesia, and Slouching Toward Bedlam (the last notable also for its setting in the übergeek steampunk milieu). In fact, for many geeks, interactive fiction provided our intro to the world of programming (this author remembers writing choose-your-own adventures in BASIC, circa 1986). Consider exploring the composing environment of Inform, created in 1993 by Graham Nelson, which allows immediate and intuitive access to the IF framework, allowing you to focus on creating your environment and plot.

Once you have engineered/written your masterpiece, submit it to the yearly IF competition at the site www.ifcomp.org (where you can download contest rules and past winning stories).

VASIMR

LABORATORY EXPERIMENT

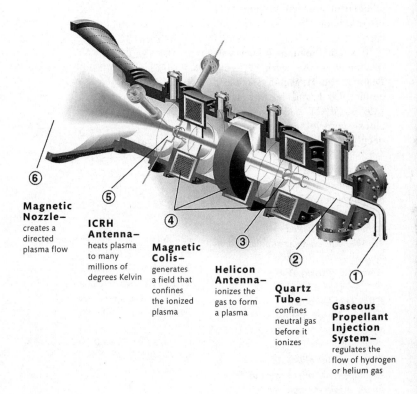

⑥ Magnetic Nozzle— creates a directed plasma flow

⑤ ICRH Antenna— heats plasma to many millions of degrees Kelvin

④ Magnetic Colis— generates a field that confines the ionized plasma

③ Helicon Antenna— ionizes the gas to form a plasma

② Quartz Tube— confines neutral gas before it ionizes

① Gaseous Propellant Injection System— regulates the flow of hydrogen or helium gas

SPAM HAIKU

The art of haiku poetry originated in Japan, with roots stretching back to the ninth century or earlier. According to the U.S. Census of 2000, people of pure Japanese descent make up 16.7 percent of the population of Hawaii. Residents of Hawaii annually consume nearly seven million cans of SPAM, or about six cans per capita.

If you do the math, it leads you inevitably to the work of Keola Beamer, the Hawaiian slack-key guitar player and leading advocate of SPAM haiku, who graciously contributed the following, deeply moving verses:*

Silent, former pig
One communal awareness
Myriad pink bricks

In mud you frolicked
Till they cut, cleaned and canned
* you*
How now, ground sow?

Pinky beef temptress
I can no longer remain
Vegetarian

Twist, pull the sharp lid
Jerks and cuts me deeply but
Spam, aaah, my poultice

"Slow down," she whispered
now guiding my trembling hands
"Turn the key slowly."

I put my shoes on
But remember far too late
My secret Spam stash.

BLINKENLIGHTS: COURTESY OF IBM, 1955

ACHTUNG!

ALLES TURISTEN UND NONTEKNISCHEN LOOKENPEEPERS!

DAS KOMPUTERMASCHINE IST NICHT FÜR DER GEFINGERPOKEN UND MITTENGRABEN! ODERWISE IST EASY TO SCHNAPPEN DER SPRINGENWERK, BLOWENFUSEN UND POPPENCORKEN MIT SPITZENSPARKSEN.

IST NICHT FÜR GEWERKEN BEI DUMMKOPFEN. DER RUBBERNECKEN SIGHTSEEREN KEEPEN DAS COTTONPICKEN HÄNDER IN DAS POCKETS MUSS.

ZO RELAXEN UND WATSCHEN DER BLINKENLICHTEN.

*With contributions of friends and fans of kbeamer.com.

BEER'S CONTRIBUTION TO THE FIELD OF STATISTICS

William Sealy Gosset was best known to his contemporaries in early-1900s Ireland by his pseudonym Student. This is because the Guinness Brewery, where he was employed, disallowed its biochemists and statisticians to publish papers after a previous employee leaked brewery secrets (think *Charlie and the Chocolate Factory*). Thus Gosset's most famous statistical achievement is known today as Student's t-distribution. This distribution allows one to estimate the mean in a population of small sample size. In other words (and with obvious irony) Guinness beer is responsible for your professors' ability to estimate the standard deviation on a prelim using only the small sample size of students who took the test. Without beer, there would be no grading on the curve.

THE ROCK, PAPER, SCISSORS MATING STRATEGY OF THE SIDE-BLOTCHED LIZARD

If you are a side-blotched lizard (*Uta stansburiana*), then you have an orange, a yellow, or a blue throat (easily determined by looking in mirror). If your throat is orange, then you will easily kick the ass of anyone with a blue throat and steal his lady lizards. If your throat is blue, you can still defend your women against the überwussy yellow-throats. If your throat is yellow, you are weak but deft and can sneak among the meatheaded orange-throaters and covertly snog their women (but the blue-throated lizards are too smart and will ferret out your clever ruse and give you a thumping). Thus, orange trumps blue, blue trumps yellow, and yellow trumps orange.

HEAD PICKLING THE OLD-FASHIONED WAY

The traditions of most cultures include the transformation of everyday things into sacred objects. For some cultures this takes the (somewhat) benign form of holiday fruitcake; other cultures, such as South America's Jivaro, prefer head shrinking. Here's how it's done:

1. Kill enemy.

2. Cut off head.

3. Carefully pull skull out through neck hole, leaving bag of head flesh.

4. Place red seeds under eyelids; sew shut.

5. Pin mouth shut using three palm stakes.

6. Boil flesh in tannin-rich water.

7. Dry with hot rocks and sand.

8. Be careful not to lose pleasing pseudohuman shape! Remold if necessary.

9. Rub with charcoal and decorate festively.

WORLD LEADERS WHO ALSO HAPPEN TO BE HOT

Inclusion on this list depends on having reached a threshold of combined power and pulchritude; thus Elizabeth Kucinich and French Prime Minister Nicolas Sarkozy's wife, the former Italian model Carla Bruni, don't quite make the list (underpowered), while Dick Cheney misses by only a hair (a face fit for cackling maniacally while stroking a hairless cat, not flashing a dashing come-hither). Note: both Putin and Medvedev made this list due to the author's wish to avoid polonium-210 radiation poisoning; and about Ahmadinejad: has anyone in the act of denying the Holocaust ever looked so dapper?

Vladimir "the Impaler" Putin **LEADER OF RUSSIA** 	Dmitri "Don't call me a puppet" Medvedev **RUSSIAN PRESIDENT**  Courtesy of World Economic Forum	Mahmoud Ahmadinejad **JEWISH PHILANTHROPIST**  Courtesy of Daniella Zalcom
Belinda Stronach **CANADIAN MP**  Courtesy of ycanada_news	Evo Morales **PRESIDENT OF BOLIVIA**  Courtesy of Allain Bachellier	Yulia Tymoshenko **PRIME MINISTER OF UKRAINE** 
Queen Rania **OF JORDAN**  Courtesy of World Economic Forum	Anders Fogh Rasmussen **PRIME MINISTER OF DENMARK**  Courtesy of World Economic Forum	Hamid Karzai **PRESIDENT OF AFGHANISTAN**  Courtesy of World Economic Forum

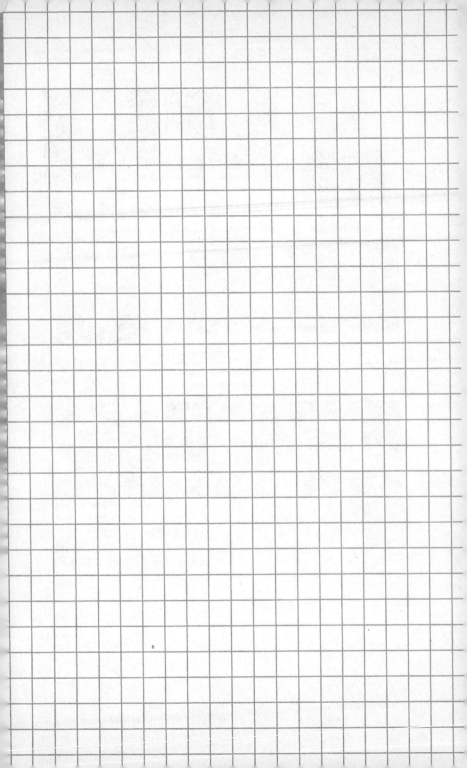

APPENDIX:

VERY GEEKY PUZZLE ANSWERS

"PROOF" THAT 2 = 1
(p. 2)

To get from the proof's fourth line to its fifth requires dividing by (a − b). If a = b, then a − b = 0, and dividing by zero is verboten.

A SAM LOYD PICTURE PUZZLE
(p. 13)

A SAM LOYD ALGEBRA PUZZLE
(p. 19)

In the second picture, imagine adding three cubes to each side. Now the only difference between the first and second pictures is that in the second, four cubes replace four marbles—thus a marble equals a cube, and it will take *nine* marbles to balance the top.

THREE REAL-WORLD PROBLEMS YOU CAN SOLVE WITH THE PYTHAGOREAN THEOREM ($A^2 + B^2 = C^2$)
(p. 19)

1. 127 feet (and change)

2. 104.8 inches

3. 7.4 feet

A SAM LOYD PICTURE PUZZLE
(p. 34)

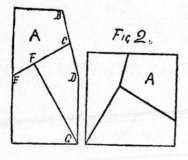

A SAM LOYD LOGIC PUZZLE
(p. 50)

The solution requires thirty-two moves: The first engine (F, labeling the cars alphabetically from left to right) passes alone through the switch via C, B, A (two moves), pulls the other engine (E) to D, and then passes through the switch again via C, B, and A. It then pulls car D to track D, pushing out engine E and again traveling through the switch. It repeats with G, B, and A before passing through the switch (seventeen moves; the left train is now pointing forward, through the switch). Engine F goes to the right, then draws all cars left, and then backs G onto the switch; draws A, B, C, D, and E to the left, then backs them right; goes to the left alone, backs up on the switch at A and takes G to the left; goes to the right, then takes everything out left, backs H and I onto switch; pulls G, A, B, C, D, and E out left, backs them to the right, then takes F to the right, backs up to the switch, and connects G to H and I; and is now prepared to go ahead on the thirty-second move.

SUDOKU STRATEGY
(p. 58)

Upper-right box of question #6:

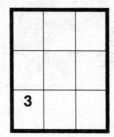

A SAM LOYD
PICTURE PUZZLE
(p. 60)

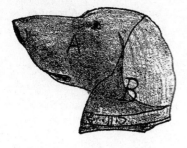

THE CLASSIC
LOGIC PROBLEM
(p. 65)

Tom = knee, soccer
Fred = concussions, curling
Bill = shoulder, baseball
Andy = wrist, basketball
Carl = hip, football

A SAM LOYD
LOGIC PUZZLE
(p. 75)

Top row: Matthew, Alfred,
Eastman. Second row:
Richard, Theodore, Luke,
Oom. Bottom row: Hisswald,
Shirmer, Fletcher, Arthur,
Alden.

A SAM LOYD
MATHEMATICS PUZZLE
(p. 92)

17 + 17 + 17 + 17 + 16 + 16 =
100

A SAM LOYD
PICTURE PUZZLE
(p. 109)

The lost star is in the lower
right, as shown.

A SAM LOYD
MATHEMATICS PUZZLE
(p. 120)

The cat wins, with exactly
one hundred leaps. The dog
must make sixty-eight leaps
(traveling 102 feet each way),

but makes them only two thirds as rapidly.

SIX SOMEWHAT FIENDISH CHESS PROBLEMS
(p. 124)

1. cxb6 e.p. (Black's only possible previous move is b7-b5.)

2. gxf6 e.p. (Black's only possible previous move is f7-f5.)

3. This is very tricky! Retrograde analysis shows that Black has castled illegally on the previous move and must thus replace the Rook at h8 and, by rule, must move the King. If Kxd7, then Bxc6 mate; if Kf8, then Rxh8 mate.

4. Qd3 and Bb8 mate.

5. Assuming Black cannot castle, Rxa6 and Ra8 mate, or Rd2 and Rd8 mate.

6. Assuming Black cannot castle, Rxa7 and Ra8 mate.

A SAM LOYD MATHEMATICS PUZZLE
(p. 129)

Exactly 8 hours, 18 minutes, and $27\frac{9}{13}$ seconds.

MORSE CODE
(p. 134)

If you can read this, then you are within this book's stated target market.

A SAM LOYD MATHEMATICS PUZZLE
(p. 137)

Lady is 135 pounds; Baby is 25 pounds; Dog is 10 pounds.

A SAM LOYD MATHEMATICS PUZZLE
(p. 146)

The girls weigh 56, 58, 60, 64, and 65 pounds.

A SAM LOYD MATHEMATICS PROBLEM
(p. 154)

This is tricky. In mathematics notation, a dot over a decimal number fills the same purpose as a straight line, making the decimal infinitely repeat. Thus (replacing repeat-dots with lines for clarity):

$$\begin{array}{r} 80 \\ .\overline{5} \\ .\overline{97} \\ + .\overline{46} \\ \hline 82 \end{array}$$

CHEMICAL EQUATION PUZZLES: IF THESE ARE FUN, YOU ARE A GEEK
(p. 163)

$3H_2 + N_2 \rightarrow 2NH_3$	$2NH_3 + 2O_2 \rightarrow NO + 3H_2O$
$2NaCl + BeF_2 \rightarrow 2NaF + BeCl_2$	$2FeCl_3 + Be_3(PO_4)_2 \rightarrow 3BeCl_2 + 2FePO_4$
$3Ca(OH)_2 + 2H_3PO_4 \rightarrow Ca_3(PO_4)_2 + 6H_2O$	$2C_2H_6 + 7O_2 \rightarrow 4CO_2 + 6H_2O$

A SAM LOYD
PICTURE PUZZLE
(p. 175)

A SAM LOYD
LOGIC PUZZLE
(p. 189)

Rip should knock out pin number six, dividing the pins into groups of one, three, and seven, thus ensuring his victory no matter his opponent's next play.

A SAM LOYD
LOGIC PUZZLE
(p. 205)

There are a several best moves, all of which use the strategy of waiting instead of scoring all possible boxes. One way is by marking G–H (opponent follows with J–K), then marking K–O and P–L, then playing the waiting move L–H instead of scoring the two remaining possible boxes. The opponent scores these two boxes, leaving the first player to score the remaining five boxes.

SPECIES IN D&D,
MIDDLE-EARTH,
WINNIE-THE-POOH, AND
MAGIC: THE GATHERING
(p. 223)

D&D—abishai, beholder, blink dog, bugbear, chaos beast, doppelgänger, drow, eladrin, frost worm, hell hound, phasm, purple worm, winter wolf, yugoloth.

Middle-earth—Balrog, Barrow-wight, Ent, fell beast, great spiders, Hobbit, Nazgûl, Uruk-hai, Valar.

Winnie-the-Pooh— heffalump.

Magic: The Gathering: Myr, Saproling, Skulk, Thrull

A SAM LOYD SLIDING-TILE PUZZLE
(p. 226)

The sequence of movements is: whisky flask, scrubbing brush, flatiron, whisky flask, pepperbox, mousetrap, whisky flask, flatiron, scrubbing brush, pepperbox, flatiron, whisky bottle, mousetrap, flatiron, pepperbox, scrubbing brush, whisky bottle.

[The following pages have been allotted for the true geek, who will need this space to jot down diagrams, quadratic equations, and sketches of Boba Fett's heavily modified Kuat Systems interceptor.]